Contents

THE
Complete
WOMAN

Mary Ann Mayo
Joseph L. Mayo, M.D.

Marshall Pickering

THE COMPLETE WOMAN

Copyright © 1987 by Harvest House Publishers under the title 'The Sexual Woman' Eugene, Oregon 97402

First published in the UK in 1989 by Marshall Morgan and Scott Publications Ltd Part of Marshall Pickering Holdings Group.

ISBN 0-551-01787-2

Printed and bound in Great Britain by Anchor Press Ltd, Tiptree, Essex

DEDICATION

Thank You, Lord, for our special women friends:

—of new memories, Jane and Miriam
—of lasting memories, Vee and Molly
—of irreplaceable memories, our mothers, Frances and Mary Jo
—a friend in eternity, Craig Zappia

THE
Complete
WOMAN

Preface

The Complete Woman was written to help Christian women understand emotional and general sexual and gynecological health. The style is intended to be readable and enjoyable, yet educational. Ultimately the book seeks to motivate women to take an active role in maintaining their sexual and gynecological well-being. It seeks to demystify the workings of the body as well as to demonstrate God's hand in the marvel of the female design.

This book is not intended to cover in depth every facet of a woman's health. There are a number of excellent books on the market that effectively accomplish this. Our purpose is to present in a clear and interesting way the most common medical and sexual concerns which the average woman faces.

Since we wish to affirm God's divine purpose in making two sexes, we have given much attention to the expression of female sexuality and a woman's relationship with men. It is our hope that informed and confident women will contribute to the stability of monogamous marriage as well as live wholesomely and comfortably with their femininity while single.

We have enjoyed combining our areas of expertise in supporting today's woman. Our interest has been motivated by the confusing and rapidly changing roles and expectations for women, the pain and suffering we have shared with patients and clients, and our own personal struggles as a married couple.

Our thanks and blessing go to Eileen Mason and Bill Jensen, whose enthusiasm and vision gave us the courage to risk such an undertaking and to continue to squeeze writing between deliveries, speaking engagements, being Mom and Dad, and taking the time necessary to minister to our personal needs as husband and wife.

Special thanks to Melanie Schiebout for excellent suggestions and for never tiring of correcting comma errors! Sincere appreciation is offered to the members of Redlands First Baptist Church, our family in the Lord, and for the special support and prayers of our pastor and his wife, Dan and Miriam Wingerd.

Chapter One

The Christian Woman As a Complete Woman

> *. . . worth more than precious gems.*
>
> *—Proverbs 31:10 TLB*

The sun was beginning to set, and finally there was a promise of relief from the oppressive heat of the day. She scurried about the garden making sure everything had been placed just as she had ordered. The fragrance of spices and perfume of flowers wafted across the marble pillars and silk-lined couches. Two goblets, the most beautiful she had been able to find, sat majestically by a plate of refreshing fruit.

Everything ready, her attention turned to herself. The dressmaker had done a beautiful job. The gossamer-thin fabric hinted seductively at her trim figure, and the handwork, exquisite in its delicacy, softened her own strong features. Her dark complexion, if not like that of the other ladies, provided a look of vitality and health, which, she reminded herself, he seemed to appreciate.

At last he was home! Her heart quickened as she ran to greet him. Her dreams of him never came close to the reality of his good looks and mighty presence. Their kiss hinted at the longing and promise of what was to come.

Undisturbed, and in their own private world, their words of adoration made the time apart seem insignificant. They shared gifts: his, a special perfume that hinted of the freshness of the vineyard after a rain; hers, a dance that left no doubt of her willingness to be his lover.

Well, what do you think? Maybe the first page out of a Harlequin romance novel? No, the story is taken from the Christian marriage manual, the Song of Solomon, minus the poetry and with a little updated vocabulary.

What does this have to do with a book about Christian women? The description of a sensuous woman seems far removed from the usual

12

Christian stereotype. Taking responsibility for oneself, whether as a sexual person within one's male-female relationships or with one's health, is not usually presented within the Christian community as the goal of the spiritual woman.

The market is filled with books that extol the value of taking charge of one's life, but in most cases God's will, help, or plan are not presented as a necessary part of the goal. As with original sin, men and women are asked to believe that they can achieve whatever they wish as long as they learn and use the right technical knowledge or skill.

Christian women are to trust in the Lord and yet be willing to take responsibility for themselves in ways that are in line with God's plan for victory in their lives. This book asks Christian women to reexamine their sexuality, health, and relationships with men, since passive behavior in these areas will not contribute to God's plan for them. Like Gideon's troops, they must choose to bring their special characteristics and strengths to the battle.

First Things First

The book of Genesis introduces God's purpose in creating two sexes. Mankind's understanding of this fact is usually misinformed, ignored, or used to justify wrong behavior. In this opening chapter we will consider God's desire as it relates to the plan, purpose, and aspiration of genital sexuality.

Song of Solomon, with its poetic intensity, serves to remind Christians that for most of us our marital sexual relationships do not measure up to the divine model so lovingly intended for us. We opt instead for a much more "proper" version practiced with dampened enthusiasm. Setting aside special time for a sexual interlude and erotic dances is not in the repertoire of many married Christian couples.

It appears that God does not have the hesitancy and embarrassment about the physical expression of our marital love that we do. That makes sense, since God is the author and designer of sex. It was His idea that our marital bond be enriched, enjoined, and sealed by genital sexual expression.

No book in the Bible makes this intention more clear than the Song of Solomon, which describes the issues of sexuality of courtship and marriage through poetic love poems. Though not in strict sequence, the poems reveal the passion and longing meant to be found in courtship and marriage. Tradition suggests that they tell the story of King Solomon and a lovely Shulamite maiden. Shulamith (Shulamite) can be interpreted as a feminine form of Shelomo (Solomon), a play on names that suggests the unity of the couple.

From Song of Solomon the image of a sexually responsible, sensuous woman emerges. Her verbal expressions of love and desire outnumber his two-to-one. Even 3000 years ago women were more talkative than men! Not only did Shulamith communicate her desires and set aside time for sex, but she allowed herself to prepare for time together by fantasizing.

She understood that sexual desire is not something that springs out of an uncorked bottle. It generally builds slowly as the situation, the individual involved, and one's own body responses are taken into account.

Energy must be expended and willful choices made even under the most romantic circumstances. Heightened arousal results from effort on the part of both men and women.

Passive receptivity, by contrast, does not culminate in an experience of unbridled passion. It contributes instead to the feeling of being used and of being a "sex object." Convincing women that they are sexually passive is a Western idea not found in Mideastern or Eastern cultures or in the Bible. The development of the mindset which suggested that women don't enjoy sex has a history dating back to some of the early church fathers.

In the beginning years of the church there was much confusion over the part which marriage and sex were to play in the new order of Christianity. Bewilderment over one's ability to be sexual and spiritual at the same time was the source of much misinterpretation. The tradition of viewing the mind and body as two separate entities resulted in the decision that procreation and marriage were good but that sex was bad. This tradition, which has persisted throughout history, prevents seeing the body, one's spiritual life, and marital relations as part of the same whole.

Although today we may intellectually understand God's true message of sex, it is still difficult to unhook emotionally from an underlying feeling that something is inherently wrong with enjoying sex.

The vagina's lack of mobility has also contributed to the idea of the "passive" female. (Freud made much of the woman being the "receiver.") But this is a mistaken idea not based on fact. As sexual excitement increases, the vagina opens slightly to allow greater access to the penis. With continued excitement it pulsates, lubricates profusely, and contracts down on the penis to heighten excitement for both partners. Internally, organs shift and move and respiration increases; externally, the nipples become erect, sweating may occur, and the toes curl. This is hardly a picture of passivity!

What's Right?

Ambivalence characterizes our current attitude toward sex. Although both sexes have accepted the correctness of sexual intercourse in marriage, few are comfortable with the idea of being sensuous. Sensuousness suggests something that seems beyond control. Christians understand intellectually their right to express themselves sexually, but they experience emotional bondage when they attempt to do so.

Shulamith, like women of today, responded to her husband when he was romantic and sensitive to her needs (Song of Solomon 6:4-10). In return, she met his needs by being as physically assertive and as appealing as possible (Song of Solomon 7:1-9). Both stretched beyond the usual desires of their gender in such a way that the other person would find it appealing.

Shulamith allowed herself to think sexual thoughts. She recalled King Solomon's attributes, sometimes quite graphically: "His lips are like lilies dripping with myrrh. . . . His body is like polished ivory decorated with sapphires" (Song 5:13b,14b). We get the point—she insured desire by thinking of him and of their love life.

Submit to One Another

In Song of Solomon the declaration is repeated, "My lover is mine and I am his" (Song 2:16; 6:3). Nowhere in the Bible is the sexual relationship defined in terms other than that of mutuality. "The wife's body does not belong to her alone but also to her husband. In the same way, the husband's body does not belong to him alone but also to his wife" (1 Corinthians 7:4). ". . . in this matter no one should wrong his brother or take advantage of him" (1 Thessalonians 4:6).

Married couples are to conscientiously try to meet the sexual desires of their spouse. Often, as illustrated in Song of Solomon, this means acting in a way that at first seems unnatural to one's sex or personality. Many people have been raised in homes which suggested that sex or certain sexual practices are demeaning even within the sanctity of marriage. Time and patience enable most people to break free of those preconceived notions and participate in sexual activities that result in pleasure and feelings of unity.

Does this mean that whatever the spouse desires must be enjoyed or at least endured? Certainly not, for sex is based on mutually submitting to one another and, as 1 Thessalonians so aptly states, "not wronging or taking advantage of anyone." A person whose sexual expression has been hampered because of his or her upbringing and/or experiences will be wronged if forced to participate in something which he or she has difficulty tolerating or feeling comfortable with. Although such a person has a responsibility to grow to please her partner, her particular sensitivities must be considered. On the other hand, a spouse is obliged to face, resolve, and reeducate himself or herself if his or her sexual education has resulted in practices that do not contribute to feelings of oneness, involve pain, or are perversions of the spirit of tenderness, love, and romance that are to characterize "making love."

Does God Know About This?

Christian couples often fail to meet each other's sexual needs for fear of offending God. They fear misusing their sexuality. Song of Solomon provides assurance for married partners, along with the above passages, that relating in a sensuous way that each finds pleasurable, unifying, and enhancing of their self-image is glorifying to God. The measure of what is moral sexual behavior is not its passion or particular expression, but whether it takes place in a covenant relationship sealed with marital love that has as its base a philosophy of giving rather than getting.

Theologians do the same thing they accuse others of when by providing legalistic lists of do's and don't's: They reduce sex to its narrowest sense. Proper sexual expression is then misjudged by what is done with the genitals instead of whether the encounter results in a sense of oneness and unity as a result of bodies being shared in a way that meets the needs of each partner.

A good performance is not loving if intimacy and bonding does not occur. If having one's own needs met inevitably takes precedence over the desires and needs of the spouse, then the sexual act, no matter how strictly defined as "properly expressed genital intercourse," brings no honor to God. Honoring God through the sexual relationship depends far more on positive answers to the following questions than on whether we participate in a specific act. Are our partner's needs considered? Will our sexual expression result in greater unity? Are we committed to a lifelong relationship? Is the relationship characterized by a willingness to trust and take the risk of being emotionally vulnerable?

Concern over what is decent sexually depends in most cases on the heart motivation. Specifically the Bible speaks against bestiality (Exodus 22:19), incest (Deuteronomy 22:30), prostitution (Ephesians 5:5), male homosexuality, and lesbianism (Romans 1:26,27). Oral sex and masturbation are not mentioned. Anal sex is specified in reference to homosexuality.

What's a Woman to Do?

The chance of doing what is expected increases enormously by the simple act of understanding clearly what those expectations are. The Bible spells out what is to characterize our marital partnerships. Both men and women are to leave, cleave, and work for unity (Genesis 2:24) within their covenant relationship. They are to give themselves with abandon to each other sexually (1 Corinthians 7:2-5). The words they share are to be truthful, appropriate, and designed to build up rather than tear down (Ephesians 4:25-32).

How are you doing so far? Working for "unity" and "words designed to build up rather than tear down" could be a major stumbling block. After all, men aren't to be trusted—there is a war going on. Isn't the old saying true that women live with men merely because they can't live without them? Does God really say that men and women are supposed to get along?

Too often a woman's experience, coupled with her formal and informal upbringing, makes her doubtful that something better exists. But the original design and plan promises a relationship that surpasses the pseudoromanticism of "Dynasty," "Dallas," or any other soap opera. We were designed for more.

Individually, the husband is told to love and lead (Ephesians 5:25-33) and to understand and protect his wife, treating her as an equal heir to the kingdom (1 Peter 3:7). A wife is to love and submit (Ephesians 5:22-24). These are simple, straightforward statements that somehow in their application to practical life lose their simplicity. How does a man lead with love? How does a woman submit without resentment?

All Things Through Him

When I was a little girl, I went to Sunday school regularly. My mother was the teacher. Inevitably I was cast as Mary in every Christmas pageant. I memorized biblical verses. I concluded I must be a Christian.

When a person has based his Christianity on such a poor foundation, it is inevitable that it will be dismissed as meaningless and replaced with worldly "wisdom." It took only until my first semester in college and a philosophy-of-religion class until I had found an "updated" ideology.

My husband's understanding of religion revolved around harassment and alienation for not being the predominant religion in his small town. Only 4 percent of the population professed a belief system that varied from that one religious expression. At age 12 he won a Bible for perfect attendance at Sunday school, which attested more to his compulsive nature than to any genuine interest.

Our marriage took place in a lovely church just off campus. We believed that God existed, and it seemed only fitting that the serious step of matrimony should take place in His house. That He was to be part of our life after the ceremony was not suggested by the minister or anyone else.

Our life progressed as we settled in at new schools and places of work. Our son was born six years later and a lovely daughter adopted 4½ years after that. Degrees rolled in, offices opened, and the long-awaited financial reward enabled us to purchase a house and cars and to take family vacations. We had arrived, and we did it "our way."

But a funny thing happened on the road to success. To quote a much wiser man, "Yet when I surveyed all that my hands had done and what I had toiled to achieve, everything was meaningless, a chasing after the wind; nothing was gained under the sun" (Ecclesiastes 2:11). The emptiness we felt was hard to define. More degrees, more money, and more prestige did nothing to abate it. Yoga, meditation, baking our own bread, therapy, granola, and hot tubs rotated through our life. Commitment to the community and service to others helped but could not alter the fact that life in all its abundance was appearing increasingly pointless.

If one could have a sound marriage, healthy children, wealth, and public acclaim but still not have inner peace, what was life all about? How curious that our willingness to search and experiment never included a serious look at the Bible! But God was patient. His perfect timing set into motion a series of events that resulted in our coming to know Him as our personal Savior.

It wasn't easy. Our immature concept of God as a mean daddy had the possibility of conversion tied up with grim scenes of Africa, living in poverty, and being scoffed at by our friends. We didn't know that God would never ask us to do something He didn't prepare us for. We didn't understand that He wanted only the very best for us. We didn't grasp that His yoke was going to be found light.

How faithful He has been to bring sound biblical teaching into our lives! How He has groomed and protected us! The hunger which He has instilled in us to know Him engulfs our lives and sheds light on each and every facet of what we do. For the first time we are living lives of reality—lives with God in them.

Gone are the days when sharing with friends "this spiritual thing" brought embarrassment and hesitation. The desire to integrate our faith into our lives has become a major undertaking. I suspect that it is the chief task of most sincere Christians.

This book undertakes to help you do that, at least in the area of your sexuality, health, and relationship with men. Nothing is more basic than learning how to live out your womanhood as God's person. With billions of sperm available, as well as hundreds of thousands of potential eggs, along with the vicissitudes and chances of intercourse, the particular match that is *you* is no accident! You are a wanted and loved child of the God who knew you before you were born (Psalm 139).

How Can This Book Help?

Information is no longer difficult to obtain. A quick trip to the library or brief phone call to Tele-Med provides more material than we can digest. But integrating the information into our lives is quite another matter. How to do this in the area of sexuality and Christianity is difficult indeed.

Our efforts can be likened to our being capsized in the middle of a lake. We grab desperately for anything that meanders by in an attempt to stay afloat. The world sends items that look like they will save us but in the end are found lacking. The church sends out a life vest, but when we try to use it we discover that it has been put together by people with good intentions who didn't read the instructions. As a result, some of us manage to limp into shore with the help of the life vest, but most of us struggle, become frustrated, and simply give up. Yet God not only sends a life vest but provides a new boat. We need only get on board and read the instructions!

The reluctance of the vast majority of women to do so is a motivating force behind *The Sexual Woman*. In my practice as a marriage and family counselor and my husband's as an obstetrician-gynecologist, we have seen firsthand the same emptiness which we experienced before God became Lord of our lives—including our sexual lives. We want to examine how a man leads with love and a woman submits without resentment. We want to help as many people as possible to recognize and responsibly climb into God's boat and make it safely to shore.

Taking Responsibility

God has made men and women sexual creatures. He never intended for us to exclude Him from our bedrooms or from matters involving the intimacies of our bodies. It is by inviting Him in as Lord of our sexual natures that we learn the part which sex is to play in who we are as males and females. Continued exclusion of God only perpetuates the current sexual practices and viewpoints that bring such defeat, frustration, and unhappiness to so many of God's people. Married or single, we are God's sexual person. We challenge you to take the risk of becoming all you were meant to be. It is your responsibility to choose: "The wise woman builds her house, but with her own hands the foolish one tears hers down" (Proverbs 14:1).

Chapter Two

The Complete Woman and the Men in Her Life

Praise her for the many fine things she does.

—Proverbs 31:31 TLB

It is not easy growing up in the eighties, even if you are no longer a child. At no time in history has the balance between men and women been in greater flux. Many people are so accustomed to the way things have been that they harbor an unconscious ideology which makes it difficult for them to distinguish traits that are deeply imbibed in their natures from those that are merely traditionally assigned to one sex or the other. Out of confusion, fear, and sheer necessity our nation since the sixties has been in a desperate search for a "new order."

As a result of this search polarization has occurred, leaving the vast majority of people floundering somewhere between two extremes. It is now time to move on, yet moving on will require that women and men look back. Their understanding and experience biblically, historically, and personally are factors in reconsidering who they were meant to be. Accepting this responsibility provides a sense of purpose and vision unobtainable in any other way.

How Would You Go on a Field Trip?

I have not been a Christian all my life. I like the freshness which I can bring to the Bible, unencumbered by preconceived notions. I am grateful for the excitement I feel with each new insight as I continue to grow in God's Word. I hate the time wasted that cannot be recovered to do His work. I resent the effort and energy I spent on the thousand-and-one spiritual bunny trails that enticingly promised "the way." I thank God that our slowness at hearing and accepting the truth is not held against us! I praise the Lord that He uses each of us according to our own particular makeup and in His own special timing.

As for me, "individual" is probably an apt description. Having made a god of striving to be the best I could be, the bunny trail of the women's movement seemed made for me, even if it came along a little late. My high school dreams of being a geologist or paleontologist were dismissed by my school counselor with a cryptic "How would you go on a field trip? There are no facilities for women!" Becoming a stewardess, I was informed, was choosing to be a "glorified waitress," and entering the Army was not even worth discussing. A teacher, though . . . yes, a teacher—now there was a suitable profession for a white Anglo-Saxon Protestant middle-class lady!

And ironically, it was. I loved teaching and sensed the responsibility involved in having a part in preparing the next generation. But it was not enough. The hole in my soul was not filled. I determined to listen more closely to the rhetoric of other women that were then making headlines by burning bras and demanding equal rights.

My first exposure to "women's libbers" proved a relief. They looked and talked like me. They liked children. They just wanted a fair chance in a male-dominated world. I was hooked; my course was set. Equality and acceptance were to be mine, and so was the elusive happiness that mystically kept just out of my reach.

My odyssey with the women's movement, along with teaching a course on the psychology of women, proved to be both positive and negative. These contributed to a greater understanding of the uniqueness of women and (for the first time in my life) an enhanced appreciation of my fellow females. Paradoxically, the more I began to love and recognize a woman's value, the more I found myself at odds with the prevailing practice of feminism. No one else at the time seemed bothered by the fact that pursuing male goals was tantamount to admitting they were the only goals worth achieving. Values seen as feminine, such as peace, balance, and nurturing, were dismissed by men and women alike as weak and secondary in importance.

My husband, an ob-gyn resident at the time, worked hard to stretch and be comfortable with the new and better balance that was to liberate us both. Always graciously supporting my efforts to grow, he encouraged my pursuit of graduate school. The years that followed were marked by some of the most turbulent times of our marriage.

I was determined to be strong and independent. No perceived putdown could be ignored, no opportunity for further "growth" overlooked. My guilt over leaving my children with caretakers was matched

22

by my rage at not being able to pursue a Ph.D. Anger characterized my days as I moped and moaned at the unfairness of life in limiting my desires. Somehow I could not ignore my "duty" as mother and wife. If only my husband had been a little rotten, maybe then I could have broken away. Every day was filled with perceived sacrifices on my part—all, I felt, unjustly deserved.

Have you been there? Are you there now? I hope not. Many women in the mid-eighties have competed with men on masculine terms long enough to have discovered the futility and emptiness of such a pursuit. It is gratifying to see some of the more mature feminist leaders now having the courage to say they made a mistake. Liberation is the freedom to be the individual you were made to be; it is not the freedom to be someone else.

True Liberation

Who was woman made to be? Certainly defining her as a person capable only of secondary positions or specific jobs is not accurate. But we can proclaim this fact with certainty: A woman was not meant to be a man.

In an era when eliminating the differences between men and women has been the emphasis, studies focusing on the distinctions between the sexes have not been popular. Yet cross-cultural work has confirmed some verifiable differences. For example, child care and child socialization is almost universally female. A recent anthropological study of 201 societies found that women were cooks in 158 of these. Only five societies reported men cooking exclusively. Group dominance and intergroup aggression is almost entirely male. Women tend to be more modest in displaying their genitals and less apt to engage in premarital and extramarital intercourse, even in societies where women are considered to have a higher sex drive than men.

Mothers generally carry infants on their left side (where the infant can hear the heartbeat), and they approach and handle babies in a very standardized fashion. When looking at a newborn child, the mother's eyes will dilate but not the father's. Most important, however, is the different way in which information is gathered and problems solved.

I have heard the uniqueness of a woman's and a man's outlook described as the difference between a floodlight and a flashlight. Men frequently see the details of a situation, just as the flashlight pinpoints an area of focus, whereas women will grasp the overall picture, just as a floodlight spreads its illumination over the entire area. Each view "sheds light" in a special way. More important than the specific job is the distinctive contribution which each sex can make to it.

To deny that our physical differences (including brain organization, reproductive capacity, and musculature) does not also affect our emotional and thinking capabilities is to be very shortsighted. The totality of who we are influences the way we approach and fulfill our responsibilities and social relationships. This does not mean, of course, that traits found more strongly in one sex cannot be found in the other sex or that a man or woman must be denied access to certain roles because of such traits.

Our basic design as a man or woman motivates us to cognitively and effectively look at life through different glasses. Far from being seen as a weakness, such variation in viewpoints should be viewed as a strength, for it enables men and women to achieve a more complete and balanced view.

And this appears to be God's intent as well. Genesis 2:18 declares that women are to be "helpers" to men. Nowhere in the Bible does this word imply inferiority. In fact, it often refers to God helping His people. It can be thought of in the same sense of a physician ministering to his or her patient.

The woman is a "helper" declared "fit for him." A perfect match is implied, as is harmony, a partnership, and companionship. The current acceptance of a "war between the sexes" was not the original design. Our different natures were intended to enable us to complete one another in areas other than in childbearing.

Man was "not good" until there was woman. The image of God is reflected in humanity through the cooperative partnership of men and women. God is a God of relationship, and we are people of relationship: "Woman is not independent of man, nor is man independent of woman" (1 Corinthians 11:11). The original plan had our lives bound up with one another; our cooperation was not limited to procreation or marriage. To view one another so narrowly as to exclude other aspects of relationship is to reduce people to mere sex objects.

The ultimate partnership and cooperation is supposed to be demonstrated in marriage. A woman who is reluctant to prepare herself to give the best she can to the partnership, or a man who fails to encourage her or actually discourages her, is limiting what she can add to their shared life. On the other hand, striving for sameness and equality has the same sad result. The covenant love of marriage should nurture the uniqueness of both husband and wife.

The Best-Laid Plans

If man and woman were made to be interdependent, the dissonance and disruption which some of us find in our marriages is not what God meant to be. The message of Genesis chapters 1 and 2 is that humanity and sexuality were created *good*. Together the two sexes were to be productive and creative in their care of the world, and together they were to reflect the image of God. Ideas of supremacy, subordination, and the resulting alienation and suffering experienced between men and women came about after the entrance of sin.

Arguments that the female is inherently inferior do not hold up to close scrutiny of God's original plan in Genesis. A lower status based on secondary creation does not make sense when one observes that the sequence of creation is from lower to higher forms.

That the woman was taken from man reflects the unity of the male and female. Indeed, the very meaning of the Hebrew word for man acknowledges woman as someone made for him, someone from the same substance who, like him, owes her life to God. No animal mate was created in the same way.

After the entrance of sin Adam named his wife Eve, providing a symbolic seal on the conflict and competition that was to follow. Neither person escaped the judgment of the Lord for his or her disobedience. Clearly, active initiation and passive compliance with sin was looked on as equally deplorable. But as a result of God's grace neither person was cursed (although the serpent and ground were), their lives were spared, and God's compassion was demonstrated as He supplied clothing to cover them.

What Does This Mean to You?

Did you ever buy a pair of shoes that was too cute to pass up but didn't fit exactly right? Perhaps you developed a corn or your whole body and demeanor reflected your pain every time you wore the shoes. Trying on a lifestyle that doesn't fit can be just as uncomfortable, but with far worse effects. The liberation promised in the women's movement didn't fit; in fact it nearly destroyed my marriage. Equally devastating was the liberation I looked for in a legalistic rendering of Christ's Word—it nearly destroyed me. Clearly, fitting into a stereotypic Christian mold was not the answer either.

I had been missing the point. Our God is a creative God, and each one of us reflects His creativity. That hole in my soul was indeed filled by liberation, but by the only *true* liberation—the freedom to be the woman God made me to be.

There is no shortcut to the study, prayer, and fresh perspective which a woman must bring to the effort of being open to God's plan for her. Yet the reward is great: It is discovering that she is a person of worth because she is a child of God and a person of significance because she has a job to do—a job that is unique because of her womanhood and her particular embodiment of it. How well this meshes with Paul's comments in Romans 12! Each of us, within the framework of our masculinity or femininity, has a task that is uniquely ours to be lived out through our own personality, ability, and faith.

A woman who accepts her femininity and expresses it within her particular calling enriches the created order. Utilizing her God-given strengths enables her to add a dimension to our current existence that is in short supply in a world dominated by the male perspective. A woman, by acknowledging, accepting, and affirming her ability to bear children, by her sensitivity to preserving life, by her relationship focus, and by her concern for the quality of life, reminds men and society that children, family, and relationships deserve equal time with the Dow-Jones average.

A Fine Example

Did you ever think how radical Jesus' attitude toward women was in His day? In a climate that declared a man "unpure" as a result of even an accidental touch by a woman, Jesus interacted with women openly. He healed them and allowed them to touch Him, and they followed Him. The motion picture *Yentl* tells the story of a young Jewish girl so hungry to know the Word of God that she masqueraded as a boy. Jesus, unlike the rabbis, had no such hesitancy to teach women. He spoke regularly to and with women.

In the stories of Martha and Mary (Luke 10:38-42; John 11:20-33), Mary's desire for spiritual growth is affirmed and declared to be the right choice. Martha demonstrates spiritual discernment when she understands and proclaims who Jesus is. In Matthew 15:21-28 and John 4:7-15 a theological discussion is carried on with women.

Women were an integral part of Jesus' ministry. Mary understood the significance of her actions in anointing Jesus in Matthew 26:6-13. In contrast to rabbinical practice, they were spoken of in parables and included in teaching services (Luke 10:39; John 11:28). For those who believe that women and men are unable to work together without sexual compromises, we are reminded of the group of women who traveled and worked with the disciples without a hint of scandal in a most restrictive age.

Women were present at the crucifixion. They were the first to hear and speak of the resurrection—the first to see the risen Lord. Women, therefore, were important witnesses to major theological events, a role never assigned them in the Jewish mainstream.

Salvation for women, then as now, depended solely on the individual act of asking the Lord to enter one's heart. Unlike other religions requiring an intermediary, a sacrifice, or a husband's intervention on her behalf, she alone could take the necessary steps. In the sight of the Lord, a woman's full personhood gave her the right to approach the King.

The Balancing Act

There is no question that in the eyes of God all men and women have the same standing: "You are all sons of God through faith in Christ Jesus, for all of you who were baptized into Christ have clothed yourselves with Christ. There is neither Jew nor Greek, slave nor free, male nor female, for you are all one in Christ Jesus. If you belong to Christ, then you are Abraham's seed, and heirs according to the promise" (Galatians 3:26-29).

Genesis speaks to the interrelatedness of men and women and the mutual task and goals set aside for mankind. Jesus' actions declared a consideration and acceptance of women as persons of value, respect, and capabilities unheard of in the culture of His day. Paul and other New Testament writers added practical advice for living out our Christian witness in our day-by-day existence.

Confusion abounds when the reader fails to carefully distinguish God's original intent from the effects of the fall. If one concludes that God set up a hierarchy, it is easy to interpret words like "submission," "helper," and "authority" in the light of superiority and inferiority. But when one sees a partnership that is to be lived out for the betterment of the created order, such words lose their sting.

The New Testament and particularly the letters of Paul speak to the issue of how to live the Christian life. The reference point for Paul is always the community. Many of his more difficult passages regarding women, those that suggest to some people the right of male authority at the cost of justice for the female, are less harsh when viewed from the perspective of whether the behavior in question resulted in a building up or tearing down of the body of believers. Paul's overall goal in 1 Corinthians, in which several problematic passages appear, is not whether women should hide in the woodwork or wear their hair braided, but how Christians as new people in Christ were to create a community of mutual love and harmonious and orderly relationships. That is still the goal and challenge within our modern church community.

The emphasis on two or three passages, no matter how difficult, is no excuse for ignoring Paul's overall positive attitude toward women. In the beginning, the New Testament church gave a status to women which they had never before achieved. In the book of Acts Paul clearly states his gratitude to individual women whose contributions included teaching and providing leadership and support for both the local church and missionaries.

Is Headship Sexist?

If both men and women have been charged with the responsibility of filling and subduing the earth and together are made in God's image, how do we explain the headship that is given to the man? The plan for two sexes has within it predispositions for each sex that have throughout the centuries motivated the male to claim economic, political, and aggressive roles and the female to take the chief role in childrearing. One might conclude that this is simply a manifestation of God's design.

But human relations are never so simple. God's plan for authority implied in headship is a concept whose expression is difficult to understand unless it is seen from the perspective of the One who designed it. Paul's understanding of authority is right in line with that of Jesus: A man's leadership in his home is as that of a *shepherd*. It is not insisting on the final say but is a willingness to serve the members of his family, his flock, in a way that leads to their betterment and happiness. Jesus demonstrated this when He washed the disciples' feet.

The authority of a husband is expressed when he serves the needs of his wife. Misuse of leadership can be frightening and pits men against women, race against race, and social order against social order. Practiced in a fallen world, leadership is flawed, but it is still imperative that we try to make leadership what it was intended to be.

Most husbands and wives recognize the mutuality called for in the sexual relationship. A man who insensitively demands that his wife respond in a passionate way without any consideration of her physical and emotional needs discovers that she becomes less responsive. The resentment which she feels and the lack of physical input she finds pleasurable effectively dampens her ardor. On the other hand, the husband discovers that his own sexual enjoyment is enhanced when he helps meet his wife's needs so that she too enjoys the sexual experience and is responsive to him. Additionally, his sensitivity to her helps her feel more confident that "submitting" to him is safe and that she can risk it in other areas of her life. Those men and women who perceive authority only as obeying commands can learn much from the sexual relationship.

Authority in a military situation may work with little consideration of the individual, but it is destructive in personal relationships. A shepherd recognizes the vulnerability of his sheep. A sheep will not rest if it thinks it is in danger, if it is being bothered by pests, or if it is hungry. It needs its own space and plenty of water. If it finds itself in the position of being unable to right itself, it must be helped to do so. Being a good shepherd requires ultimate commitment to knowing the sheep and their needs. It requires exercising authority as Jesus did—through service.

God's kingdom is not a democracy. Headship and authority are clearly spoken of in contexts other than the husband/wife relationship. Leadership can be a source of order and meaning, but the exercise of leadership never involves exploitation.

When an impasse occurs between a couple, it can be a disquieting experience. If prayer, counsel, and study does not reveal a solution, James Hurley in his book *Man and Woman in Biblical Perspective* suggests the following prayer: Husband: "Not because I am inherently wiser or more righteous, nor because I am right (although I do believe I am or I would not stand firm), but because it is finally my responsibility before God, we will take the course which I believe right. If I am being sinfully stubborn, may God forgive me and give me the grace to yield to you."

Wife: "Not because I believe you are wiser in this matter (I don't) or more righteous, nor because I accept that you are right (because I don't or I would not oppose you), but because I am a servant of God who has called me to honor your headship, I willingly yield to your decision. If I am wrong, may God show me. If you are wrong, may He give you grace to acknowledge it and to change."

The purpose of headship is to provide direction within our homes in order that they may become the models of respect, love, and spiritual growth which they were intended to be. Power of this sort is not to be taken lightly or practiced without love. The authority which a husband holds over his wife is to be wielded with understanding, compassion, and genuine concern for her welfare and that of the family. It is a task which can be burdensome and which is rife with responsibility.

A man who loves his wife as himself does not mistreat her (Ephesians 5:28). God is quite aware of the misuse of power. His admonitions to the husband to imitate the Lord's willingness to love and care for the church—to the point of death—is a powerful metaphor. The husband is never ordered to force his wife to submit.

Submitting is a voluntary act on the woman's part and thus requires her active choice. She is to submit because she respects Christ and the order He has declared (Ephesians 5:21), not because the husband is superior, has all the answers, or has the highest-paying job. Submission is based on theology, not cultural vicissitudes.

Let's Make It Simple

A comparison of the various ideologies regarding women is shown in the following chart, which was inspired by the writing of Donald Bloesch in his book *Is the Bible Sexist?*

The biblical view of the sexual woman stands up well against systems of beliefs such as Patriarchism, Hedonism, Feminism, and Romanticism. Briefly, Patriarchism seeks to define headship as a dictatorial, autocratic system based on the natural superiority of men. Many critics accuse Christians of seeking to return to patriarchal views, and indeed some Christians misinterpret biblical commands in a very patriarchal light.

Contrary to the call of the alarmist, who suggests that Romanticism and Hedonism are new phenomena related to the degeneration of our time, these views have been around for ages. Romanticism relativizes romantic love. In other words, true love can be experienced only under certain conditions and is identified by a "feeling" of being in love. The excitement of the illicit affair, for example, would indicate to the Romantic that real love existed. A Hedonistic view sees marriage only as a means of regular sex. The TV message that says "If it feels good do it" is a good illustration of this ideology.

Finally, Feminism seeks to convince men and women that there are no significant differences between them and that women have no unique responsibility to men and children in determining how they live their lives.

Taking Responsibility

When a woman accepts herself as the person God intends her to be, she has not resigned herself to insignificance or sold herself out as indistinguishable from man. Her heritage as a female promises that she is to impact the world.

The fear, disrespect, and hostility toward men which so characterizes many women's lives is wrong on two counts. First, it is not reflective of the attitude of love and high regard which Christians are to have for one another. Second, it absolutely defeats the design defined in Genesis in which women are to be the helpmates suitable for man in the task of ordering the world.

A woman may or may not be a mother, but this should not affect her propensity to view life with a lifegiving vision. She may stay home and raise her children or run a major corporation, and she may be married or single. Whatever she does, she is a person of significance and worth because God made her so. Her gift of femininity has the potential to add richness and meaning to anyone whose life touches hers. In partnership with men, her fellow caretakers of the earth, she has a contribution to make.

Each woman has a responsibility to know who she is. Roles and worth have become so tragically intertwined that many women have found the task a difficult one. The starting place must be God's original aim. Don't rely on past understanding or what your mother or pastor has always told you. Go to the Bible and search the Scriptures. Read commentaries and supplementary materials of various persuasions, and make your foundation firm.

"Why do you call me 'Lord, Lord' and do not do what I say? I will show you what he is like who comes to me and hears my words and puts them into practice. He is like a [woman] building a house, who dug down deep and laid the foundation on rock. When a flood came, the torrent struck that house but could not shake it, because it was well built" (Luke 6:46-48).

IDEOLOGIES REGARDING WOMEN

Model	Personal View of Women	Relationship to Men	Salvation	Marriage	Church
Patriarchism	Brood mare	Property of man	By Childbearing	Necessity	Separates men and women; women have no authority
Hedonism	Playboy "Bunny"	Sex partner	By orgasm	Convenience	
Feminism	Self-sufficient career woman	Rival of man	By asserting independence	Contract to serve ambitions	Irrelevant; looks down on women taking traditional roles
Romanticism	Fairy princess	Object of men's dreams	Possessed by "knight"	Possibly a threat (if it interferes with true love)	
Bible	Partner in Ministry (and Christian mother)	Helpmate	By grace for a lifetime of service	Partnership to build kingdom	Partnership; common commitment to Christian community

Chapter Three

The Complete Woman by God's Design

Why have you made me like this?

—Romans 9:20 TLB

The silence of sleep is broken by the jangle of the phone. For the third time on this rainy night a new baby is ready to be born. Tired eyes are opened, clothes are grabbed, and the way down the dark stairs and to the car is somehow accomplished.

While driving to the hospital thoughts of becoming a dermatologist (who rarely have night calls) filter through my mind. Upon arrival at labor and delivery, sounds of panting, an occasional scream, and sometimes a few expletives fill the corridor. A brief examination reveals that delivery is imminent, and the patient, no longer the well-coiffed, well-rested, controlled lady seen countless times in the office, is moved to the delivery room.

And then the miracle occurs. What seemed so cruel, futile, and unbearable minutes before is already becoming a distant memory. As mother and father bask in the wonder of their newborn, I'm moved to reflect, even after 4000 deliveries, on the wonder of it all.

As for me, having a baby is well left to the female. I've frequently told my childbirth classes that if men were to have babies, the world would have zero population growth. I would request a pain-relieving anesthetic at the moment of the first false labor! But fortunately God knew what He was doing, and women are remarkably adapted to childbearing.

The woman's wider pelvis and her superior endurance make even the most difficult birth possible. Equally important is the phenomenon that, even though most women remember the labor and delivery as being laborious, they rarely recall how truly miserable it was.

God's remarkable design extends beyond birth into a man and woman's sexual life. Humankind is the only animal that makes love face-to-face. How important that is! Even the newborn locks onto his or her mother's facial expressions in order for bonding to occur. The desire for sex is not limited to estrus cycles as found in the animal kingdom. Sex in humans can occur when there is little possibility of conception. One must conclude that its significance for mankind lies outside the mere realm of procreation.

More Alike Than Different

While a resident at Stanford, I was introduced to one of the most attractive females I had ever seen, a tall, curvaceous blonde who appeared to be the picture of health. A medical workup (done to reveal the reason for her lack of menstruation) divulged that she had no uterus, tubes, or ovaries, but that she did have male gonads. Our female was a chromosomal male!

The importance of such rare occurrences is that they remind us that men and women are designed for interdependence even on the most basic physical level. Contrary to the male dominance found in society, on the biological level the female rules.

At conception the embryo is female. It is not until the seventh week that gonad (and thus sexual) differentiation occurs. If the "Y" chromosome of the male does not direct the increased production of male hormone, the "male" will fail to develop masculine traits. Such input is critical at several developmental stages, providing an explanation for the greater number of gender difficulties found in men.

Both sexes have estrogen and testosterone hormones. Females have a greater amount of estrogen, while in males testosterone predominates. The cells that become the scrotum in the male develop into the vulva in the female. The glans of the penis is equivalent to the clitoris. Some internal remnants of our shared inheritance are the Wolffian and Müllerian ducts. These ducts are of concern when the Wolffian fail to atrophy in the female causing cysts to develop which can lead to uncomfortable intercourse and other complications.

The Jewel in the Jade Temple

Rarely do women appreciate or understand the intricacy of design of the female anatomy. The lack of esteem in which women hold their genitalia is evident in their vocabulary. Many women refer to "down there" or studiously avoid any name at all. By contrast, the Chinese refer to the vagina variously as the Jade Gate or Jade Pavilion and the clitoris as the Pearl of the Jade Gate.

There is no standard of beauty for a woman's genitalia. There is as great a variety of shapes, sizes, and characteristics as there are combinations of facial features. To conclude that a person has "ugly" or "disgusting" genitals makes no sense. One must question why an area declared so repulsive is the object of such constant attention.

The external portion of the genitalia is collectively known as the vulva. In the past it was referred to as the pudendum, the "thing of shame." It includes the mons pubis (the mount of Venus), the major and minor labia (lips), the clitoris, and the vaginal opening. This area is directly and indirectly involved with reproduction, menstruation, and sexual activity. Its obvious function is protection of the sensitive internal organs.

Before childbirth the labia cover the vaginal opening; after childbirth they usually remain separated, revealing the opening. While the external lips have hair, the inner lips are hairless. The apex of the inner lips join to form the hood of the clitoris. The inner lips may extend beyond the outer labia, although they usually are not seen in women who have not had children. Both sets are sensitive to touch, and swell and darken during sexual arousal. Any woman or young girl who has ever slipped while riding a bicycle with a crossbar has known the pain of bruised labia. As a woman ages, the labia majora atrophy due to fat absorption.

Facts About What?

Adjacent to the vulva are two important areas: the perineum and the anus. The perineum is composed of muscle and fascia which support the pelvic floor (the anus and vagina). During childbirth it is sometimes necessary to make an incision in this area to provide more room for the birth. This incision is called an episiotomy.

The anus, the opening from the lower digestive tract, has no reproductive function. It may be affected during childbirth by tears and bruising. Sometimes it is a source of infections of the urinary or vaginal areas. There are nerve endings which can produce sensations during sex which some people find pleasurable. Anal intercourse does not damage the anal sphincter muscle, but inserting the penis directly from the rectum to the vagina can cause severe infections.

The Hidden Parts

During the Middle Ages the lords of the manor magnanimously volunteered to "deflower" young virgins before their marriage. The purpose was to protect the groom from evil spirits caused by tearing the hymen. Variations on such myths have persisted throughout time.

When dowries were important to marriage, proof of unused "goods" was vital. As a consequence many curious rituals prevailed. In Italy, bloodstained sheets were displayed outside the window of the marriage chamber. Even today in Morocco the bride's "bloomers" are paraded on a pillow in front of the wedding guests. In Japan such importance is placed on virginity that a procedure for restoring the hymen has been developed.

The assumption that an intact hymen is an accurate measure of virginity is not valid. Often the hymen is broken in young athletic women, sometimes without their knowledge. The hymen is a mucous membrane that has many configurations. It is located about one-half inch into the vagina and covers the opening. Few hymens lack an opening. Those that do are often diagnosed when menstruation begins and abdominal and pelvic pain occurs due to the retention of the menstrual products. The simple procedure for correcting this is called a hymenotomy.

Tampons can cause the hymen to stretch but not tear. The myth that young, virginal girls should never use tampons is not true. Remnants of the hymen can be mistaken for polyps or papillomas by women. A hymenal remnant sometimes causes difficulty when a vestige is pulled across the vagina as it expands with sexual arousal, resulting in painful intercourse.

Above the hymen is the urethral opening through which urine flows. Around this opening are the Skene's glands. They are noticeable only when they are infected. They have no known purpose. Below the hymen lie two Bartholin's glands. They too can become infected, forming large, painful abscesses which can be treated medically if recognized early enough or surgically by incision and drainage. There is some speculation that these glands produce a subtle odor that attracts the male, although their secretion has no function in the sex act.

A Source of Pleasure

Under the protective hood formed by the labia minora lies the clitoris. It has no function other than pleasure. On more than one occasion women have made appointments convinced they have a cancerous growth. Examination reveals that what they had determined to be a tumor was their clitoris. How tragic! Not only have they worried needlessly, but they were apparently unaware of a major source of their sexual pleasure. This is not surprising when one reflects on the way we teach children about their bodies. Our practice is to ignore the clitoris. The majority of women have never been taught that it exists. Such an obvious oversight suggests to the child that this appendage is "unmentionable" and therefore nasty or evil.

The clitoris is one-fourth to one inch in length and very sensitive. Like the penis, it has many nerve endings and vessels. In many women direct stimulation of the clitoris is not pleasurable. It is stimulated indirectly during intercourse by the pulling of the mons pubis above it. Many men who enjoy the direct manipulation of their penis have difficulty understanding the discomfort which such intense focus causes women.

At the height of arousal the clitoris retracts under its hood. This is a normal occurrence which nonetheless has brought some couples to sexual therapists convinced that something is wrong. A recent fad involved the surgical cutting or removing of the hood with the purpose of increasing sensation. Most medical organizations consider this procedure to be unnecessary and even harmful, and forbid its use by their membership. Occasionally small bands of tissue called adhesions form, fusing the hood to the clitoris. In rare instances release of the adhesions might be beneficial for improving sexual response.

A Collapsed Tube

The vagina functions as a reproductive, menstrual, and sexual organ. It is a collapsed tube that accommodates a penis or baby as required. It has three layers: muscular, connective tissue, and mucosal. Lubrication occurs directly through the vaginal wall. This "weeping" is the first sign of sexual arousal for the female. The mucosal layer becomes very thin and frail in menopausal women.

The vast majority of nerve endings are located in the lower one-third of the vagina. It appears that many women have clusters of nerve endings, most commonly on the anterior wall, that heighten sexual pleasure. These clusters are often referred as the "G" spot (from "Grafenberg"). For some women they provide the major source of sexual excitement, while for others they prove irritating or simply have no effect.

A Most Unusual Muscle

The uterus is another of God's miracles. It has a complex muscle pattern which includes muscle fibers in a figure-eight configuration. These are the fibers that contract around blood vessels after delivery to prevent hemorrhage. Unlike other muscles that relax and return to a precontraction state, this muscle never completely relaxes, resulting in a propulsion effect that continually moves the baby forward, dilating the cervix.

The uterus is shaped like a hollow inverted pear. The size may vary from quite small to the size of a closed fist. Most often it is tilted forward (anteverted), although it is a normal variation to be in a mid-position or even to tilt backward (retroverted). The blood, lymphatic, and nerve supply is abundant.

The uterus is divided into three sections: the fundus, the corpus, and the cervix. The fundus is the top section which contracts during labor and has the Fallopian tubes attached to it. The largest section is the corpus, which is the main body. This area is usually the implantation site of the fertilized ovum.

The cervix is the long, narrow end of the uterus which connects with the vagina. After childbirth a woman may become aware of the penis or tampon hitting and glancing off the cervix. This may cause some physical discomfort or bleeding after intercourse. If bleeding or pain becomes too troublesome there are ways to alleviate the problem.

The Fallopian tubes are funnel-shaped structures commonly referred to as "tubes" in reference to sterilization procedures, ectopic pregnancies, or infections. They are responsible for transferring the egg from ovary to uterus and are the usual site of fertilization. The fertilized ovum takes three to five days to enter the uterine cavity. Cilia provide a gentle waving motion that directs the egg through the tube, whose opening is no larger than the period at the end of this sentence.

The final portion of the female reproductive system is the almond-sized ovaries. They are held in the upper pelvic cavity by ligaments that attach to the sidewall. At birth the ovaries usually house 400,000 eggs. In addition to the eggs, they produce estrogen and progesterone.

The Most Obvious Part

Our son is 19 years old. He was born before the natural childbirth emphasis. Breast-feeding was considered unusual if not downright crazy for white, well-educated women. My wife's decision to breast-feed was a source of gossip to many people and repulsive to others. We were told by one of the medical school classmates that we would not be welcome at her home if she intended to nurse the baby there.

How sad that the purpose and function of the breast had become so perverted! It is good to see the emphasis on breast-feeding return. The baby benefits through being held closely and by natural antibodies found in mother's milk. The mother benefits by the stimulation of the uterine muscle to contract, decreasing the amount of blood loss.

Breasts can be highly sensitive to touch. During arousal the nipple will become erect. It is not unusual for nursing mothers to experience orgasm from the suckling action of their infants. Some studies suggest that nursing mothers are more anxious to return to sexual relations with their husbands than those who do not nurse. Breast-feeding women can experience less lubrication during sexual arousal because of hormone suppression.

The nipple is erectile tissue usually one-fourth to one-half inch long. There are 15 to 20 ducts opening on its surface through which milk is expelled. Surrounding the nipple is the section known as the areola. A small reservoir for milk storage exists under the areola. (This is why women have leakage between feedings.) This pigmented area can range from one to four inches in diameter. It contains small sebaceous glands (Montgomery glands) that give a bumpy appearance and secrete a fatty material that lubricates and protects the nipple during breast-feeding.

During pregnancy the areola becomes much darker. The usual color of the areola varies with the individual and from race to race. For example, in redheads or blondes the areola is pink, in brunettes generally dark brown, in Orientals dark rose, and in blacks darker than the surrounding skin.

Whether a woman breast-feeds or not, the breasts lose size after pregnancy. Creams and other means to prevent stretchmarks are futile, since their cause is related to loss of collagen and genetics. A good-fitting bra is helpful, although a woman must take the time to learn exactly how a bra is to fit.

Who's in Control Here?

The reproductive and sexual systems are controlled far from their sites: The master control areas are located in the brain. The reproductive functions are regulated by the pituitary gland, and the sexual functions have their ultimate origin within the hypothalamus.

Taking Responsibility

How much we take for granted! The order and creative design found elsewhere in God's world is nowhere better demonstrated than in the intricacy of the body. That so few people love, cherish, and care for it as the temple it was designed to be must be a great frustration for the Lord. Rarely do we hear a person affirm the gift of his or her body. Most of us spend our days bemoaning our aches, wrinkles, and fat.

The remarkable creature that is woman is so complex that medical science still lacks complete understanding of her functions. Biologically and socially she is perfectly matched for her partnership with man. No part of her design has escaped God's watchful presence.

"For [God] created [her] innermost being; [He] knit [her] together in [her] mother's womb. [We] praise you because [she] is fearfully and wonderfully made; your works are wonderful, [we] know that full well" (Psalm 139:13,14).

Chapter Four

The Complete Woman and the Single Passage

I have learned to be content whatever the circumstances.

—Philippians 4:11

In the Old Testament days everyone married. During World War I, 98 percent of all Americans were married. Being single is a relatively new phenomenon—and growing. Statistically there are now more single-headed households than the traditional man-and-woman-two-children type that make up the stereotype of the average American home.

Gone are the days when one married at 14 or 15 and died at 42. Although morality in the past was not always as chaste as we are sometimes led to believe, it is clear that the unmarried did not face the pressure to act on their sexuality everywhere they turned. Times have indeed changed, and adapting our lifestyles to the modern world has presented many new problems and questions.

Worrying About Tomorrow

God made men and women sexual creatures. If a woman is single or single again because of divorce or the death of her husband her sexual nature is not to be denied but lived out in a manner that honors God. No one is promised marriage or remarriage. If life is lived looking for someone to marry, the focus is wrong. A Christian's first priority is to love God with all his or her heart, soul, and mind (Matthew 22:37). What happens tomorrow and whether it includes marriage is not where energy need be directed. No one has to be reminded that there are plenty of things to worry about today (Matthew 6:33,34).

The hurry to marry is sometimes motivated in a person's imperative to feel "O.K." A proper self-image, however, can only be assured by the God who created us and gives our lives purpose. Some singles find that loneliness pushes them into a commitment which they are not emotionally ready to make. Loneliness does not kill, and is not the exclusive domain of the unmarried. Well-meaning friends and relatives may pressure for remarriage, but their motivation sometimes stems from their own misunderstandings about the single life.

But I'm Divorced

Amidst loneliness, exhaustion, and lowered self-esteem, it is indeed hard to view being single again as a gift (1 Corinthians 7:7). The decision to end a marriage is always painful, although the mourning may have taken place years before. Such singleness is nothing less than piercing surgery decided upon as a final stratagem.

Such a sharp incision is usually done in hopes of removing decay, deadness, and/or dishonesty so that healing, health, and happiness can proceed. Whether or not this actually happens depends greatly on an individual's attitude. If instead of leading to new beginnings, life is viewed as being on hold, the surgery will not cure but merely sustain life. Actually, many people view the results of such a drastic measure ambivalently, longing for the type of intimacy which marriage offers but experiencing relief over not being accountable to a spouse.

The reluctance to date or think of remarriage shortly after divorce is a protective device that should be heeded; movement toward remarriage should be a slow process. Studies indicate that it takes an average of two years before a person is in a healthy enough recovery phase to consider remarriage. This is not surprising, since divorce is mentioned second in a list of the most stressful life events—only the death of a spouse preempts it.

The willingness of pastors and others in leadership roles to prepare the recently divorced for life as a single-again can help to facilitate a righteous and peaceful lifestyle. There are no easy answers on how to live as a single, but the process is aided by open discussion and teaching. The opportunity to be heard makes one feel less alone. In addition to the support in living a Christian lifestyle, other practical considerations, such as temporary relief from parenting and inclusion in activities, can be important outreaches to single-agains.

All too often pastoral counseling is available only after the single-again has struggled unsuccessfully to live without the genital sexuality that he or she has become accustomed to. By then guilt compounds the problem. Support groups are helpful because other people in the same situation share the burden and can help forestall behavior that provides a momentary but improper solution to a problem that must be faced daily.

Balancing Friendships

All people are sexual. All enjoy the nurturing touch of others. The book of Genesis declares that the yearning for relatedness with the opposite sex is "good." Until there were two sexes man was "not good" in his aloneness. Being single does not preclude the need to relate as a male or female simply because one does not have a specific mate. The most prominent part of our personality is our maleness or our femaleness; it is through this reflection of our personality that we communicate.

All people desire intimacy. We are people of relationship because our God is a God of relationship and we are created in His image. Intimacy takes time and thrives with an undergirding of commitment. Society, however, believes that intimacy is brought about, supported, and defined by genital sexuality. Such a message results in confusion and places a stumbling block in the pathway of fulfilling friendships between men and women.

More than ever before, men and women are allowed the freedom of association. Any friendship that involves a degree of intimacy must deal with its sexual component. Most of the time this is an unconscious process that acknowledges, "I'm a woman and you're a man, and we could allow this to become a sexual relationship. In order to insure that this does not happen, this is how I intend to handle myself and my feelings." Sometimes this needs to be brought into the open. Occasionally it is appropriate to discuss and diffuse feelings directly with the person. Sometimes it is best to make oneself accountable to a trusted friend.

Saying no to unhealthy and unrighteous sexual involvements takes effort, a conscious decision, and honesty. No one ever becomes involved with another person "out of the blue"; the decision results from a series of small "yesses" that finally culminates in one big YES. Evil desires, as James so aptly points out (1:13-15), begin in our hearts—not from the devil or as an adverse test from God.

Our male/female friendships will glorify the Lord when the agenda includes uplifting and loving our friend before our own selfish desires, moving (as in marriage) from "What's in this for me?" to "How can I serve this person?"

Sometimes maintaining friendships requires getting our feelings under control and accepting the fact that certain aspects of our lifestyle and thought processes need changing. For example, if time is spent daydreaming about an "off-limits" friend or an "in-limits" one in the wrong way, thought-stopping can be used to "renew the mind." An individual may need to reevaluate the types of books she is reading, movies she is attending, or activities she is participating in with her friend. Just as hanging around a bar is not wise for the alcoholic, hanging around certain people and activities is not wise for anyone trying to stay away from harmful behaviors.

Celibacy As a Choice

Deciding not to remarry because of fear of establishing a relationship with the opposite sex is not acceptable behavior, though celibacy is a viable option if it is chosen for the right reasons.

Most people have gone on a diet only to come crashing off it by eating the most forbidden nondiet item they could get their hands on! Remember the movie your parents forbade you to see? You spent the night at your friend's house and saw it anyway. Feelings of deprivation frequently result in an obsessive pursuit of the very things we should be avoiding.

Sexuality is no different. When our unmarried condition requires that we abstain, this is easily looked upon as deprivation, and our desire for sex can become all-consuming. More help needs to be given by churches and pastors to singles so that they can discern the reason for their celibacy. Understanding the purpose of their celibacy gives meaning to their decision to refuse genital sexuality. When the absence of sex is viewed as meaningless and a source of deprivation, there appears to be no logical reason to say no. This makes the resolve to do so very tough.

"If God's purpose for us is good, why is remaining celibate so hard?" God indeed acts in us for good (Philippians 2:13). Remaining celibate is not a perverse test. A person will not be harmed physically or mentally by the decision to remain celibate. In contrast, the self-discipline which celibacy requires has many positive aspects. It enables a person to focus on other than self-centered needs. Righteousness and rewards are a promise of both the future and now. Much is gained psychologically and spiritually when it is clear that the individual is ruling the sexual life rather than the sexual life ruling him or her.

The impact of taking the "easy" way results in physical pleasure, but in many other pains as well. The most fulfilling sex is found in healthy marriages. Diseases affecting our life, future fertility, and health are no longer something that "other" people get. Emotionally, a woman can be devastated when she discovers a discrepancy between her investment in a relationship and her lover's. Feelings of being unworthy, empty, and even used do not help the single or single-again cope with the many pressures already on her. In addition, no one can sin and be honest about it without feeling separated from God.

God expects singles and singles-again to admit to and control their sexuality. Yet the vast majority choose not to do so because it is the difficult thing to do. In Philippians 4:11 Paul reminds us that he learned to be content in whatever circumstance he found himself. The first step in control is learning to be content with the gift of singleness, knowing that it is for a good, God-given purpose. The alternative is a half-life and deprivation.

Colleen has to be careful of situations she finds herself in. As a teenager she mislearned that touch equals sex, and has spent a lifetime reinforcing this skewed message by nurturing the arousal felt when someone hugs or caresses her. Her Christian walk has become the primary focus of her life, so Colleen has found that staying out of intimate one-on-one situations is an absolute priority for her. She prefers group dates and activities and is careful about the movies she goes to and books she reads. Her high sexual tension is kept in tow by occasional masturbation.

Vicki has little problem controlling her sexual feelings. Her life is filled with activity and friends. Being in an intimate setting with close friends of the opposite sex is nurturing and important to her. She is able to handle such physical and emotional closeness easily and righteously.

Colleen and Vicki are typical of the variety found in people in regard to their need for sexual expression. Just as a person has been blessed with a nose and eyes unique to herself, the biological sexual drive is also specific. However, learning has a powerful influence on the way a person handles his or her natural drives.

Such drives are easily sidetracked. A four-year-old appearing at the door at the height of sexual arousal quickly dampens ardor. A person can be starving only to be distracted by a phone call from an old friend and forget about eating. Preoccupation with other events, activities, and mindsets helps keep our feelings of arousal on the back burner. Psychologists call this "sublimation." We can find the concept of focusing on new thoughts in order to change the direction of life in the concept of "renewing of the mind" (Romans 12:2).

Sublimation is a legitimate and healthy way to help keep sexual arousal under control. By contrast, repression, the denial of sexual feelings, is a poor choice.

Linda loved the Lord, and her life seemed as if it couldn't get better. Her new job was challenging and fun, and her boss was a wonderful man. His encouragement motivated her to work hard and produce superior work.

It was necessary for Linda to accompany him on an out-of-town job. They were elated when their business went well, and Linda was singled out for accolades. That night Linda did not return to her room. She and her married boss had sexual intercourse.

No one could have been more shocked, ashamed, and disgusted with herself than Linda. Linda's denial of the mounting feelings she was experiencing made her vulnerable to the emotions and opportunity of this otherwise outstanding day. She was overwhelmed with the intensity of her emotional and sexual feelings. Because she had no plan of action, she simply went along.

Honesty and awareness of feelings enables a person to face and control these feelings. Acknowledging strong sexual and emotional feelings does not mean that they must be acted upon; the option exists to defuse them. The Lord's sacrifice insured freedom from having to sin: "For sin shall not be your master, because you are not under law, but under grace" (Romans 6:14). Linda needed Colleen's sensitivity to her personal arousal system and her confidence that sexual feelings could be controlled.

Knowing one's vulnerabilities and drawing arbitrary lines of behavior does not totally address the problem, however. Jesus was always concerned with the heart motivation. Remember the guidelines from 1 Thessalonians chapter 4? God wants us to remain pure, setting our standards by Him and not the world. Singles and singles-again must ask themselves if their behavior is the loving thing to do. Is the relationship one of equals? Are they more interested in physical satisfaction, discovering who they are, or proving their sex appeal than they are in what is right for a partner, family, or God? Are they realistic, or are they functioning on a fantasy model of the way they would like things to be? Are they using sex as a salve for the pain and sorrow in their lives?

Keeping a Standard

Maintaining a standard of purity for singles begins by taking God at His Word and trusting that His plan for their lives is good. This helps them view the lack of genital sexuality as having purpose and reason, enabling singles to see their state as other than one of deprivation. (No one gets everything she wants.) There is a commitment to convictions that have been clearly thought through and are biblically supported. Goals are set, work done attentively, and solid friendships shared. By understanding their nature, singles can be sensitive to what they must avoid. As with the alcoholic, maintenance of sexual purity must be accomplished one day at a time. If such a plan of action seems impossible, singles and singles-again need to remember that God is on their side!

A trusted friend or counselor can help keep a person accountable, but ultimately it is God who will be there: "He will not let you be tempted beyond what you can bear. But when you are tempted, he will also provide a way out so that you can stand up under it" (1 Corinthians 10:13).

And what if they fail? Jesus' sacrifice was made not because people are so wonderful but because they are sinners. As the Master Surgeon, Jesus cuts sin away, leaving no malevolent cells to fester again. A scar may remain, but healing is complete.

Taking Responsibility

Singles or singles-again, like married Christians, can search for self-worth outside of the only consistent and dependable source—our Lord Jesus Christ—or they can acknowledge that their value is in relationship with Him. Their status is in no way diminished by not being married. It is *society* that suggests such ideas, not Scripture.

Living a righteous and complete life is within the grasp of the single person who accepts the fact that God is in charge and who refuses to succumb to a spirit of deprivation.

Being single in a sex-saturated society is not easy. When resolve fails, our Lord is there with open arms for any who take responsibility for their actions and resolve to begin anew, refreshed and clean.

"Put your hope in the Lord, for with the Lord is unfailing love and with him is full redemption" (Psalm 130:7).

Chapter Five

The Complete Woman and the Reproductive Years

Many are the plans in a . . . heart, but it is the Lord's purpose that prevails.

—Proverbs 19:21

We are an enlightened society. We've seen the surface of Jupiter, we've watched the miracle of conception in test tubes, and we're mastering the language of the computer. Yet an appalling number of people lack understanding of even the most elementary processes of the body and its accompanying sociological and psychological adaptations. The next three chapters define stages of a woman's development: the reproductive years, adolescence, and maturity.

These stages will be examined from three perspectives: the social, the physical, and the sexual. The social perspective encompasses a wide variety of material. For example, the major psychological tasks that must be accomplished in order for a woman to reach maturity will be discussed as they affect her adjustment to her role in society. The overriding external factors that shape and influence her life in each developmental stage will also be pointed out.

The social factors are greatly affected by physical changes that are unique to each stage of development. During the reproductive years the body may be called on to adjust to pregnancy and nursing. In adolescence menstrual cycles are begun and a female's childlike frame must make the necessary adaptations to prepare it for the possibility of childbirth. The years of maturity introduce physical changes that poignantly affect the individual woman's view of her role in society and the family.

During each developmental stage a woman's understanding of her sexual nature makes new and significant adjustments necessary. The meaning and effect which her sexual nature has on the way she lives her life is profound. Her femininity and how she views it is the most pervading aspect of her personality.

The Reproductive Years

The time between the onset and the ending of the menstrual periods is likely to be the busiest and most active of a woman's life. They are years filled with great changes and challenge. Joy and sadness are sprinkled together like sweet and pungent spices, the particular combination giving to each life an aroma and flavor unique to the bearer.

Our modern lady has more options than women have ever had. If choices were the root of happiness, women in their reproductive years living at this time in history should be in their zenith. Instead, many are overwhelmed. Besides leading to confusion over a new place in society, having access to a man's world has opened the door to men's diseases and emotional problems.

Depression over limited options has been replaced by pressure to get more accomplished in the multiple roles of wife, mother, worker, and volunteer. Stress and its manifestations keep doctors as well as entrepreneurs busy. Stress has been called "the disease of the eighties." Although it can reveal itself through outright anxiety, stress more often masks itself behind other symptoms or escalates existing problems.

When I had a full-time therapy practice, I also had a chronic backache. An aching back had plagued me off and on since age 15, when spondylolisthesis was diagnosed. I began to keep track of when my back felt worse. There was a pattern, and it didn't take long for me to connect my worst pain with those days on which I saw my most "difficult" clients. Something is wrong with therapy when the therapist works harder than the client! My tendency to take responsibility for making the therapy work, and the helplessness I felt with certain people when it didn't, left me physically immobilized!

The relationship between stress, illness, and accidents is shown numerically in charts like the Holmes-Rahe Stress Test. If you have had a high stress trauma occur in your life (divorce, for example), your chance of becoming seriously ill within the next year or two increases by one-third. Clearly, our new lifestyle is taking its toll.

The changing roles of women have resulted in changing habits. Increased smoking by women led to the lung cancer rate in 1985 surpassing breast cancer as the number one cause of cancer death among women, despite leveling off for black men and dropping among white men. Heart attacks and other vascular diseases have increased among females. (There is a definite link between smoking and arteriosclerosis.) Alcoholism among women has increased considerably.

While no one wants to return to the days when women were denied their full personhood, learning to be God's woman in these transition times is far from easy. Women who work outside the home find that such work, no matter how fulfilling it may be, is also rife with hassles. While in the past females returned to the work force after their child entered school, today many women find themselves returning to work shortly after delivery of the child. They must solve the incredible logistics required for day care, household responsibilities, jobs, and marriage. The sheer magnitude of the operation leaves many of them overwhelmed and depressed.

Yet many of their sisters who exercise their option to stay home are not much better off either. Their choice to affirm the value of their children is not supported by society, while at the same time they may elevate their job of mothering to the point that they alone can do it. You see them in church, at the movies, and in meetings struggling to make an uncomfortable infant unnaturally quiet while they attempt to carry on life as usual, Supermom style. With no support system and no break from the constant demands of their infants, they (like their "working" counterparts) are overwhelmed and depressed.

Complaints of boredom and depression despite "having it all" are the most frequently heard problems in my husband's obstetrician and gynecological practice. A woman in the reproductive years is more vulnerable to depression, especially after childbirth, than at any other time in her life. Most nervous breakdowns occur before 45. This puts a new perspective on our commonly held misconception that menopause is the time of life most prone to emotional upheaval.

Social Factors

Let's examine those factors and pressures that mold the lives of women within the span of years that are known as the "childbearing years." Although the ability to bear children is a focusing point, there are many questions and much decision-making for each woman regardless of whether she has children.

Christian women have an additional set of concerns not experienced with the same intensity by other women: "How can I balance God's plan for me to properly run my household and also spend eight hours a day out of the home?" "I earn more than my husband; should I give up my salary to insure his headship?" "How does a Christian woman handle male friendships?" "What do I do with sexual feelings now that I'm divorced?"

While the adolescent finds herself in an accelerated time of preparation in order to acquire a sense of self and competence as a social person, and the woman of menopause is expanding the competence she has acquired, the years of young adulthood revolve around changes that result in attaining an occupational skill, an established personality, and an outlook on life. The woman of reproductive age is organized and motivated by a vision that is hers alone. Education, marriage, jobs, and relationships are planned around making the vision a reality. For example, a woman whose dream is to be a lawyer spends the greatest amount of her time pursuing educational goals, and she may avoid emotional entanglements that interfere with her overall quest.

A woman of this age is concerned with the impact she makes as well as with attaining external and material goals. Learning to be intimate (versus isolating self) is a major developmental task for her. The question "Who am I?" would normally have been uncovered in adolescence, but sharing "who I am" with another person in an open, supportive relationship is the goal of continuing healthy maturation.

An important element in being able to share ourselves is being secure in who we are. Mature people move on and reach a new level of development by being able to consider and meet the needs of others.

A woman who doesn't make this transition becomes locked into herself. Failure to see beyond personal needs and desires prevents experiences of caring and trust that lead to intimacy. A woman who fails to move beyond self-absorption may seem to function satisfactorily in a practical way, but many needs remain unfulfilled.

As the end of the reproductive years approaches, changes become more subtle. Sometimes there is a relearning that takes place, often due to experience. This may be accompanied by a questioning of the goals she originally set, before a final settling-in occurs. The older the woman becomes, the more involved in roles of parent, job-holder, and citizen she is, and the less likely she is to plunge headlong into a new venture. Security begins to win out over challenge.

Developmental changes occur over a lifespan. They are predictable and fall in sequence. Two-year-olds are not the only ones who go through a "stage." This is important to know when a woman hits those natural times of uncertainty and begins to question her life choices. A proper perspective can be maintained if we understand that part of our unrest is a natural phenomenon of development, and will pass.

Making the Right Choices

"Whatever you do, work at it with all your heart, as working for the Lord, not for men . . ." (Colossians 3:23). It is so easy in our land-of-many-options to forget that whatever we do, it is to be for the Lord's pleasure. We agonize that God's will and ours might not coincide and at the same time ignore the serious plight of conducting our lives as if compartmentalized areas of it do not fall under His jurisdiction.

The busy woman of Proverbs 31 illustrates on a practical level the types of work a woman may rightfully involve herself in. This feminine ideal was into merchandising, manufacturing, administration, farming, real estate, the garment industry, teaching, and philanthropy—as well as her jobs of mothering and being a good wife. What is left out? Very little.

Was her husband threatened by all this? No, he was proud of her. She had the right attitude: Work was not for the personal power, wealth, and prestige it gave, but was a way to serve her family, community, and Lord.

Although we like to think that our assignment of roles to one sex or the other is theologically based, in truth most of the time we associate certain jobs with men or women because that is what we have always done. A Christian woman's role is determined not by her womanness but by her faith.

Asking if there is anything she can't do is the wrong question. It is her motivation, her sense of responsibility to others, and the balance she maintains that determines if she is in the Lord's will. Women have been freed to be fellow workers in the kingdom; they have not been liberated for a life of autonomy and independence.

Freedom to serve one another also gives us the right to select the balance in life that has been uniquely prepared for us. Not all women have the physical stamina to keep up with the Proverbs 31 prototype!

We have been uniquely made by God to serve according to our gifts and skills. The emphasis is not on fitting a stereotype but on what we do with what we have been given. Matthew 25:14-30 refers to "talents" given and God's displeasure when they are not used wisely. Luke 12:48 speaks to the fact that those blessed with talents and skills have much expected of them.

Being Who We Were Meant to Be

God has not made us for depression, overwork, and unhappiness; yet far too many women live lives characterized by these traits. The capacity for achievement and creativity is meant to bring light into the world, our homes, and our own lives. We can only be what we were intended to be when our personal desires and needs are in balance with those whose lives are intertwined with ours.

This is hard to achieve, for balancing our families with career goals for ourselves and our husbands requires great clarity of purpose. We need to remember that status with God outweighs the fleeting acknowledgment of a boss, community, or job. Proper balance is not simply accepting the role of "Mom" begrudgingly, but with all the creativity and enthusiasm that we can muster. It is placing our talents and propensities at the feet of the Lord to use as He desires. It is keeping in mind that our lives are detailed with seasons, each to be lived in the fullness of our abilities.

The seasons of life are short. It may not feel that way when small children make a private trip to the bathroom impossible, but ask any mother of an 18-year-old, and she will tell you that it seems like only yesterday that she was introducing carrots to a balking one-year-old! Each season is characterized by its own learning, joys, and pains.

Adulthood is not reaching a plateau on which we stay until life on this earth ends. If you are the same person you were five years ago, you have prematurely died! Life is a continually unfolding series of opportunities. The challenge of new experiences enables us to reach into our character to utilize all those talents with which we have been gifted.

We needn't buy the world's message that our full potential must be met by a particular year or else all is lost. Solomon's wisdom reminds us that there is a season for everything. Each slice of life builds upon the past and prepares us for what is to come. No experience is wasted—good, bad, or indifferent. Hindsight enables us to see that even in the wrong turns "God works for the good of those who love him, who have been called according to his purpose" (Romans 8:28). Our faithfulness to strive for contentment and to live with a joy and appreciation of the life we have been blessed with is a measure of our belief that the Lord is in control.

Be Your Own Person

There is a tendency in the Christian community to focus more on idealized Christian images than to affirm the creative hand of God in making individuals. The result of trying to live a stereotype is anxiety and depression. It is selling short who and what we could be.

But suggesting that our sexual woman be her own person does not mean that I am advocating a "do-your-own-thing" attitude, which is both unbiblical and irresponsible. Discovering the woman that God intends her to be is not an easy task for the very reason that it isn't a stereotype. Instead, it takes realistic appraisal of talents and propensities. It requires a clear understanding of responsibilities as outlined in the Bible. It means willingly submitting to a life of interdependence with other people. It requires acknowledgment and acceptance of the individual that she is now, along with a vision of who she can become. It is acknowledging that she is a person of worth because she is God's person.

Many families have celebrated Mom's completion of school (or some new self-improvement venture or business) with a diploma and a divorce. Yet the desire to improve or be stimulated is not the problem; the problem is striving to get ahead by worldly wisdom instead of by continually asking for God's method and timing. Paths chosen with worldly wisdom are shortsighted and usually self-centered.

It is not the desire to live life in its fullness that causes difficulties, since God wants that for us (John 10:10). The problem develops when we depend on our own power to provide the fullness. Not living up to the potential within God's plan for us affects our ability to establish relationships, to parent capably, and to express ourselves in the most intimate of communications—the sexual relationship.

Christ-Confidence Versus Self-Confidence

Let's take a look at four women's lives who failed to live up to the potential of God's individual plan for them. Each ignored who they were in Christ and instead allowed themselves to think less of themselves than they should have. Their decision resulted in living sexual lives that did not please either God or themselves. But sex was not the real issue. Each one sought worth through some aspect of achievement, money, power, or other commonly defined means of "success." They failed to grasp they were persons of worth because God loved them, forgave them, and provided meaning and acceptance in their lives through their relationship with Him.

Janine came to marriage counseling reluctantly. Her husband, John, was at the end of his tolerance, since Janine had admitted to her third extramarital affair. Both professed to love each other, and their relationship was basically good. Janine, however, found herself inexplicably involved with other men. She always felt terrible about it, but it seemed that she was the original model for the song "I'm Just a Girl Who Can't Say No!"

Yvonne had been married three years. Bill was a loving husband and sensitive lover, but Yvonne was unable to enjoy their lovemaking. The more she tried, the worse things seemed to get.

Mary was single, pretty, and slightly overweight. Mary had been engaged to a man who had married her best friend a month before they were to marry. Her confidence in herself had plummeted. Lately her dating behavior involved "falling in love," then a torrid affair (which somehow always came unraveled), then deep depression.

Betty felt privileged to be able to stay home with her two young children. Her prestigious job had been given up with little reluctance. But lately she found herself moping around the house and fantasizing more and more about the days when she was a high-powered career woman. Her interest in sex was nonexistent.

Depending on the world (self-confidence) as the source of their esteem and ignoring who they were in Christ (Christ-confidence) was at the heart of the problematic sexual behavior which each of these women faced. Janine had been abused by a tyrant of a father who was only affirming of her when she surrendered to his sexual demands. His complete dominance of her and her mother had resulted in a "victim mentality." She felt helpless to resist the demands of any strong man. The payoff came when her submission resulted in their treating her in a way that enabled her to feel powerful and in control.

Yvonne's family had immigrated to the United States when she was a baby. Thanks to the continual hard work of both her parents, they had become materially well-off. Yvonne was highly praised for her diligence in school and her musical ability. Except for Christmas day, she couldn't remember the family ever closing their small restaurant and taking a day off for pleasure.

Yvonne's achievements had been highly reinforced by her doting family. That a person could feel good about oneself when not working had never been suggested or demonstrated. The conflict between pleasure and work (and her belief that her self-worth depended on what she accomplished) made elusive the release which was necessary for sexual pleasure.

Mary was trying the world's solution for a damaged ego: "I'll be

all right if someone loves me." She could not have chosen a less rewarding path. No two people enter an affair with the same intentions.
Seeking to be O.K. through another person's affirmation becomes a
major gamble.

There are thousands of Bettys. They want to be good mothers and
wives, but the "tyranny of the urgent" makes them lose perspective
and become fatigued. Creativity and a sense of purpose are lost in the
demands of diapers, doctor's appointments, and three different break-
fasts daily. They become depressed and convinced that they will never
desire sex again. Their lives are out of balance—including their relationship with the Lord.

God Cares During the Trials

Responding sexually is inescapably tied to how a person feels
about himself or herself. Sometimes a poor self-concept was obtained
in childhood, and it might be essential to explore those contingencies
with an objective pastor or counselor. This is certainly true in the case
of abuse. Healing is most likely to occur when an abused person is able
to reexplore the abuse with a sense of protection, love, and caring.

Reactions to abuse are many and varied. Often they seem far
removed from the event. Frequently drug abuse and promiscuous behavior (sometimes including prostitution) appear in adolescents who
have been sexually abused. Depression and depressive symptoms (such
as feelings of guilt, self-blame, and suicidal thoughts or attempts) are
common in all ages. Difficulties with sexual functioning frequently
occur and may take many forms, from mild dysfunctions to severe
phobias. Lack of trust makes establishing or maintaining relationships
difficult for victims of abuse. A variety of other symptoms, from backache to migraines, completes the picture.

Incest or molestation outside the family has an indelible influence
on men and women alike. The long-term effects are only now beginning
to be understood. Sex in the wrong setting is frequently hidden in
complex webs that become untangled when victims determine to become survivors. Such a monumental task requires God's supernatural
touch for true healing to occur.

Statistically, sexual abuse occurs most often in eight- to 12-year
olds. Eighty-five percent of the time it involves someone the child
knows, most often a father or stepfather. Seventy-five percent of the
time the mother does nothing to stop the abuse. The vast majority of

parents will deny that abuse took place even after verifiable proof and therapy. The shame and disruption to the family system act as powerful reinforcers in parents' refusal to come to terms with the problem.

A child-abusing father is generally moralistic and rigid. It is unlikely that he would be involved in extramarital affairs or other perversions. He could be seen as a pillar of the neighborhood.

Sexual abuse has always been with us, although today there is much greater willingness to face it. There is no segment of our society that escapes its touch, including those of the Christian community. The number one reaction of the victim is self-blame. Getting well necessitates understanding that the victim is not at fault, even if there was a willingness or if pleasure resulted. The Bible is clear in stating that no one is to take advantage of another person sexually (1 Thessalonians 4:6).

There is little likelihood of recovery without help, and almost no likelihood at all if there is a refusal to face the truth. (Blocking the incident out of the mind is a very common coping device.) If unexplained behaviors or physical problems are observed, exploration of the possibility of abuse might well be in order. Estimates of sexual abuse of women run as high as 20 percent.

Sexual abuse is dramatic and no one has difficulty seeing how such an experience could take one's eyes off Christ and result in failure to live life joyously in all areas, especially the sexual.

It is easy for women whose lives have not included such trauma to lull themselves into a feeling of false security. The truth is, less severe influences can profoundly affect the quest to be God's person.

I'm Too Fat!

A woman's body image can be poor even if she has a fine physique. Nicknames and periods of overweight or underweight sometimes leave an indelible self-image that often does not match reality.

Besides our petitions to the Lord for a realistic picture of who we are, it is clearly biblical to use affirmations to change our perceptions. We are told in Romans 12 to become God's person by "renewing our minds." Transforming our lives begins very practically with a new way of thinking. We can use daily repetitions such as "God wants me to see myself as I am; I am a fine weight for my height and size."

If negative thinking threatens to undo positive affirmations, a pro-

58

cess called "thought-stopping" is highly effective if used consistently. Thought-stopping is not used to deny sin but to break negative habits of thought. The moment a demeaning thought comes into your conscious mind, pinch your wrist, snap a rubber band you have placed there, or verbally or mentally shout "Stop!" Substitute a *preplanned* positive affirmation. You may be most comfortable using Scripture. For example, God chose me (Ephesians 1:4). I am perfectly loved (1 John 4:18). The God of the universe is always with me (Joshua 1:5). Consistent use of this technique for as little as two weeks can have dramatic results in ridding a person of recurring negative thoughts.

Often a young woman will have weight problems beginning with pregnancy. There is a myth that since the woman is eating for two, she no longer has to watch what she eats. Many a young woman who takes this route regrets it later. The health concerns involved in limiting weight gain in pregnancy to 20 or 25 pounds is also wise psychologically. The addition of extra pounds with each pregnancy causes such negative feelings that a vicious cycle is set up. The woman becomes depressed over her weight and eats more, finds herself pregnant again, and repeats the cycle.

No one need strive to look like a fashion model, but staying within a reasonable weight is essential for good health and a positive mental outlook. Dieting does not provide the whole answer, however. Almost all diets work if you stick to them. The problem is not so much in *taking* weight off but in *keeping* it off. To avoid the yo-yo syndrome of losing and gaining repeatedly, most people need to alter the way they eat and exercise.

Our American diet is too rich in fats and added sugars. Although it has twice the amount of protein needed, it is deficient in fiber-rich carbohydrates, fruits, and vegetables. Most of us have been taught that starchy foods (carbohydrates) are to be avoided because they are fattening and not especially nutritious. This is simply not true. Our "lean" substitutes (steak, for example) can have up to 80 percent of their calories from fat!

With the exception of soybeans, plant foods must be combined with small amounts of animal protein (or some other plant that supplements the missing amino acids) in order to provide a complete protein. A rule of thumb for this would be consuming a legume (dried beans or peas or peanuts) with a grain (wheat, oats, rice, rye, barley, millet, buckwheat, etc.). In other words, those peanut butter sandwiches you never allow yourself anymore would make a healthful lunch!

There are health and weight advantages to eating smaller meals six times a day: Nutrients are absorbed better, blood sugar is more stable, appetite is kept under control, and stress is tolerated better.

I would guess that few best-selling diet books give such advice! Neither do they report that thin people often eat more than overweight people. Two factors are at work that makes this true. Low-calorie diets can lower the metabolic rate (the rate at which you burn food). Your body automatically protects itself from starvation by lowering this rate. Thinner people often exercise more, which speeds up their metabolism not only while they are exercising but also up to 15 hours afterward. As fat is replaced by lean muscle, there is a permanent increase in metabolism. The more efficiently you burn calories, the more your weight stays under control.

Exercise has the additional bonus of releasing a chemical (beta-endorphin) that is a natural tranquilizer. Regular exercise enables a person to endure stress better and to increase stamina so that work can be done longer and more efficiently.

Other proven weight control methods include drinking six to eight glasses of water daily (one glass before and after each meal). Contrary to what most people think, this does not cause swelling—excess salt and sugar do. A weight-reduction diet that is low in fat and rich in starches, vegetables, and fruits enables a person to eat more food and still limit calories. This type of diet also blocks the craving for sweets which builds up with high-protein, low-carbohydrate diets due to the drop of serotonin (a chemical found in the brain whose action is like that of adrenaline).

A moderate plan that an individual can live with is the key to controlling weight. No quick fix will work permanently. A mindset that includes an image of oneself at an appropriate weight, daily exercise, three meals a day (prepared with the above guidelines), and healthy snacks (if desired) cannot be improved upon even if your favorite movie star did write a book on dieting!

Physical Factors

The reproductive years are relatively peaceful when compared to puberty or menopause. The greatest physical upheaval occurs with pregnancy, yet God's plan is clearly demonstrated by a woman's marvelously adapted design. Much of this book is devoted to the cares and concerns of women in this stage of their life, and little more need be said here.

Sexual Factors

Usually it is within the reproductive years of a woman's life that she marries. The rich, enjoyable sexual sharing described in Song of Solomon did not happen overnight and did not always go smoothly. The man and woman had to put time and energy into making it happen.

But sex is natural, people say. However, this doesn't mean that a woman need not take responsibility to learn. How and when a person is to be sexual, the meaning which sex has to the rest of a woman's life, how to please a partner—all of these come about as a result of having been taught. In the first two categories the church and our families are responsible for providing education. In the third category it is the spouse who must clarify his or her needs. Healthy and gratifying sexual functioning involves seeing that our needs are met and extending ourselves to match the desires of our spouse. The only "natural" part of sex is the inborn ability to experience sexual arousal; the rest is up to us.

Many people object to taking responsibility and learning about sex for fear that the "mystery" will be lost. This certainly happens in pornography, where the sex act is reduced to only one of its many facets. Sex is greater than its parts; it is more than sharing genitals. This is illustrated the first time someone makes love. An individual may be trivialized by the setting or discover something profound, but the moment is never forgotten and may color future sexual encounters for years to come.

I worry when I hear well-meaning people suggest that we should not provide sex education with both sexes present because of the need to perpetuate the "mystery." Women, they say, are to be viewed as having a "special something" that, as long as it is kept hidden, will keep a man intrigued. There is no biblical basis for this.

The mutual sexual relationship called for in the Bible will not be achieved by women keeping their sexual feelings and desires hidden from men. Such thinking merely perpetuates the myth that men are supposed to possess a magical incantation that unlocks the secret of a woman's sexuality. Nothing could be further from the truth. Good sex

happens when both partners take responsibility to make it happen—
and that is biblical.

Our Song of Solomon couple insured their sexual desire by thinking of each other in sensuous, erotic ways. They verbalized what they
wanted; neither played "Twenty Questions" in their sexual advances.
All the following are attributed to the woman: "Let my lover come into
his garden and taste its choice fruits" (Song 4:16). One could hardly
label that communication coy! "Let us go early to the vineyards. . .
there I will give you my love. The mandrakes send out their fragrance,
and at our door is every delicacy, both new and old, that I have stored
up for you, my lover" (Song 7:12,13). Do you think there is much
chance that the man might misunderstand and think she wanted to go
bowling? "Let him kiss me with the kisses of his mouth—for your love
is more delightful than wine. Pleasing is the fragrance of your perfumes;
your name is like perfume poured out. . . . Take me away with you—
let us hurry!" (Song 1:2-4). I doubt very much if his reply would have
been, "Five minutes—I've almost got the chariot wheel oiled." Are
your invitations to your spouse as clear? Have you even asked?

Chances are that you rarely initiate sex (most women today are
uncomfortable in this role). Yet our biblical model didn't seem to be
reluctant to do so. Perhaps she understood that the initiator has a head
start, and that women need this advantage. Or is it possible that the
coded messages you send out may not be as clear to him as they are
to you? Could he have overlooked the fact that you put on an extra dab
of perfume and brushed your teeth twice as a message that you adore
him and desire his body next to yours?

Clearly we must never strip sex of its meaning, significance, and
myriad expressions, for these are the real "mysteries" of sex. Good
communication will not destroy it, but failure to understand and be
sensitive to each other's propensities as men and women may well
damage the mystery.

Coming to Terms with Dependency

Men and women were made for dependency. Dependency does
not exclude the ability to act in independent ways and have great
emotional strength. Such traits are found in both sexes, but men are
usually told to hide and/or reject their dependency. "Healthy modern
women" are encouraged to do the same. Relying and trusting oneself

and perhaps one's "inner guide" is in vogue.

It may be fashionable not to be dependent, but the vulnerability and trust that is involved in dependency is basic to good sexual functioning. The ability to let go and be emotionally and physically moved does not happen without accepting that it is safe to do so. Do you hold back? Inability to risk dependency is a factor found frequently in anorgasmic women.

Does your spouse hesitate to show that he depends on you? Many women, buying the world's message, fail to acknowledge how much men need them, except when men are ill or left with the wash! A wife who isn't supportive and respectful can undermine a man's self-image. "A worthy wife is her husband's joy and crown; the other kind corrodes his strength and tears down everything he does" (Proverbs 12:4 TLB). If he were independent of her this wouldn't be so. A man's ability to counteract the effects of aging on his sexual functioning is highly related to whether or not he has a supportive partner.

The Pressure's On

The pressure to achieve and maintain a sexual life that is pleasing to both partners becomes such a burden for some couples that they cease being sexual altogether. Their solution is not biblical. The only biblical reason given for stopping marital relations is mentioned in 1 Corinthians 7:5: "Do not deprive each other except by mutual consent and for a time, so that you may devote yourself to prayer. Then come together again so that Satan will not tempt you because of your lack of self-control." Of all the reasons I have heard for couples not having sex, I have never been told that it was to enable them to pray!

Monitoring our sexual health is as important as being in charge of our physical well-being. Song of Solomon speaks of this (2:15): "Catch for us the foxes, the little foxes that ruin the vineyards, our vineyards that are in bloom." In other words, those pesky little problems that continually crop up can make inroads into our sexual sharing by undermining our good feelings for each other. The solution is to face them and talk about them.

Allowing even small problems to go unresolved can result in two problems: lack of respect for one's spouse and/or feelings of anger. Studies tell us that lack of respect for our spouse negatively affects sexual expression even more than serious problems with communication. In Ephesians 5:33, after a magnificent discourse on the way in which husbands are to love their wives, Paul tells wives to *respect* their husbands.

When a person's mood is down, it is hard to see the good in anybody or anything. Since women in the reproductive stage of their life frequently suffer from depression, it is not difficult to see why they might find fault with their husbands. No one is perfect except our Lord, so they don't have to look far for something to complain about!

How does one break the cycle? Try praise. Each morning begin the day by thanking the Lord for specific, positive traits of your spouse. Solomon and Shulamith repeatedly recalled each other's attributes. If negative thoughts continue to creep in, try thought-stopping. Substitute an experience you have shared in which your husband pleased you. If you can't think of anything he did right anywhere or at any time, imagine a scene that reflects the type of relationship which the Lord would like for you.

Use the positive experience to evaluate the factors which made that time so special. We can't always repeat the circumstances, but often the elements within the event can be reintroduced into our lives. For example, if one of the happiest memories shared was watching the sun go down on the beach in Hawaii, one factor that made it special was the uninterrupted time spent together. How can such a situation be set up to happen again?

Anger seriously affects sexual expression. It is physiologically impossible to have loving, sexual feelings while filled with anger. Our body limits us to one set of sensations at a time. Body tension labeled by the brain as anger in one situation involves the same muscles and nerves but is labeled as erotic feelings in another situation. A body that is tense with anger blocks sexual feelings both mentally and physically. For this very reason much of sexual counseling focuses on relaxing the body.

Keeping Things on Simmer

Because of the ambivalence which many Christians feel about sex, there is a tendency to compartmentalize it. For instance, sex is O.K. after 11 o'clock, when all the children are in bed and the day's work is complete, although never on Sunday! To expect feelings to be aroused magically when we have decided the time is right is unrealistic and rarely succeeds. The end of the day finds the majority of women anxious only for sleep. Having placed sex out of their mind, sexual arousal begins from a cold start. The possibility of the female responding is further reduced by the fact that men often need less time to prepare for intercourse.

Some women do nurture sexual thoughts, but through soap operas or romantic novels. Such women remain open to their partner's advances, but their erotic focus is not on their husband. One of the purposes of sex in marriage is to increase the bond of unity between the husband and wife. Misdirected fantasy does not do this but centers instead on make-believe. Healthy relationships are based on *reality*. Taking the pressure off a poor relationship through misdirected fantasy does nothing to face the real problems and to make the changes that are necessary to develop a strong connection between the spouses.

Proper fantasies, however, are a part of everyday life. We run through our activities for the day, rehearse how we will run a meeting, or envision a letter or paper we must write. It is appropriate that we should fantasize about our sex life as well. Fantasy is a problem if it becomes more important than reality or if we allow our fantasies to arouse lustful thoughts about persons other than our spouse. Many couples find their sexual response heightened through use of fantasies which they share with each other.

It is important that we keep our fantasy life under control. We can start by asking the Lord to take away fantasies that are intrusive or misdirected. Thought-stopping can be a helpful adjunct in keeping our thoughts righteous.

Taking Responsibility

Keeping a sexual relationship healthy involves a number of factors. We have mentioned proper self-image, a willingness to do some honest self-evaluation, a clear understanding of what our ideal model is, ability to be dependent, and acceptance of who we are as Christ's person.

The sexual woman is in full bloom during the reproductive years. In the past, the path to womanhood was clearly drawn. Women who were poor, or who had husbands who did not work, somewhat shamefully worked outside the home. Today there are so many choices of how to live in the fullness of womanhood that women are immobilized by confusion over which to choose.

A Christian woman does not live a life of *independence* but one of *interdependence*. Life choices are determined by her acknowledgment that all she does is for the glory of God. This means that she seeks the Lord's timing, will, and direction before her own. It means that she does not live life in a stereotypic way but according to the unique plan that is hers alone.

"Where your treasure is, there your heart will be also" (Matthew 6:21).

Chapter Six

Becoming the Complete Woman

*May your father and mother be glad; may she who gave
you birth rejoice!*

—Proverbs 23:25

When I was ten years old and my body only hinted at the curves
that were to come, a training bra somehow crossed my path. I proudly
tried it on, only to determine that it looked much better with the addition
of strategically placed socks. The socks, the bra, and my thin frame
spent many an hour prancing, primping, and polishing the grown-up
visage reflected in the mirror. Three years later the "real" thing was
beginning to happen, but acknowledgment of this by my dad sent me
tearfully fleeing up the stairs in utter humiliation.

My first period occurred at age 13. In my estimation "the curse"
had been aptly named. I hurt in a way I had never hurt before. I was
convinced that everyone knew and was snickering about it behind my
back. The three years that passed before my next period seemed like
perfect timing to me. No one ever suggested that menstruation could
be viewed with joy. That it heralded a body that was fit to fulfill its
destiny had never been discussed. It was simply "the curse."

Social Factors

Experience tells me that I have not been alone. Like everyone, I
had obviously been born with the potential of deriving pleasure from
having a healthy perspective of my body. Each woman needs to realize
that underestimating the effects of an unhealthy view of the body can
result in a lifetime of difficulties.

With or without instruction, people grow and change. A family
can avoid educating, communicating, and modeling sound attitudes.
Many choose not to confront developmental issues because of fear that

they lack correct information. Others simply follow their parents' example and hope the necessary details will be transferred by some mysterious process apart from them. Avoidance, regardless of the cause, leads most people to conclude that bodies are shameful.

I decided that my body was shameful. The closest I came to regarding it positively was through athletics. Running and jumping seemed "natural" and good. Dance, on the other hand, had a sensuousness about it that stopped me from ever being more than a technically correct dancer. I can still remember those moments when I allowed myself to respond with feeling to the music. They only occurred in secret, when I was assured that no one else would see.

An attitude of modesty, no different from that of most other families of the day, characterized my home. I do remember, however, that special day when I made the connection that bodies could be moved in ways that evoke "evil." It was the day my dad covered the mirrors and my five-year-old dancing exhibition was stopped.

Developing good feelings about my body has taken a long time. My ballet is still inhibited, and I must work at being sensuous in my marriage. My parents' view of the world, particularly their understanding of a "proper woman," has colored who I am. What was the alternative? What message about your body have you received? What are you conveying to your children?

Taking responsibility for our sexual selves requires such introspection—a thinking back over the many influences on our lives that have contributed to the view of the world we hold.

Daddy's Little Girl

No one denies the significance of Mother in a child's life. Until recently, with few exceptions, Dad's importance was dismissed as "provider." If he was a decent provider, he was said to have contributed to our steadiness and good start in life. All our idiosyncrasies, however, could be attributed to Mom, who never knew when to leave well-enough alone, insisted on potty-training at too young an age, and stifled our creativity by not allowing us to draw on the walls.

Research is beginning to tell a different story. Dad, whether he was present or away, appears to have affected our lives in more ways than previously imagined. My father could certainly not be considered a "new father"—one who attends the birth, changes diapers, and feeds the baby. I rarely remember him touching me during the first five years of my life.

His theory of childrearing was to teach humility, withholding praise so the child would work harder to achieve it. And in a sense his method worked. (The unconditional love of my mother I dismissed as insignificant—too easy to attain and therefore not to be valued.) Energy, motivation, and drive were invested in whatever it took to get Dad's attention and hopefully some of his conditional love.

It was a balancing act—being enough of a tomboy to please his desire for a son, but never forgetting to be his image of the Southern lady. I became an achiever, a perfectionist who was never quite satisfied. It wasn't until I was 28 years old that I was able to face the fact that my dad, long dead, was still running my life. Being accepted, with all my imagined and real faults, by my heavenly Father has been one of the most significant events of my Christian life.

My dad worked long hours, and he did not talk much, but his impact on me was enormous. Dates with a variety of boys was acceptable, but marriage could only be considered with those young men who showed a strong sense of responsibility to care for their family. But less obviously, the image that my dad reflected to me, and his message of how men and women are to relate, have affected my actual sexual functioning.

A woman's relationship with her father has the highest and most consistent correlation of all the factors affecting her ability to be orgasmic and comfortable with her sexuality. It is Dad who teaches his daughter what it is like to be the opposite sex. He contributes to her self-esteem as a woman when he compliments her. He literally molds and shapes the way she will approach, relate, and respond to the future men in her life.

The ever-growing statistics of teenage pregnancy illustrate this as well. Anyone who works with teenage girls understands that the physical desire for sex is not the major motivating factor for their decision to become sexually involved; the young girl is looking for *love*. Statistically, the greatest chance for producing sexually promiscuous children is found in one-parent homes headed by a female.

The "new father" is the subject of much publicity today. With the average age for having the first baby up from 21 in 1970 to 25 in 1982, working women are interrupting their careers with the expectation that parenting will be shared. In reality, although there is greater participation in childbirth, the average father still spends a paltry amount of time nurturing his children. Paternity leave, where offered, is rarely taken. Since working women by necessity also have less time to spend with their children, many are being left on their own—and to TV—to figure out how to relate emotionally and sexually as men and women.

Christians must not lose sight of the fact that developing healthy sexuality, in both a broad and narrow sense, is a task set up by God to require two sexes. Having children without thinking through the seriousness of parenting (including the practical point of view) is irresponsible. Now that 50 percent of our marriages are failing, the church has no choice but to step in and do what it can toward helping to develop healthy and godly children. Personally each of us must reach out, particularly to those children who are missing the influence of one parent or another, and provide solace, relief, and guidance.

Influencing Teens Spiritually

Familiarity with the Word is unquestionably a Christian mandate, but we all know people whose knowledge makes little impact on the way they run their lives. Acknowledging that the Bible has relevance in our lives is important if we are to influence anyone spiritually. John 13:35 teaches us, "All men will know that you are my disciples if you love one another."

Imparting Christianity requires living it. God is shown to be present through loving and caring relationships. Faith must be integrated into one's lifestyle. (Kids do not expect our total perfection in this, since they know how easy it is to fail.)

Being an example necessitates sharing how God ministers to you. What kinds of things do you struggle with and seek His Word for? What doubts do you wrestle with? When good things happen, who gets the praise? Words become credible when they speak of a reality that kids know and live with. What are they struggling with? How are they seeking answers? Is a habit being established of looking to the Bible, or instead to the world?

My son Joey once enjoyed being the biblical expert in our home. He relished the role of teaching Mom and Dad about the Bible. As our faith and knowledge grew, it was clear that he resented giving up his role of resident scholar. The consequence has been a real reluctance on his part to tolerate biblical reproof and correction from us. The particular factors are unique to our home, but the solution applies to every Christian home: Expose your children to other loving, Christian adults.

A healthy and necessary part of adolescent behavior is for them to become their own person. Sometimes this process makes it difficult for them to accept admonition from their parents. Mature and responsible adult friends, youth pastors, and counselors are an invaluable aid in spiritual growth.

Sound personal belief also plays a crucial part in a person's understanding of who he or she is as a sexual person. The wholesome self-concept brought about by children knowing that they are children of the King causes them to care what is done to and with their body. But they also understand why they have been created sexual. Sex has meaning within the context of the totality of their lives. Teens who have a sincere belief system are among the most morally responsible adolescents.

Straight Lines to Curves

Your daughter is 12 years old. She's having some minor gynecological problems. Who do you make the appointment with—the pediatrician or the gynecologist? Your perplexity reflects society's dilemma of what to do with the adolescent. The whole idea of an age between childhood and adulthood is a new concept.

Reaching adulthood in America requires many years of technical education, training, and sophistication. By contrast, bodies are maturing faster than ever. The onset of menstruation has dropped five years since the 1800's. Yet our children's well-developed facade hides their immature social and emotional condition. It is hard to remember that they are still children when they appear to be young adults. It is not uncommon to have 12- and 13-year-old girls passed off as sophisticated women in fashion magazines. In California an unemancipated female is required to have written consent from her parents in order to receive medical treatment. More than once my medical colleagues have been surprised when a mature-looking woman turned in a permission slip from Mom.

This is the "too-much generation." There is too much closeness before adequate personal development has been accomplished, too much exposure to too many things before a strong value system is solidified. There are too many choices, which leads to too many problems.

The result is a difficult and unsettled life for teens today. The mature appearance coupled with little respect for authority tempts parents to bail out of what appears to be an increasingly futile job. But the complexity of this "tween" time is the very reason that parents must try harder to stay involved in their adolescent's life.

Teenage suicide has never been higher, and neither have teen pregnancy and substance abuse. As it does in every facet of life, the Bible offers clear direction: "Train a child in the way he should go, and when he is old he will not turn from it" (Proverbs 22:6). Although "the way he should go" is often viewed as meaning "according to the truth," this phrase can also be rendered "Train up a child in keeping with his or her characteristics, and when he is old he will not turn from it."

Parents must be sensitive to the uniqueness of their teen and train (teach, discipline, model, and relate) according to the nature of the child. It is tempting to have a preconceived notion of the child's destiny and of childrearing techniques that fit comfortably with parental desires. But this proverb reminds us that cut-and-dried or "that's the way my dad did it" approaches to raising children will not work for everyone. This is true even within the same household.

Each child is unique and cannot be compared with another. Where does this individuality come from? A look at Psalm 139:13-16 gives us the answer. Parents are not to mold their child into their own image (or one of their choosing) because God has already created each child with an image that is his or hers alone. Psalm 139:13 says, "You created my inmost being." Our modern equivalent would be "You created my heart, my character." Verses 15 and 16 say, "My frame was not hidden from you . . . I was woven together . . . your eyes saw my unformed body." Today we would say, "You know my physical appearance . . . You put me together . . . You knew me as an embryo."

Not only does the Lord create each child according to His own agenda, but we are told in verse 16, "All the days ordained for me were written in your book before one of them came to be." The length of our children's lives is known! Since God has been so intimately involved in the formation of each life, the burden is on us to attempt to understand, treasure, and enhance our child's nature.

Nature can be difficult to comprehend when it appears to shift as frequently as the wind. This in-between age is, however, the appropriate time for experimenting with new behaviors and personalities. Childhood ways of coping are being jettisoned before new adult standards have been incorporated, and the maddening swing between immature and mature behavior results.

The older teen, with hormones mostly under control and most experimentation with new personalities behind him or her, begins to relate in a more stable fashion. Yet this does not mean that the growth process is complete. Most seriously lacking is a sense of "futurity," the ability to relate one's current actions to the future. Its effect on sound decision-making is dramatized by teen pregnancy and substance-abuse. Parents must remember that their teens lack the developmental ability to consider future consequences, and must help them by talking this out and bringing it to their attention.

Recently a very distraught mother brought her 14-year-old daughter in because of vaginal discomfort. The diagnosis was herpes. The mother became increasingly upset as she realized the lifelong consequences which her daughter faced. The aplomb with which this young girl revealed the story of having been challenged by her boyfriend to prove her love by having sex with five of his best friends was incredible. The consequence of what she had done to herself emotionally and physically had not yet registered beyond what it would be if she had been diagnosed with a cold. This is a perfect example of lack of futurity.

The struggle over finding one's identity remains the chief task of social development. The new, beautiful adult body is not matched with adult responsibilities and privileges, causing major conflicts between society, parents, and the teen. Slowly, with parental love and guidance, a clear sense of self emerges, along with the ability to hold moral principles that are independent of anyone else's enforcement.

When my son was born I believed that he would learn how to behave by watching the correct behavior of other people. I soon learned that values and correct behavior not only need to be *taught* but need to be reinforced again and again. We Christians have been incredibly naive to think that the Christian message of sex and what it means to be an adult will somehow take hold in our children without any effort on our part.

Perhaps it is more accurate to say that Christians have expected Christian values to be conveyed when they themselves are not completely clear on what those values are, having never bothered to discover the actual biblical message. Fulfilling our responsibility to adolescents must involve aiding them in the development of a personal faith that is based soundly on an accurate biblical message.

Babies Raising Babies

One often hears the statement, "Now that she's pregnant, she'll grow up in a hurry." Unfortunately for most teen moms, it doesn't turn out that way. Early pregnancy disrupts education, goals, and the completion of adolescence. Girls who prematurely find themselves in sexual relationships often isolate themselves from friends and activities that provide social maturity. Instead, the focus is on boys whose continuing attention is insured by "proof" of her love.

When the relationship ends, negative feelings of having given away something precious haunt even the irreligious. The damage that results is sometimes salved by the attentions of a new relationship. The gradual acceptance of one's role as a sexual woman and what this means is telescoped into a short period of time.

The long-range result of not taking time to put sex in its proper perspective is to affect future relationships. Fears and guilt are reinforced. An infant can be a tangible sign of an event associated with pain and shame. The immaturity that allowed an unwed pregnancy still operates to cause additional pregnancies. A recent study found that of 100 girls who had gotten pregnant by age 15, only five had not had a second pregnancy before age 20!

Many unwed teen moms feel locked into a lifestyle of deprivation. Hopes of higher education, rewarding jobs, and happy marriages are left for others to dream about. In poor families, lack of hope in the future further adds to the futility of deferring gratification and planning.

There are physical complications as well. Teen mothers have an increased rate of birth complications and defects. They are subject to a 15 percent higher chance of toxemia, 92 percent higher chance of anemia, and 23 percent higher chance of premature birth. Their babies are nearly twice as likely to die during the first year. The maternal mortality rate is also greater.

Although adolescents must begin to think for themselves, to abandon them to the process of reaching maturity in light of the complexities of our world is irresponsible and unbiblical. Being strong moral examples, accepting our teaching roles, viewing adolescents as made under God's direction, and keeping the lines of communication open are unshirkable responsibilities of mature adults. This is true even if our son towers over us by a foot and our daughter looks like a beauty queen—and both see our help as unnecessary!

Physical Factors

All the changes which a young girl experiences as she matures are orchestrated by substances in her bloodstream called hormones. The most important of these include follicle-stimulating hormone (FSH), luteinizing hormone (LH), estrogen, and progesterone. The final processes of puberty begin in the brain as a result of commands given by the maturing hypothalamus. The pituitary receives the chemical orders and produces FSH and LH. Progesterone and estrogen originate chiefly from the ovaries.

The very first sign of puberty, the eruption of breast buds, occurs somewhere between the ages of nine and 11 for most girls. The last sign, the menarche, or period, begins from age ten to 16 (following the growth spurt). While estrogen has been at work several years before the period begins, it is with the menses that the intricacy of hormonal action is best demonstrated and begins functioning in a truly adult fashion.

The first two weeks of a cycle are known as the "proliferative" phase. During this time only FSH travels through the blood to the ovaries. As a result of the FSH a follicle containing an egg enlarges and produces increasing amounts of estrogen. Generally only one follicle will mature a month, whereas a thousand will degenerate.

About midmonth, but prior to ovulation, the increased estrogen in the bloodstream causes the hypothalamus to order the pituitary gland to produce a surge of LH. LH stimulates the follicle to release its egg within ten to 12 hours.

Throughout the first half of the cycle, estrogen has caused the lining of the uterus to increase in depth. Further buildup occurs after ovulation, when the empty follicle becomes a corpus luteum that produces progesterone. Progesterone prompts the lining of the uterus, the endometrium, to become even more lush in anticipation of implantation. If pregnancy does not occur, the corpus luteum deteriorates within eight to ten days. Without the support of progesterone the lining sloughs off. If pregnancy occurs, the corpus luteum continues to sustain the rich lining on which the implanted egg is growing. This second half of the cycle is known as the "secretory" phase.

With the onset of menstruation the reproductive system has finally matured. This end result has been proceeded by several years in which estrogen has literally reformed the body. The transformation begins with the breasts. It is not unusual for each breast to have its own timetable for development. In some girls one breast bud may precede the other by several months. This is a normal variation. A difference in size may continue throughout the woman's lifetime.

The original growth of the breast is basically glandular in nature. Later the shape and size is primarily related to fatty deposits. Genetics and nutrition also contribute to the final shape. Size is affected by obesity and fluid retention. By age 16 breast development is complete for most girls. Inverted nipples may be psychologically distressing but should be considered a normal variation. Breast-feeding may prove difficult for some women with this problem, but most have no trouble at all.

Large breasts or early breast development cause many problems for the teenage girl. Her curvaceous shape attracts men and boys of all ages, putting tremendous pressure on her to handle attentions that she is most likely not prepared to cope with. Extra parental guidance, awareness, and support is crucially necessary in preventing serious emotional and behavioral repercussions.

Whether or not a bra is worn is strictly a matter of cosmetics and comfort. Unsupported heavy breasts can stretch the Cowper's ligaments, causing the breasts to droop. Stretchmarks result from excess weight gain (or loss) and pregnancy. The propensity to get stretchmarks is genetically determined by the amount of collagen in the tissue. No oils, lotions, or magic potions can prevent stretchmarks.

Breast bud development is followed by the appearance of pubic and axillary hair. Some adolescents find this "disgusting." The fact that adulthood is around the corner seems heralded by this particular event even though most adolescents are only 11 or 12 at the time. When pubic hair thickens and becomes coarser, menses will usually follow within six months.

Estrogen also stimulates bone growth, causing a growth spurt. During this time the pelvis enlarges in preparation for future child-bearing, and the hips become more rounded. Both the internal and external genitalia enlarge. The vaginal walls become thicker and more resilient. Menstruation occurs after the majority of these changes have taken place.

General Concerns of Puberty

Like many things in life, the process of puberty varies according to a bell-shaped curve. The majority of girls will experience the pubescent changes between ages ten and 16. Of those who fall outside the middle range, 75 percent are perfectly normal and are simply subject to different timing.

Young girls are frequently motivated to come in for an evaluation when all their friends have begun developing but they haven't. Sometimes it is the mother who is most concerned. If signs of puberty are present, the problem is often timing. An imperforate hymen is not common but can explain failure to menstruate, especially if there has been abdominal pain. A physical exam can assure the mother and daughter that things appear to be in order, if they are. Good history-taking might reveal anorexia nervosa or bulimia, excessive dieting, or athletic activities which can affect menses.

If some signs of puberty are present but the period has not begun, reassurance and waiting are all that need be done. If by age 16 the breasts have matured and there is still no period, an evaluation would be in order. By 18 there is true cause for concern. Patience is what is usually called for, since the total process takes at least 4½ years, and two stages must be completed: the bodily maturation and the release of the egg.

Less frequent but equally disconcerting is precocious puberty. Puberty is labeled "precocious" if it begins before age ten. If bleeding occurs, physical trauma must be ruled out; then thyroid problems and the possibility of a tumor must be considered. Again, 75 percent of the time the cause is poor timing.

The major physical problem with precocious puberty is that it causes a person to be short. Several techniques exist by which the process can be slowed to allow as much growth as possible. The most difficult aspect, however, is the psychological reality of a child having to deal with a woman's body. Counseling can be very helpful by preparing both child and parents for the problems that this phenomenon sometimes creates.

Concern may also be expressed by adolescents over excess hair growth on the face and body. Although the possibility of a tumor of the ovary or adrenal gland must be considered, the most significant factor at work is the genetic history of the family (familial hirsutism).

Family history is a determinant of the "normality" of the period itself. The beginning of menses as well as the time between periods and the length and amount of flow are influenced by inheritance. Approximately 95 percent of all women have periods ranging from 21 to 42 days. The flow ranges from three to six days and is considered normal within one to seven days. Although the volume of flow varies from period to period among teens, one to three ounces of blood is average, which should necessitate no more than six to eight pads per day.

It is common for teenagers to have atypical periods. Irregular timing is not unusual and should not be a cause of concern unless the periods have been regular for at least a year and suddenly become erratic. The most likely cause is irregular ovulation, but dieting, obesity, exercise, stress, or travel must be considered. Severe bleeding might require regulation through the use of birth control pills or oral or injectable progesterone and/or estrogen. Teens often suffer from heavy and long periods because of their irregular ovulation and the increased length of time which the tissue has to grow before it is shed. Painful periods (dysmenorrhea) are feared as being abnormal by young girls, but usually only people who ovulate have the problem. Sometimes teenagers complain of severe pain, having heard that birth control pills are the treatment of choice. Obtaining pills in this way enables them to avoid admitting, sometimes even to themselves, that they have decided to become sexually active.

Severe cramping due to uterine contractions, plus a vague heavy feeling, headaches, vomiting, and diarrhea, are all caused by increased prostaglandins. New antiprostaglandin drugs on the market effectively relieve most of the symptoms which women in the past had to endure.

Menstruation is a sign of health, not of sickness. When should the doctor be called? If bleeding occurs more than six to eight days, requires more than six to eight well-soaked pads per day, is abnormal for the individual, and/or disrupts normal life.

There is confusion over whether tampons are recommended for teens, as discussed in Chapter 3, because their insertion merely stretches the hymen out of the way, there is no physical reason for them not to be used by any person. They offer several advantages. Unquestionably, they are more hygienic and provide increased freedom. Of greater importance is the physical and emotional teaching they provide. Proper insertion requires learning, looking at, and touching an area of the body often studiously avoided as "dirty." Superabsorbent varieties are to be avoided. The risk of toxic shock is minimized with frequent changes every four to six hours and alternating with pads at night or when the flow is light.

Establish the Patterns

Our adolescent daughter is sometimes hurried along by the rest of the family. "Spur-of-the-moment" is not in her vocabulary. Our curiosity has been piqued to check out the mysterious and time-consuming ways she can find to spend her time. To our surprise, much of her attention is given to carefully and meticulously practicing good health habits.

She applies lotion liberally, conscientiously soaks her contact lenses, and judiciously cares for skin that without the slightest provocation has a tendency to break out. She is a rarity! Although teens spend hours getting makeup just right, few give much thought to good health habits. But this is the time when good hygiene and health-care routines should be established for a lifetime of health.

A pattern of regular health care can be begun as a result of a sensitively performed first gynecological exam that has been informative and not intimidating. A teenager should be asked privately if she wants her mother in the examination room with her. Any communication with the mother should be done in the girl's presence.

Having an exam when nothing is known to be wrong is good policy. However, most people experience their first exam when they are already worried about some facet of their reproductive health. Girls of mothers who have been exposed to DES (diethylstilbestrol) should begin annual exams with the onset of menses or by age 14. They are at increased risk of vaginal cancer and a number of other benign abnormalities of the vagina and cervix.

A pelvic exam is not always necessary and in very young girls is done under anesthesia to lessen the emotional trauma. When a pelvic exam is decided upon, anxiety is relieved when the girl is given the chance to examine the speculum and has been told exactly what will be done and why.

While the exam is performed, each step should be explained and the opportunity given, with the aid of a mirror, to pinpoint the location of the various portions of the genitalia. A breast exam can be demonstrated and instruction given to examine the breast monthly about a week after the first day of menstruation. Any young girl who is sexually active should be given a Pap smear because of her increased risk of cancer.

Doctors have been known to create panic in young girls and their mothers by such terms as "infantile uterus," "underdeveloped uterus," and "hard time getting pregnant." There is a considerable difference in size between the uterus in the infant, at puberty, and at maturity. The body of the uterus (the fundus) and the tip of the uterus (the cervix) are about the same size in the adolescent. In adulthood, the fundus is three times as large as the cervix. The uterus of the adolescent girl is normally and naturally small.

Sexual Factors

Recently an acquaintance of mine said that he had a solution to the sex-education controversy currently in the news. The whole problem would disappear if we just preached one message: a simple "NO." My friend would be surprised to learn that our Christian message is far more positive than negative. Unfortunately, the only kind of sex that makes the news or warrants the time of our pastors and teachers seems to be misused or maladaptive sex.

With the increased revelations of sexual abuse and the expanded awareness of the repercussions of AIDS, this one-sided approach is a cause of concern. I fear that Christians will finally overcome their reluctance to speak of sex, but their children will be no better off because the message of sex as a gift designed to increase unity in the marital relationship and provide pleasure will still be ignored.

Teaching the concept of sex as a gift to be used for God's glory is the chief task of sex education. This involves much more than simply knowing what to avoid. It is a mindset or attitude which enables a person to accept one's maleness or femaleness and to live wholesomely with sexual feelings and sensuousness.

This definition of sex education points out the folly of thinking that sharing a few facts of anatomy constitutes sex education. Some parents have insisted on a gynecological exam for their teens in hopes that the doctor will provide the sex education which the parents are too shy or reluctant to share. Although a doctor can provide information, nothing substitutes for the influence of a parent.

Parents, even if they have not spoken openly about sex, have been conveying a message affirming their belief system and practice since their child's infancy. Observation of the husband-wife interaction provides a major sex-education message. The details which a doctor might add are in reality the "simplest" part of the teaching. What sex means in an individual man or woman's life and the way it is meant to be expressed has been determined already through observation within the home.

It follows that the most sexually responsible children are those from homes where there are two parents, a semblance of order is maintained, values are verbalized, and each member feels loved. If a faith is practiced that appears real and relevant and is accepted by the teen, there is even more chance for high moral standards.

Even when our teens appear to reject our values, our expression of them is important because it has a positive effect on sexual responsibility. Not sharing negates this effect and gives unfair advantage to a world system that screams its philosophy from the rooftops. When parents refrain from condemnation, home can be a place where debate and evaluation takes place.

Listening to our adolescent's concerns, dreams, and philosophies earns us the right to be listened to. Most sons and daughters do not know what their parents think about sexual issues. The more a parent verbalizes, the more influence he or she has. This does not imply the right to "preach to." Forcing acceptance of an ideology doesn't work; compliance is done out of fear, guilt, or concern over disappointing the parent. Values are internalized when discussions, exploration, and questions have allowed the teen to internalize a belief system.

The argument that discussing sexual matters merely raises sexual interest has no basis in fact. By contrast, inadequate information stimulates curiosity and sends kids scurrying to discover the "truth" for themselves. Incarcerated sex offenders invariably have backgrounds in which their early sex education was deplorably misdirected or who had almost no exposure to normal sexual information.

This argument also perpetuates the myth that sexual feelings once aroused are uncontrollable. God didn't give us bodies that we can't control. No one suggests that control is easy, but we can do anything through the Lord who strengthens us (Philippians 4:13).

Healthy sex education begins with a solid spiritual foundation which can be demonstrated through a strong husband/wife relationship. The rise in single-parent homes creates new complications and can produce an atmosphere which gives rise to teens who accept the media standard for sexual behavior. Lack of supervision, time pressures on the parent, and the modeling of "breakable" sexual commitments are some of the factors involved. But in many cases the behavior of the parent in bringing home sleepover dates or parading multiple partners in front of the children makes highly untenable any credible plea for responsible sexuality. As conniving as teen behavior can sometimes be, hypocrisy is something which teens simply do not tolerate in adults.

We must not make the mistake of giving up because our home situation is not ideal. We all know of exceptions where "good kids from good homes" have gotten into trouble by violating God's admonitions. It can and does happen to anyone. The single parent, however, must be especially aware of the messages within the home and be careful that she (he) and/or other people provide the information, attention, and role-modeling which the individual child needs.

Having a Plan

A first step toward control is knowing what we are doing. A person is far more likely to handle a situation well when he or she knows what to expect and has a plan of action. No effective plan can be developed without considerable discussion of all the relevant issues. At least as much time as is spent determining career plans should be devoted to determining how one expects to conduct his or her sexual life.

Telling someone to avoid situations in which strong sexual feelings are likely to occur is good advice. Yet sometimes those situations develop unexpectedly or when we have miscalculated the intensity of a particular setting. It is at such a moment that we can recall a well-formulated plan, but not invent a new one. We must have an existing standard by which we can judge the situation. "If this situation continues, will the outcome be one that is in line with my plan?" "How will I view myself, my partner, and my relationship with Christ?" "Is this how I imagined my genital sexual life would begin?" "Is this what I want to look back on?"

Abstaining from improper sex is not the easy way, but it is the best way. It takes courage in a world which suggests that self-discipline when applied to sex is impossible and/or sick-minded. Choosing to abstain enables each partner to appreciate the fullness of who he is as a whole—not just his sexual nature. It preserves self-respect and gives clues as to the kind of marriage partner each will be. Unquestionably it contributes to a better relationship with the earthly parents and the heavenly Father.

I have written elsewhere that having sex is not like eating a Big . Mac. Whether participated in with someone we care about or someone for recreational purposes, no one gets up and walks away untouched. No single act has a more profound effect on our basic sense of femininity or masculinity. The sense of violation experienced during and after a rape attests to the powerful meaning beyond even the physical that sex holds for us.

It is true that a young woman misses a lot by remaining sexually chaste—has no chance of getting any of the 27 different sexually transmitted diseases! She also never needs to deal with the heart-wrenching choices involved in mothering a baby. She escapes the guilt of having violated the standards of God, self, and parents.

Relating and Dating

My son appeared at the door in obvious crisis. His new girlfriend's mother had decided they could not date because he was too old for her. Things had been progressing well until he had given her a ride home and she had proudly worn his letterman jacket into her house. I knew exactly what her mother was thinking. It was her daughter's first year of high school (we have a three-year high school in our town). The fellow who had brought her daughter home was no pimply-faced kid but was a 6-foot-3½-inch grown man who had his own car.

Our discussion explored his various alternatives. He concluded that a personal talk where he could define his intentions was worth the risk. I was relieved when his girlfriend's mother agreed to listen.

I was confident that Joey's intent was not one of manipulation. I knew that he had carefully thought out the circumstances under which he wished to be sexual. And I had seen him handle his propensity to be open and touching with a real understanding of his personal limits of vulnerability. He meant what he said.

The meeting went fine. He assured both parents that his intentions while dating their daughter included affection but would not involve genital sexuality. If they were more comfortable, he would make sure that all dates took place with another couple present. He concluded with, "I'm sure you have much to think and talk about, so don't give me an answer today."

Recently I checked with him to see how he was handling his sexual feelings now that he and his girlfriend had dated several months. His reply conveyed a little-known truth: "We're doing fine, Mom. It's easy when you've made up your mind." He has learned what some people never learn: Once the decision to abstain has been made, it can be a liberating experience. My question was still important, for it gave him an opening to talk if they had been having difficulty.

This is not to say that I have a perfect son. There are other areas in his life where his resolve is inadequate or he is immature. In fact I learned an important lesson from one of them. It was only at the end of several months of experimentation with drugs, and after quitting, that his father and I discovered the facts about his experience.

Our horror that he would experiment with something so deadly motivated us to see that counseling was made available to him. A policeman friend also told him a few of the realities of drug use, and we followed up with periodic and unexpected urine tests. One day as I was helping him organize a paper he was writing on drug-abuse, I asked him what we might have done to prevent the whole episode. He replied, "Mother, you didn't mess up—I did. It was my choice." Then, after a pause and with an obvious need to comfort me, he added, "You've done a great job on sex!"

I laughed, but I also began evaluating the different way we had approached each possibility. Knowing how little support males in our society get for choosing to be celibate, we had always made sure that we verbally and repeatedly reinforced his decision. Many a dinner conversation had included the difficulties and advantages of taking such a stand. TV shows and record lyrics had been used to provide teachable moments. On the other hand, experimentation with drugs seemed such a remote possibility that the usual perfunctory statements had been made but far less discussion and emphasis had been placed on the danger of even mild flirtation with drugs.

Determining proper dating behavior is much easier before a teenager has met the boy or girl of his or her dreams. In fact, guidelines work best when they are drawn up through a family counsel before dating age. Moral principles introduced at an impressionable age make sense. They can be internalized and accepted when the need to be independent is not so primary. Reevaluation is always in order through the same system. Parents have been setting and helping their children set limits and guidelines since the child was born, so this is not the time to stop.

Sometimes the guideline which a teenage girl needs is permission to say no and examples of how to do this. More often than we imagine girls don't know they have a choice because no one has ever told them they do. Learning how to get oneself out of awkward situations is part of what is to be acquired through dating. Fast responses provide humorous ways to get out of compromising situations. Sol Gordon, a sex educator, suggests the following: Line: "Everybody does it!" Reply:

"That's nice—you won't have trouble finding someone else." Line: "I'd like to know you mind, body, and soul." Reply: "Great! Take Psychology 206, Biology 101, and Religion 203." Line: "Don't you know men can't go two days without sex?" Reply: "Come back in two days."

Parents sometimes fear teaching against premarital sex. They worry that it is old-fashioned or can't be done. Yet such teaching is fully time-tested, though rarely done without the help of Christ. God's plan for us to be in a stable, monogamous relationship is nowhere better demonstrated than in the emotional and physical hardships of a woman who begins her sexual life too soon and with a multitude of partners. Teaching our young men and women to respect God's plan requires a willingness to vocalize and teach it and a concerted effort to increase the understanding of our children so that they value their body enough to protect it.

How Do We Say It?

One of the most effective ways to teach is to share personal experience. Jesus often told stories to make His point. Your struggles and triumphs will help your teens identify with you and enable you to have a greater impact in their lives. Who can identify with someone who never made a mistake? This does not mean that you must reveal every aspect of your sex life. Some things are private. "Whether I had sex before marriage is private. I'll be glad to share with you what I have learned and think about sex."

Because direct questioning can be uncomfortable, general questions can be used to reveal how a teen feels and what he or she is concerned or confused about. "When I was your age the kids were curious about homosexuals. What are they saying today?" "Do you think people fall in love as quickly as that couple on TV did?" "Another child has been reported molested. What are the kids saying these days about things like that?"

More important than any teaching is developing an atmosphere in which kids are willing to risk giving their opinion and seeking yours. Healthy sexuality is rare in a society that refuses to teach it but allows the misuse of sex to be the mainstay of advertisers and other media outlets.

Realistically, it is the rare parent who succeeds in shielding a child from the secular media message. It is more realistic for a parent to develop independent thinking and evaluation of material from a biblical perspective. Children who have learned to be discerning—to look with a critical eye at what they hear and see, will be able to handle the bombarding that will inevitably cross their path.

Adolescents are concerned that they be "normal." They fear they may be homosexual if a relative or friend is "gay" or if they have had a crush on or dreamed about a same-sex person. Assurance can be given only if there is a willingness to talk with teens about these issues. They wonder what an orgasm feels like and if they will be able to experience it with someone they love. Questions about virginity are asked as they seek to define whether or not they are "virgins."

Taking Responsibility

The ability to have sex is in no way a measure of the appropriateness of doing so. The mature facade of our teenagers and our society's message that no healthy, capable person is to say no belies the fact that the human body was not designed to withstand multiple partners without consequence, and that childbearing at too young an age can create lifelong physical and emotional problems for mother and child.

Good health habits are learned from the mother's example and attitude and from her commitment to teach such habits. Fathers provide a unique influence on their daughters' sexuality and their acceptance of themselves as female. Together they contribute the influences that determine a lifetime of their children's conscious and unconscious choices.

There is indeed too much exposure to sex—the immoral variety— but not enough instruction on moral sex. Conscientious acceptance and planning of the parental role in this area is as vital as any other aspect of planning for a child's life.

The physical, sexual, and religious health of children depends on parents choosing to accept the gift of their children and training them "in the way they should go." The know-it-all attitude of some teens should not deter the mature adult/parent from actively teaching the next generation positive attitudes about their body and the plan it was designed for, since someone else will do it if they don't!

Chapter Seven

The Complete Woman at Maturity

> *. . . no fear of old age.*
>
> —*Proverbs 31:25 TLB*

The speaker had been controversial but thought-provoking. The crowd of women began to file out, but Cindy and Mona remained in their seats. Their animated discussion reviewed and dissected the speaker's remarks about when life begins. Cindy boldly volunteered that, in her belief system, life began when an infant could survive on its own outside the womb. Mona was livid in responding, "No, that simply isn't so! Life begins when the sperm and egg unite!" Mrs. Bradford couldn't resist a comment as she passed them. "Ladies," the sweet and innocent-looking grandmother interjected, "life truly begins when the dog dies and the children leave home."

We have explored the social, physical, and sexual changes during the reproductive and adolescent years of a woman's life in the previous two chapters. We turn now to the effects of aging on those three elements. It is our opinion that far too many women dread "midlife" as a time of diminishing pleasure and fulfillment. How accurate is their assessment? Let's take note of the role which aging plays in the life of today's sexual woman.

The quality of a woman's life as she ages depends on her attitude, her general health, and the overall satisfaction she feels with the way she has lived her life. People like Mrs. Bradford and a local heroine by the name of Hulda Crooks (who began mountain-climbing in her eighties and who has scaled Mount Whitney annually ever since) become inspirations by virtue of their rarity. If the Bible is to be believed, one would expect the age of maturity to be lived in a unique and especially fulfilling way, for "is not wisdom found among the aged? Does not long life bring understanding?" (Job 12:12).

Social Factors

In this chapter we will focus on the years after childbearing has ceased or is coming to an end. The greatest emphasis will be on what is commonly referred to as middle age, the years from 35 to 65.

Unlike the adolescent, who sees a year as a monumental length of time, a woman of middle age is highly aware of time's passing. Ferris wheel rides have lost their appeal—she senses her mortality. For many a woman there is a shift from *attaining* goals to maintaining and strengthening whatever position she has already achieved. Another woman might make a hurried examination to determine whether there is enough time to risk change, for there may be regret about certain aspects of her life.

Psychologically one attempts to resolve the tension between "generativity" and "stagnation." Energy is directed less at "doing" and more toward teaching the next generation: "Teach the older women to be reverent in the way they live, not to be slanderers or addicted to much wine, but to teach what is good. Then they can train the younger women . . ." (Titus 2:3,4). Contrary to the misconceptions of many, there is no generalized intellectual decline with aging. Many women find themselves entering school and/or the work force for the first time and proving themselves productive and creative.

Stagnation occurs when life is allowed to become a rut (a grave with both ends kicked out). Failure to grow or expose oneself to stimulation results in increasing self-absorption. Life becomes dull and uninteresting. Menopause is seen as an end to one's family obligations and the heralder of old age.

But even among "well-adjusted" generative types, middle age is often a time when they are less happy and more anxious. Life is recognized as the complex entity that it is. There are social and physical losses. Women find this stage especially difficult if they have received attention and reinforcement for their beauty and/or ability to have and raise children. It is still noteworthy in our society when an older female newscaster is featured, for it is the young who are featured as not only having all the fun but also all the answers!

Well-adjusted middle-aged people have most likely attained some occupational success and made a marriage work. Romans 12:3 reminds us not to think more highly of ourselves than we should but to use "sober judgment" in our personal evaluations. In other words, we are to be realistic. Adjusting to reality, knowing how and when to compromise, contributes to a healthy middle age. Some women refuse to face the facts of aging and suffer because of their denial. Willingness to overcome monotony and fear of change can convert the middle-aged woman's life into an open book of adventure.

Beyond age 65 the greatest concerns and changes are usually physical. The developmental task is to achieve "ego integrity" versus settling for "despair." Ego integrity means being able to view one's life as having been worthwhile. It is saying to oneself, "I've lived the best life I could under the circumstances." Despair, on the other hand, is reviewing one's life and concluding that it lacks value. The older woman shifts her interest from the outside world to the inner world. Spiritual matters become increasingly important, which explains why older people often renew their interest in religion. Those who remain active are the most satisfied with life, while the least active are the least content. Accepting one's life and developing a healthy point of view about death contribute to overall pleasure.

Perhaps with the aging of our population, older people will develop a mental attitude that recognizes the richness that can be theirs in every aspect of their existence. After menopause a full third of life is left to live! Any female who has experienced menopause after 1977 can expect another 30 years of life. Menopause is just a marker of life—not the end of the line.

Physical Factors

Perhaps you remember when Archie Bunker told Edith on "All In The Family" that if her "groinocologist" insisted that she go through the menopause, she could, and he would give her 30 seconds to complete the process. It has been suggested that this is a good solution for adolescence! Unfortunately, menopausal and adolescent changes don't run their gamut in the wink of an eye, despite our wishes that the metamorphosis of our loved ones would be quick and painless.

Americans are used to the concept of "built-in obsolescence." When a woman reaches the age of menopause, her tendency is to view herself as a spent and useless object. Many problems result from this acceptance of society's evaluation that middle age is a declining time of life for a woman.

What is commonly referred to as the "change of life" is called medically the "climacteric." The word stems from the Greek and means "rung of the ladder." This implies another step of healthy development. The climacteric includes the menopause and takes a number of years to complete. The menopause actually refers only to the last menstrual period, although it is usual for people to refer to the whole change of life as "the menopause."

Cessation of menses may occur any time between ages 41 and 51. Although the age of the first menstruation has dropped, the age of menopause has remained the same, averaging 51 years. It is preceded by "premenopause," which may take two to six years. Around 38 to 42 years of age egg production is diminished and the remaining eggs are more resistant to complete development. As the eggs degenerate, there is less and less estrogen production. The periods may become erratic, be light or heavy, or missed entirely. PMS-like symptoms may appear due to the estrogen and progesterone deficiencies.

When menopause occurs under the age of 40 it is considered premature. About 3 to 5 percent of all women have early menopause. Treatment for these women is by estrogen replacement. Twelve months after her last period a woman is felt to be "postmenopausal." Fifteen percent manage to menstruate even after this.

If a woman wants to know if she is truly postmenopausal, she can have a blood test called a serum FSH (follicle-stimulating hormone). This will indicate that the pituitary is ordering production of large amounts of FSH to force egg production. When the hormone measures are beyond a certain level, the physician can assure the woman that she is no longer releasing eggs and can safely quit using birth control.

What's Happening to Me—Again?

The initiation of menopause and the other climacteric changes is unknown. At a particular time in a woman's life, her ovaries begin to respond less to her hormones and fewer ova mature. The ones that do are released irregularly. The reducing amounts of estrogen and progestrogen eventually fail to stimulate the endometrium to develop, and periods cease. A woman who has great difficulty during this period of her life is probably more genetically sensitive to estrogen withdrawal and perhaps psychologically dreads facing this era of her life.

Symptoms of the Change of Life

Some women have reported that menopause has been the best time of their life. Others state that portions of it were miserable but brief.

A final group expresses a desire to "rob banks, shoot in-laws, and leave home for Rio." Despite rumors to the contrary, the change of life does not cause major psychiatric symptoms.

There are symptoms that are common but unrelated to hormonal changes during this stage of life. They include the following: insomnia, numbness and tingling sensations, fatigue and weakness, irritability, mood swings and/or personality changes, and apprehension (fright and anxiety). The cardiovascular system is affected, and a woman may experience heart poundings, chest pains, shortness of breath, varicose veins, and swollen ankles.

Estrogen depletion is responsible for a number of problems, particularly if the depletion is rapid. The early symptoms of menopause include menstrual changes and night sweats or hot flashes. A true hot flash is a rather sudden occurrence that involves feelings of warmth from the chest to the head which may be mild or intense. Some women say it feels like a blowtorch has been turned on their upper body. The feeling may last for just seconds or up to an hour and may be followed by a rapid chill. Three out of four women will experience hot flashes or their night equivalent—night sweats. Some women may have three to five episodes a day, but it varies within and between women. Only one in five find this condition so incapacitating that hormone treatment is necessary for this symptom alone. Sometimes vitamin E (400 I.U. per day) gives relief. No permanent damage is caused by hot flashes.

As the climacteric continues and estrogen is further reduced, a woman will notice other changes. The skin becomes drier and itchy, loses its elasticity, and bruises more easily. There may also be an increase in facial hair. The thinning of the tissues of the bladder and urethra cause increased frequency and urgency. The affected tissue is less able to combat infection, as are the vulva and vagina. They too become thin, delicate, and dry. Intercourse may cause bleeding and tearing and be painful. Breasts become smaller and softer and, if large, may sag.

As a woman's hormonal composition more closely resembles the older male, her risk of heart attack and stroke increases dramatically.

Osteoporosis: A Disease to Prevent

Mrs. Brown had almost canceled her appointment. It was raining and she feared falling on a slippery surface. It didn't take much for her to break a bone. Her "dowager's hump" had her so stooped that she needed a walker to keep her balance. The disease had resulted in a loss of six inches in height. She delighted the staff as she good-humoredly reported on the small world directly below her gaze. "Do you know your carpet has a small tear?" "Today a little bug has come in to see Dr. Mayo for a checkup. Is Miss Lady Bug on your schedule?"

Early intervention certainly would have decreased the severity of Mrs. Brown's osteoporosis. The disease begins invisibly between the ages of 30 and 35, but it symptoms may not be diagnosed until the sixties. The best prevention for the disease is to build strong bones at a young age. This is accomplished by good exercise and an adequate diet including plenty of calcium. Care must be taken in dieting not to exclude foods rich in calcium. Excess protein and fat will accelerate calcium excretion, as will soft drinks (diet and regular), coffee, alcohol, and cigarettes.

Although damage to the skeletal system cannot be undone, further progression can be slowed or halted. A calcium-rich diet and calcium supplements started in the thirties are very important. Taking half the calcium needed at night and half at breakfast or lunch is most efficient. Lack of exercise also contributes to bone mass loss. The first astronauts showed bone loss after a short time in space. Many patients have been discouraged after cast removal to find their limb a "shadow of its former self." Exercise which involves an upright position, such as walking, jogging, or aerobics, builds bone mass.

By age 90 a woman loses two-thirds of her bone thickness. The primary complication of such osteoporosis is hip fractures. Fifteen to 20 percent of affected women will die within the first three months of a hip fracture; one out of five will never return home. Twenty percent of women with hip fractures will have another osteoporosis-related fracture within one to two years.

Light-skinned Caucasian women, Oriental women, and those with small frames have the greatest risk of developing this largely prevent-able condition. Osteoporosis is rightfully a major consideration in the decision for estrogen-replacement therapy after menopause.

Estrogen Replacement

When a woman no longer produces estrogen through the natural process of menopause or undergoes surgical menopause, it is the current practice to replace the estrogen through medication. With few exceptions, the complications that can occur are far outweighed by the benefits. This does not mean that every woman must accept estrogen replacement or will need it. Estrogen-replacement therapy (ERT) does not increase a woman's risk of cancer of the vagina, cervix, ovary, breast, or gastrointestinal system, as feared and reported in the media.

Some precautions must be taken, however. Women who suffer from unscheduled, undiagnosed vaginal bleeding and thromboembolic disorders of the circulatory system should not participate in ERT programs. It has been accepted practice not to prescribe ERT if there are any known or suspected estrogen-sensitive tumors of the breast or uterus. Recent studies, however, indicate that even though the risk of endometrial cancer is increased with estrogen alone, estrogen in combination with progestin reduces the chance of endometrial cancer. There are side effects of ERT, none of which occur in over 1 percent of the population taking hormone replacement. They include the following: minor skin changes, headaches, migraines, nausea, bloating, and minor vision changes.

In determining whether estrogen replacement is right for any individual woman, she and her doctor must evaluate a number of factors. First, what is her risk of osteoporosis? The danger of dying from a broken hip outweighs dying from endometrial cancer 16 times. Is there a history of heart disease? ERT results in a significantly lower incidence of ischemic heart disease. There is also some indication that a protective effect against breast disease results when estrogen and progestin are taken together. Unquestionably life can be more pleasant and useful when a woman does not have to deal with the symptoms commonly associated with menopause. For some women, symptom relief may motivate them to undergo surgery to enable them to use replacement hormones. An example would be a woman with fibroids whose hot flashes are so severe that they interfere with her normal daily functioning.

The bottom line may be that without estrogen replacement she will have more problems than if she takes the hormones. Most of the time estrogen is given over a three- to four-week period and progestin is added during the last seven to 14 days. No medication is given for five to seven days, during which 80 percent of the women will have one or more periods annually. The bleeding will be light and painless. Occasionally estrogen creams which are inserted vaginally and sometimes rubbed into the vulva are necessary.

Since estrogen is absorbed through the skin, some doctors are using estrogen in a "skin patch" form. Estrogen administered this way is absorbed directly into the bloodstream; a smaller dose is effective and fewer side effects are experienced.

Sexual Factors

Midlife and old age are significant transition times in the sexual life of men and women. The actual adjustments are usually less traumatic than our society suggests they will be. Each couple responds to sex as they age in their own unique way.

Gladys and Peter have been married for 40 years. They glow when they are together. They have nurtured mutual interests, have been careful of their diet and exercise habits, and have continued to find pleasure, tension release, and unity through an active and positively regarded sex life. They are the first to state that their sexual relationship is better now than in their youth.

The natural process of aging has necessitated changes in their sexual patterns, but those adjustments seem only to have increased their pleasure. Gladys has found that she must use estrogen creams regularly because her vagina has become dry and especially sensitive to friction. After some experimentation they discovered a lubricant that both found pleasurable and nonirritating.

Peter has been honest and clear about his need for more physical and visual stimulation. He likes to see Gladys in lovely lingerie. Looking for and selecting special items that appeal to them has proven to be fun and stimulating. Neither is concerned about the fact that they actually make love less. Peter needs more recovery time between sexual encounters. If Gladys needs sexual release, Peter is thrilled to provide pleasure to her manually or orally.

They never attempt lovemaking when they are fatigued or stressed. The leisurely atmosphere takes pressure off Peter. Like other men of his age, he needs more time to achieve an erection. Both understand and accept the fact that less-rigid erections and reduced volume and force of ejaculate are no reflection on his desire for his wife.

The Perfect Couple

Everyone in their church knows Charlene and Joe. They are active on their respective boards, committees, and fund-raisers, and they sing in the choir. Like Gladys and Peter, they have been married for 40 years. However, the spark so evident between Gladys and Peter is not evident in their relationship. No one ever hears them argue—in fact they are considered a model Christian couple—but Charlene and Joe no longer share a sexual relationship.

Occasionally Joe will approach Charlene, but such attempts are becoming less frequent because they have proven so frustrating. Charlene finds penetration extremely painful. With infrequent coitus the vagina becomes dryer and decreases in size. (Successful sex with aging is highly related to the frequency and continuity of the sex life.) They are too embarrassed to try lubrication or seek medical advice.

Their sexual difficulties did not begin with aging. Joe began to overindulge in food and alcohol in his forties. Advancement in his job demanded considerable entertaining and extended hours from home and family. Charlene became increasingly consumed with church and community activities. At 45 she had a hysterectomy, with removal of the ovaries, for an early uterine cancer.

Sex had always been a sensitive area in their relationship and one in which they would not communicate. Their perfunctory sexual routines could only be described as boring. Neither one worried about the other leaving the marriage because of problems with sex, however, because of their strong Christian commitment. They did not realize how much they were taking each other for granted. Being taken for granted does nothing to encourage sexual feelings.

The hysterectomy provided a welcome excuse for both Joe and Charlene to place sex on the back burner. Their ever-increasing church involvement and continued spiritual growth provided further evidence to them that sex was really an unnecessary distraction. Although they were sensitive about their Christian witness, they seriously underestimated the impact which their lack of intimacy had on other people. Most importantly, neither Joe nor Charlene could put his or her finger on what was missing personally in their lives. Externally everything appeared fine, but internally they both sensed a confusing emptiness.

A Time for Sabotage

Penny and Ken were referred by their pastor to a counselor who specialized in sexual problems. Ken was a successful businessman who had recently retired. Penny had raised four children, been a superb hostess for many of Ken's business obligations, and generally kept the home operating without his emotional or physical support. The degree of resentment she felt had never been expressed and was unclear even to Penny.

Retirement was difficult for Ken. He missed being in charge of a growing and dynamic business. He had cultivated few outside interests during his working years and had become quite dependent on Penny to help him cope with his free time. Like many men his age, Ken had less physical capacity for lovemaking than previously but an even greater psychological desire for sex. His need for increased physical and psychic stimuli before he could become erect made him vulnerable to his wife.

Penny dealt with his revived sexual interest in the way she had dealt with him on other conflicting issues throughout their marriage: There was no direct confrontation, anger and frustration were expressed through passive-aggressive techniques. She appeared to go along with his desires, but her stimulation of him was done in a way that implied disinterest on her part. She refused to buy new nightgowns, pretending outrage at the cost or subtly implying, "He didn't used to need such things." Often her bedtime conversations involved worry over the children or taxes or whether they were going to make it now that he wasn't earning a big income.

It wasn't long before Ken began to have difficulty achieving erections. Having lived his life as a high-performance, competitive type, he began to panic. His lifelong habit of placing too much emphasis on appearance and the meaning of special sexual performance rendered him at high risk for a dysfunction. A year after his retirement he was unable to maintain an erection long enough for penetration.

A thorough history revealed that Ken had frequent and firm night erections. He was taking no medication, nor drinking or smoking or indulging in other behaviors that would effect his physical potency. The therapist wisely recognized that before sexual counseling could be done, there were some relationship factors that had to be explored. Neither Penny nor Ken was conscious of the connection between Ken's problems and Penny's sabotage. In the beginning neither was aware of the anger Penny felt over the neglect and insensitivity she had endured for so many years. The fact that they were in the midst of a power struggle had to be pointed out to them.

Good counseling enabled them to understand and cope with their problems. As insights were clarified, sexual counseling techniques were used to reintroduce a positive and healthy sexual pattern. Understanding alone does not miraculously fix all sexual problems; behavioral successes and new ways of being together must also be included.

A Time of Vulnerability

Realizing that their men are vulnerable to them, some women find the temptation overwhelming to misuse power they are perhaps experiencing for the first time. They can sabotage by being passive, withholding the direct stimulation which their husband now needs to function. They can undermine with little remarks or by ceasing to look attractive. A woman may decide to stay up late, talk on the phone all night, refuse to listen to him talk about his day, or eat excessively.

Our society places such pressure on men to be "sexually potent" that many are very insecure about their sexual functioning. Few connect their failure to perform with sabotage or with their own callous, detached current behavior or with past hostile behavior. They may react to their new dependency on their wife by seeing her as their mother, and may feel confused at their ambivalence in wanting to be with her but also independent of her. They may have an affair with someone who is not "Mother" or become anxious, desperate, and obsessive in trying to please her.

If neurotic or unresolved problems exist before reaching midlife or old age, a couple is at greater risk for developing problems. Depression, stress disease, loss of purpose, addiction to drugs or alcohol, food, work, or sports are at the root of many marital and sexual problems. Well-integrated men with loving, supportive wives and healthy marriages have minimal sexual adjustments as they age.

Making Midlife Sex Better Than Ever

Midlife sex has the potential of being the best sex of a couple's life. They are not fumbling around trying to figure out what to do, but are comfortable with their bodies and sharing them. Little children and careers are no longer leaving the couple in a frazzled heap by the end of the day. And best of all, men have become better lovers! Their increased maturity, physical vulnerability, and lessened sexual urgency make them far more sensitive—and consequently better lovers—than in their youth.

Sex can be a gratifying experience for both partners. Lovemaking becomes more artful and varied when the couple feels secure and is open to the wife's greater involvement. The focus shifts from performance to pleasure. In summary, sex changes from "what works" to "lovemaking."

To insure that this becomes true for you and your relationship, avoid boredom. The brain is able to overcome the deadness that comes with familiarity. Be open to new ideas, places, and times for making love. Don't take your mate for granted. (If you were only allowed to see each other once every five years, is this how you would dress or act?) As we get older, it is more important than ever to recognize sex as a priority by being rested and making appropriate time available for it. Even though an older couple may be spending more time than ever together, it is still important that they set aside time to talk about other than mundane matters.

Accept the fact that your spouse may have a different value system from yours, but recognize your call to make a sincere attempt to meet his or her desires. Surveys show that Christian women who consider themselves "very religious" often report greater satisfaction with the sexual aspect of their marriage than do other women. There are probably two reasons for this: 1) They see marital love as *giving*, and thus there is a willingness not to demand sexual pleasure for themselves as a first criterion; and 2) the security of a convenant commitment allows them to risk being the sexual person they were meant to be.

Since natural vaginal lubrication is reduced and slower, sensuous oils are important to use at the beginning of sex for both the man and the woman. As orgasm becomes more difficult, a couple may add variety and stimulation with a vibrator. There are many types on the market, and it may require some experimentation before the couple finds the right one for them. No one questions our use of glasses or a cane to make life more pleasurable or to aid in normal functioning. In the same way, a vibrator should not be considered inappropriate if it helps a couple maintain a fulfilling and intimate sex life.

With old and young alike it is important that we broaden the definition of sex to more appropriately meet our sexual appetite: Sex is not just intercourse. Mutual masturbation as a prelude to coitus or enjoyed just for itself should be a possibility. Intercourse sometimes takes more psychic and physical *energy* than a person can muster, and yet he or she longs for sexual intimacy. Sometimes it takes pressure off the male if the female has already had an orgasm and the remaining time can be spent pleasuring and taking the time needed for him to achieve an erection.

Oral sex is a highly practiced sexual variation among the young. Many older people worry about its biblical sanction. It is not specifically mentioned in the Bible. Often the desire for oral sex increases as a couple adapts to the natural changes of aging. Ejaculate is not harmful, and no physical damage can occur with the practice.

The Best of Seasons

When we watch TV we see older people advertising refrigerators and denture cream but never touching one another. No wonder so many people dread getting older! The proliferation of aging females without mates states to the older sexual woman, "I'm not supposed to be sexual."

Clearly, older people must give themselves permission to be sexual, or more accurately, sensuous. Don't hesitate to luxuriate in a bath, lather yourself with lotion and oils, or read a love story or poetry. Allow yourself to wear clothing that feels sensuous. Leave the "granny gowns" to the seven-year-olds!

Even without a partner, allow for touch by maintaining a social life that includes good friends who love to hug. Make appointments for facials, pedicures, and massages. Join the local health club and enjoy the sauna and Jacuzzi. Keep alive the sexual woman that God made you to be!

Going in for Help

It is much harder for an older person to seek help for sexual problems than a younger one. A health professional or a pastor may have discouraged the older person from seeking assistance by suggesting that he "act his age." Many older people simply become "asexual," while others deny their problem and try to convince themselves that things are getting better.

The dropout rate for older people in therapy is high. Facing relationship problems which they have sought to deny for decades is simply too large a task. There may be fear that if sexual problems are resolved, the mate will seek a new partner.

Those who risk therapy are often people ending a relationship through death or divorce. Some are facing dating for the first time in years. Others simply need appropriate facts. They need to know that their desire for sex is normal and God-given. Sometimes the goal is to receive a diagnosis and not a prescription, and the couple is happy in understanding the dynamics of what is going on mentally and/or physically.

With few exceptions, a woman can continue to have intercourse throughout her life. Men, however, must be able to acquire and sustain an erection. Because they are subject to a number of physical problems that can interfere with this process, careful diagnosis must be done to eliminate a psychogenic origin. This is especially true if the man is considering vascular surgery, papaverine injections, or penile implants. Great progress has been made in overcoming physical impotency. But any of the treatments require high motivation, realistic expectations, and reasonable health.

Taking Responsibility

We have all heard the expression "Life is what you make it." There is no portion of a woman's life when this is more true than during the "change of life." Although one cannot deny the physical adjustments that must be made, it is the *mental outlook* that sets the tone for a full third of the mature woman's life.

Sexually it can be a time to "bail out" or shift power—or else to experience a sexual relationship that is better than ever. A majority of women find that their interest in sex increases, perhaps due to the drop in estrogen and unopposed androgen. There is no reason to avoid sexuality, especially as the older woman becomes free from previous problems and concerns.

In perfect alignment with God's truth, the mature sexual woman is called to pass on her wisdom and experience to the next generation. The alternative is to stagnate.

"Age in a virtuous person, of either sex, carries in it an authority which makes it preferable to all the pleasures of youth" (Sir Richard Steele).

Chapter Eight

The Complete Woman

*My lover spoke and said to me, "Arise, my darling, my
beautiful one, and come with me."*

—*Song of Songs 2:10*

Life moves along whether we determine to let things slide or take
an active part in making things happen. It is sad that any persuasion is
needed to convince people that a little effort expended on behalf of their
sexual health and well-being is worth it. In this chapter we will urge the
complete woman to take responsibility in keeping the sexual aspect of
marriage alive and well.

Looking at Sex in Marriages That Work

Pastor and author Tim Timmons has remarked that if God made
marriage, He ought to know how to make it work. This is a valid
observation, for there are many people whose marital experiences have
made them wonder if marriage in the twentieth century is really viable.
Television suggests that real love is found before marriage and within
extramarital affairs. A content analysis of soap operas conducted over
a six-month period revealed eight divorces, two cases of bigamy, four
separations, six divorces being planned, 21 couples living or sleeping
out of wedlock, two women with more than one bed partner, and several
children conceived with questionable identity of the father.

Only 6 percent of the sex on television involves marital partners,
leaving a viewer with the obvious message that the best sex is not found
in marriage. Research doesn't support such a message, however.
People involved in extramarital sex often find themselves less free and
less functional. It is in marriage that we find the most sex, the greatest
variety, and the most orgasms. It is in covenantal marriage that we can
be totally free to be ourselves sexually without worrying that when

"feelings" change we will be deserted by our partner.

Long-term relationships in which husband and wife still have positive, loving, and romantic feelings for each other provide the best source of information on the factors that make such relationships healthy. This is a more logical approach than focusing on the factors that destroy a marriage (which is almost the total concentration of conventional research).

Psychologist Bernie Zilbergeld has looked on the positive side and has made some observations on the characteristics of sexual functioning in healthy, long-term marriages. One finding was that couples who give a high priority to their sexual relationship have a more satisfying sex life than other couples. This does not mean, of course, that sex takes precedence over everything else. It does mean that sexual considerations are not shoved to the back of the list—a perfunctory act performed at the end of the day when everything else has been accomplished.

Giving sex proper priority means that time is made for sexual interludes, for rest, and for just being together. It means that other activities are placed aside if necessary. In other words, even though it would be nice to get all the ironing done for the week (or the car polished), now that the kids will be gone for an hour the opportunity can be seized to make love before 11 at night.

It is sometimes difficult for couples to see that time together without distractions—just visiting—improves sex when it does occur. Dates and dinners together send a message that being with each other is important. (One of the things so enticing about an affair is the feeling that the person you are involved with finds you special.)

Short vacations without children or a hectic sight-seeing schedule can provide an atmosphere in which love can flourish. Sometimes work, school, and pressures of children make such a vacation a reward that carries a couple through hectic times. Couples who fail to prioritize such time forget what can be, lose their sense of intimacy, and drift apart.

Good sexual relationships are found in long-term marriages in which there is a sincere effort to maintain harmony. In accordance with 1 Corinthians 13, such relationships "always hope," "always persevere," and are "not easily angered." Because they choose to "keep no record of wrongs," such couples can have good times together even if there are aspects of their shared life that are unsettled or unresolved. If an opportunity to share an experience that will increase closeness or enable them to have fun presents itself, they do not allow pride to prevent them from seizing the moment. Such practice works well because it employs the elements of real love and not just the "good feeling" kind.

Most of us have a "touching quotient" that must be met in order for us to feel good. Anyone who thinks he doesn't should work to reintroduce into his life a comfort level that includes touching. Infants die and old people languish away without touch. Our skin is our biggest sex organ. Hugs, kisses, and touching that are spontaneously and sincerely given keep alive a feeling of sensuousness between people. Think of how the simmering teapot, kept on low heat all day, takes little energy to reach the boiling point. How do couples keep their sexual relationship on simmer? They touch each other in passing, sit by each other, and work in the same room.

Like Solomon, they understand the need for romance, and they make contact with each other during the day through calls, notes, flowers, or other tokens that say "I'm thinking of you." In my own marriage of 25 years I have received poems written especially for me, apart from special events. My birthday and Christmas presents always reflect personal consideration. There may be a new household appliance, but it is accompanied by a gift that is strictly personal—lingerie, roses, or perhaps a special piece of jewelry. The essence of romance is doing what isn't expected or essential to one's needs, but that reflects a special type of caring above and beyond the mundane.

Contrary to the stereotype, men thrive on such caring as well. Emilie Barnes in her book *More Hours in My Day* talks of preparing "love baskets," which are essentially intimate dinner for two in the bedroom or a motel that convey the message "You are worth this special effort." A wife who wishes that her husband would be more romantic will become more successful by her own example. When someone does something special for another person, it is natural to want to do something in return. Within marriage this desire arises not out of guilt or social obligation but from the warm and caring feelings that have been generated by husband and wife.

Sex has been called adult play. Certainly there should be an element of fun in it. A sense of humor is essential because funny things happen and things go wrong—children make unexpected visits, beds break and squeak, and strange noises emanating from the genitals can break the mood.

A preconceived notion of how the sexual experience should go is rarely found in sexually compatible, long-term marriages. The reality of how things actually are is accepted rather than insistence that sex match up with a fantasy model. Such couples understand that sex is always different. Sometimes it is mostly for the pleasure of only one of the partners. Occasionally there is an element of anger to it, or one of softness. It can be loud, or languid, or over quickly. Sex can do, feel, and say whatever the couple wants and needs at the moment. This frees the couple from having to set up a scenario where sex is always tender, or physical, or overwhelming.

Sexual satisfaction is related to talking about sex. Being able to communicate helps resolve problems by providing feedback and reinforcement. Often the best and easiest time to speak is after a sexual encounter. The peace and contentment, as well as the feeling of oneness which the couple experiences, make it a profitable time for sharing both what went well and what might be done the next time to make the experience even better.

For some couples married for a long time, sharing appropriate fantasies, books, and other romantic materials provides variety. This may be the least significant factor and must be approached with caution. The comfort level of individuals, particularly in sharing fantasies, varies considerably. As Christians, this is an area where we must be sensitive to our heart motivation and the offensive and demeaning exploitation that can be found in some of the "romantic" media materials.

Studies have found that sexual enjoyment deteriorates with every child born—until they leave home. Kids make us feel like a family, but their effect on our view of ourselves as sensuous, responsive men and women is mostly negative. The time and energy needed to raise a child well, coupled with the demands of a job outside the home, make this a very real and complex problem that faces the vast majority of couples.

Children need to be taught that parents have "private times" which may be used for sharing, making love, or just being alone together. Rather than feel excluded, the children can learn the valuable lesson that marriage requires special attention and time alone between husband and wife.

Adaptations can be made, especially when children are young, to help keep sex alive and well through this difficult time. Learning to make love with children awake elsewhere in the house may be a necessity and can even be fun when done with the right attitude. This solution goes back to our first criterion of a successful long-range sexual relationship: giving sex proper priority. This may involve baby-sitting exchanges with others in the same situation, occasionally getting away, and hiring extra help to aid with the fatigue factor.

What's Love Got to Do with It?

No healthy person marries without a sincere desire that his or her marriage be a permanent union, but fewer and fewer people are believing that this will be the actual outcome. Part of the confusion stems from failure to understand what covenantal marital love is. Love, after all, is defined by our society as a "warm puppy" or "never having to say you are sorry." All too seldom is the biblical definition of love explained.

For many people, marriage is primarily a social convenience held together by romantic love. By contrast, biblical marriage is a covenant held together by three special and distinct kinds of love—agape, phileo, and eros. Agape love is love that enables an individual to lay aside his own desires and causes for the desires and causes of another person. It is love that remains even when the person of our affection doesn't please us. Phileo is a type of brotherly love, a love whose focus is on friendship, sharing, and fun. Eros incorporates the physical, warm-fuzzy "feeling" that we so often label as love. It is also the sexual desire that we experience for one another.

Marriage based on romantic love—love dependent on "feeling" and the possibility of having all one's needs and desires met by the other person—results in disappointment and instability. Eros or erotic love is the most common base for marriage today. When feelings wane or disappear, it is concluded that the right mate has not been found. The result is serial monogamy, as one mate is shed and a new one tries to fulfill an impossible role. Eros is clearly an important part of Christian marriage, but commitment to the union is not measured by it.

Other factors—such as the movement away from belief in a God whose plan is still in effect, and a media blitz that shouts "Look out for number one!"—perpetuate the current disillusionment with marriage. In their own homes and on television, children are not seeing God's model for marital love.

God's covenant with Abraham and with us is an unbreakable commitment sealed with unconditional love. It is difficult for most people to grasp the depth and permanence of a covenant. Mankind's understanding is of contracts "only as good as the paper they are written on," in which loopholes can always be found and which terminate when they no longer "feel" right.

Paul grasps God's meaning of covenant in Romans 8:38,39: "I am convinced that neither death nor life, neither angels nor demons, neither the present nor the future, nor any powers, neither height nor depth, nor anything else in creation, will be able to separate us from the love of God that is in Christ Jesus our Lord."

Hebrews reminds us that marriage is to be honored and the marriage bed kept pure (Hebrews 13:4). In addition to adultery, this passage speaks to other issues. Our marriage beds are honored and kept pure when Christians view marriage as the covenant commitment it was meant to be. The words "what God has joined together" (Matthew 19:6) imply more than a legal document. When God joins couples in Christian marriage, they are joined sexually, personally, and socially.

Covenant marriage and its fidelity and trust are sources of stability and permanence in an unstable world. Christians may love many people, but they are bound by their covenant to only one person. Eros is important, but it is undergirded by agape; phileo provides additional glue that bonds couples together as they delight in their friendship, mutual goals, and pleasure.

Our Problems Are Different

Remember the little foxes in Song of Solomon? Even though they were small and seemed to have limited capacity for destruction, when left alone they were capable of ruining the whole vineyard. Such is the case with sexual concerns that are ignored.

Sexual problems can be disrupting and upsetting. What follows is a plan of action for meeting the challenge of a sexual relationship that is more problematic than most.

What Do I Do When Sex Isn't Good Anymore?

When they are finally faced, sexual problems can be so frightening and overwhelming that their solution seems beyond anything we might be capable of. Our self-image is tied so closely with our feelings of masculinity or femininity that such problems inevitably leave us feeling vulnerable and frightened. Before we conclude that investigation into a dysfunction will require years of counseling or entering a nunnery or monastery, we need to look at the most obvious causes of sexual problems.

Among them we find a long and interdependent inventory of rather common factors. Upbringing, religion, extent of knowledge, fear, and guilt are highly related to a person's family setting. Stress, fatigue, preoccupation, and boredom reflect the lifestyle which an individual lives and the priority which is given to sex. Depression, a trait normally found in conjunction with sexual difficulties, may be either a cause or a result of such difficulties. Finally, relationship considerations, such as the ability to communicate and the attitude which men and women have toward each other, contribute to problems of sexual adjustment.

Stress and Preoccupation

The relationship between stress and poor sexual function has previously been pointed out. One body cannot do two things at once. A job that takes virtually everything a man or woman can give may need to be changed, for if the sexual relationship is valued, an atmosphere in which it can flourish must be maintained. Reducing stress in whatever way it occurs in a person's life is crucially important. It is true that some people become more sexual under stress, interpreting the body tension they feel as sexual arousal, but often sexual acts motivated by stress have a driven nature that becomes more pleasurable when stress is reduced.

Fatigue blocks sexual functioning in the same way stress does. Young mothers, for example, may have a sincere desire to maintain a loving relationship with their husbands, but the energy required to chase a two-year-old and get up with a new baby may make "the spirit willing but the flesh weak." Older men and women are another group susceptible to fatigue.

Upbringing

The effect of a person's upbringing, including his or her religious background, must be thought through when a dysfunction exists. Often self-awareness can be freeing, especially if it can be communicated to one's partner. A therapist or counselor is not always necessary to facilitate this process, although many people feel more comfortable and are able to take greater risks in a setting directed by another trusted person.

Eileen was the youngest in a household of girls. Her dad was deeply disappointed that she was not a boy. Although they were close while she was young, when she began to bloom in adolescence his attitude toward her became cold and rejecting. Her ambivalence about her budding femininity was reflected in her clothing. She hid her new curves under layers of unattractive clothes, wore her hair closely cropped, and rejected makeup.

In her senior year she met Dave, a nice young man who clearly saw past her disguise. They married, and their social and sexual adjustment was good until Eileen became pregnant. At this point Dave appeared to withdraw, even though he seemed delighted with the prospect of being a father. Eileen became seriously depressed. They stopped making love.

Fortunately, this family had a pastor who had let it be known that he was comfortable discussing sexual issues. Exploration in counseling revealed that Dave's apparent rejection of his wife's most feminine of conditions had hooked into Eileen's feelings of rejection of her femininity by her father. She was reliving the pain of not being accepted for the healthy, maturing person she was.

Dave was suffering from lack of knowledge. He was delighted with the pregnancy but was fearful that sexual activity would somehow harm the baby. Since his wife was sensuous and beautiful to him, he attempted to dampen his desire for her by not looking at her and minimizing their time spent together.

Dave and Eileen continued to explore the effect of her father's message on her feelings of self-esteem and ultimately her sexual functioning. Dave accompanied his wife to her next obstetrics appointment and expressed his fears to the doctor, where he received the assurance he needed.

Religion and Guilt

Almost everyone has a horror story involving the sex education attempts of poorly informed and overzealous parents. Bob sadly related how his mother, having noticed ejaculate on his pajamas from a night emission, forced him to confess his "sin" to the priest. The incident was so humiliating that he began to masturbate four or five times a day to ensure that it would never happen again. His mother had merely triggered and reinforced the very behavior she feared.

Punishing Bob for a night emission, a normal God-given function designed to reduce the buildup of sperm, is in the same category as disciplining young children for touching their genitals or playing doctor. When this happens, natural body functions or touching the body to create pleasure become sources of ambivalence and fear.

At the heart of many of these messages is a misunderstood biblical concept of sexuality that, because of the church's reluctance to talk about sex, has never had a chance to be corrected. God is not against sexual pleasure at all; what He abhors is the *misuse* of sex. He also does not place sexual sin in a category that elevates it above all other sins. It is a sin much the same as envy, greed, and malice are sins. Yet it is unique in that it is the only sin committed against our body as the temple of the Holy Spirit (1 Corinthians 6:18-20).

There is and should be legitimate guilt over sexual expression that does not glorify God. Adultery, fornication, lustful and/or obsessive behaviors, and failure to accept the mutuality in marriage or to consider one's partner's needs are all legitimate reasons for guilt.

False guilt can also be a great problem. People worry over whether they should enjoy sex or not, whether they are under- or oversexed, or whether their particular idiosyncrasies are sinful. Sometimes there is guilt, particularly among Christians, over saying no to marital sex. Unless one can be honest about one's real feelings of desire, there can be no honest yes. It is legitimate to occasionally be too tired for sex, out of the mood, or preoccupied!

Fear and Lack of Knowledge

Fear of sex obviously hampers its expression. Sexual fears can be based on fear of physical pain or can be related to traumatic experiences. The fear may be real or imagined. Lack of information (or misinformation) is the culprit in the majority of cases. An individual may be fearful that he or she won't measure up or be able to perform satisfactorily.

Among Christian singles fear can take another form. If they misunderstand sexual feelings, thinking that these are always sinful, they can get in the habit of denying and blocking arousal. When they marry, they discover that it is not easy to reprogram being open and responsive when they have worked so hard to ignore sexual feelings. God intends singles to glorify Him by remaining celibate, but denial of legitimate feelings is not His method, as we saw earlier.

A glaring example of lack of knowledge is the vast ignorance which women have of their own genitalia. Most have never looked at their genitals. Many are unaware that they possess an organ designed solely for pleasure. Parents overlook pointing out the clitoris because locating and naming it, as they have other parts of the body, would require an explanation of its purpose.

Boredom

Mr. and Mrs. Daniels fortunately had good sexual knowledge. Their sexual life had been fulfilling for most of their 20-year marriage. But lately they had found themselves making love less frequently and feeling somewhat empty after the experience. They had forgotten that anything, no matter how delightful, delicious, or delirious, can be boring if allowed to become routine. They needed to put their chief sexual organ—their brain—into operation. Their sex life had become a predictable pattern instead of a spontaneous expression of their love and delight in each other.

By using the word "spontaneous," I do not mean to imply that there can be no planning. If we waited for the perfect opportunity for wonderful, spontaneous sex, most of us would still be waiting! Usually time must be set aside or cleared for sex or else it won't happen. But what happens within that planned-for time should be spontaneous. Routines are easy and comfortable and are simple to fall into. They do not require much energy or attention. In sex they deaden our senses and our pleasure.

Having variety in one's sex life does not mean that a different position must be tried nightly. In reality, people enjoy one or two positions most frequently. It does mean that there is an openness to change in time, in location, and in the experience itself, allowing it to take on whatever face is right for that particular moment.

Depression

Along with fatigue, depression is often a cause of sexual dysfunction. Depression affects a person's self-image and his or her ability to take risks. Sex is inextricably tied to risk-taking. A person must feel confident enough to ask for sex without fear of rejection and with the belief that she can do her part in making the experience a satisfactory one. Depression affects sexual functioning most, however, by reducing the desire for sex.

Illness

An often-overlooked factor affecting sexuality is illness. Occasionally, particularly in the case of life-threatening illnesses, a benefit can result if the individual becomes interested in the quality of life and lets go of performance demands. Sex can actually be improved as a result of the reevaluation.

It may be that sex is affected by anatomical or structural alterations or physiological changes. But the psychological reactions to illness can be just as significant. When we don't feel well, we commonly become depressed and lose our desire for sex. If the illness is lengthy or chronic and affects our ability to function in our usual role, there is loss of self-image.

Sometimes illness requires dependency, and there is the fear that the loved one will withdraw. A person may brace himself from this by becoming emotionally remote or else may try too hard to monitor her sexual response for fear that her sexual performance won't be good enough to please the partner. "Spectatoring" kills sexual responsiveness.

Spectatoring is tuning out the natural sensations of the body that heighten arousal and focusing instead on how one is doing. It is asking oneself, "Will I be able to last?" "I don't think I'm going to be able to have an orgasm." "I'll bet he's going to be disappointed because I'm not responding like the girl on the soap!"

Problems due to illness may be prevented to a large extent by good communication and education. It is important that "sexual contact" be maintained. This may require a redefinition of sexual capacities. Handicapped people, for example, can have fulfilling sexual relations because they grasp the fact that it is not the mechanics of any one act that makes sex special but the sharing, pleasure, and unity which the couple experiences.

Be aware that all illnesses have an effect on sexual functioning—even a cold. People readily accept the idea that their appetite is affected, their need for sleep increased, and their digestive system upset, but they must be reminded that because sex is a natural function, it will be affected as well.

Communication and Sex

Being able to state openly and honestly what is desired sexually is one of the surest ways to ensure that we get it. Yet it is often one of the most difficult things asked of us. Rather than take responsibility for their own sexuality, many women prefer to believe the myth that men know everything about sex and thus shouldn't need to be told, especially if they really love them. This is complete foolishness, for there is no way the sexual appetite can be known without being told. Men do not have magical powers. They are not women and can't relate to the needs of a woman's body. It is unfair to expect them to do so and places enormous pressure on them.

When honest and clear communication finally occurs, most people are surprised at how cooperative their partners can be. No one marries to make another person miserable! Each partner desires to cooperate with the other, but he or she doesn't always know how to. Sexual information can be exchanged in the peaceful time after a sexual encounter, when defensiveness is reduced, or anytime when both partners are feeling positive and strong. Just before and during a sexual act is not advised.

The sexual act is the time for subtle and sensitive remarks or behavior that will prompt changes in position or any other aspect that will lead to greater responsiveness. Since at least 50 percent of all couples have sexual problems at some time in their marriage, such problems are not an accurate gauge on whether a couple is happily married.

If talking about your sexual relationship is especially difficult, you may find that you can write a letter to your spouse that will open the lines of communication. Couples sometimes find that sharing a sexual history breaks the ice for them. A number of books have models of a sexual history that include questions such as "What was said about your birth?" "Were you the sex your parents wanted?" "How did you first learn about intercourse?" "Did your parents show affection to each other?"*

Our Christian models from Song of Solomon were very verbal about their desire for each other and the endearing traits that each possessed. They understood the secret that getting what they wanted had much to do with clear communication.

What If Sex Is Still Bad?

Everyone gets sick on occasion and sometimes overeats, works too hard, or gets angry. People take medication, get bored, and find themselves under stress. Trying to operate sexually without considering the influences from the rest of their lives can result in bodies that don't

---

*Such a checklist can be found in *Parent's Guide to Sex Education*, by Mary Ann Mayo, and *Becoming Orgasmic: A Sexual Growth Program for Women*, by Heiman, LoPiccolo & Lo-Piccolo.

function properly. Usually such dysfunction is for a short period of time and will pass. If the marital relationship is healthy, factors affecting feelings of affection and arousal can be shared and will be accepted for what they are—a temporary hurdle. If either partner is insecure or immature or is suffering from some unresolved conflict or misunderstanding of sexual functioning, sexual problems may persist or escalate. Emotional reaction to a dysfunction may be so intense that a third party's intervention is clearly necessary.

What Is Sexual Counseling?

Currently the chance of finding an individual with specialized training in sexual counseling who is also a Christian is difficult. Personally I feel that any pastor who has a heart for counseling should be educating himself or herself for this very needed and important task. *A Christian Guide to Sexual Counseling: Recovering the Mystery and Reality of One Flesh* is my attempt to heighten awareness of this need. Clearly, the Christian perspective on sexuality is different from the world's. Indeed, many of our sexual concerns are not considered a problem for the non-Christian.

Many secular counselors have had some exposure to sexual therapy in their training. Large university settings often have well-run and reliable clinics for sexual dysfunctions. Do not hesitate to go to such a clinic if your sexual problem has escalated to the point that your marriage is in jeopardy, or simply if the pleasure to be derived from the physical side of marriage is not what God intended it to be.

Diane waited too long; her husband reluctantly left the marriage. Diane viewed her husband's unwillingness to make love to her on demand (and the increased foreplay he required) as proof of his disinterest in her. Her self-centered insistence that his sexual appetite equal hers ignored the work stress he was under and his age.

Diane had mistakenly assumed that sexual performance was a measure of love. Her husband's loyalty and devotion to his family were dismissed as any meaningful proof of his commitment to her. Sensing the importance which she placed on their lovemaking, he tried hard to please her. But the more he tried, the greater his fear of performance, which compounded the problem. Eventually he began to avoid sex altogether, and she retaliated by verbalizing her frustration and fear through innuendo and put-down.

If Diane had chosen to demonstrate some personal responsibility by going in for counseling, the counselor would have pointed out the fallacy of equating sexual performance and love. Since one's ability to perform is a natural function of the body, demanding that a partner's sexual appetite equal yours is equivalent to insisting that because you are hungry for apple pie your spouse must be too or else he or she doesn't love you!

She would also have learned that sexual functioning changes with age. Such changes are normal and do not reflect a lack of love or commitment to the spouse. Her husband would have been helped to overcome the habit of spectatoring—a practice that stifles sexual performance in both men and women.

Sensate Focus

Barbara and Joel had been happily married for several years, but lately Barbara found herself staying up until she was sure Joel was asleep. Sex seemed boring, and she rarely felt aroused. The disinterest in sex which Barbara felt is categorized as the number one sexual problem presented to sexual therapists in the United States. Its causes are many, but its correction (like that of other sexual problems) requires accepting responsibility to make things different.

Low-desire problems are almost always relationship problems. Barbara and Joel needed help in assessing what was going on between them. Had they been communicating their dreams, desires, and fears? What importance did each of them give to sex? Did they set aside time, allow themselves to be rested, and think about sex? Was energy devoted to varying their patterns by changing location or changing the way sex was expressed? Were they aware of any unresolved business between them?

Counseling helped Barbara get in touch with the frustration she felt over Joel's mechanical and clumsy approach to their lovemaking. Early in the marriage, the newness of sex helped her overlook his ineptitude. A Christian, she tried hard to view sex as the giving experience it was intended to be. Because of guilt over not being able to maintain that perspective, she was unable to admit to herself the disappointment and anger she felt. Her expectation of sexual expression in marriage was not the perfunctory, joyless, and sometimes painful act which she and Joel shared.

The counselor instructed this couple to reawaken their desire by practicing "sensate focus" exercises along with communication techniques designed to improve their ability to be open and candid with each other. Sensate focus works because it provides a safe environment in which to deal with avoidance or anxiety in approaching sex. Having put aside time and eliminating the threat of intercourse, they are free to concentrate on relaxing and pleasurable sensations. Old habits are broken and new ways of being together are practiced and reinforced. Even the physical environment is considered for its effect on lovemaking, just as in Song of Solomon chapter 1.

Couples are first asked to work on developing a comfort level with their nude bodies. This may involve taking a shower together or simply cuddling on a bed. A nonsexual examination of genitals is shared. Touching or caressing the genitalia in a sensual way is not allowed. Sometimes these steps require considerable time. Until the couple can be together without embarrassment, they are not to progress. The goal is to reestablish touch without anxiety, reawaken pleasure, and to begin to see their partner as someone with whom it is safe to share their sexual desires, fears, and concerns.

When a comfort level with giving and receiving pleasure is achieved, the exercise is extended to include the genitals. Orgasm is forbidden. Communication of what feels good and special creates a sense of the uniqueness of their particular relationship.

If both partners are able to be orgasmic, a new task is assigned. Each partner is asked to pleasure himself or herself in the presence of the partner. This difficult task is hard to do but infinitely releasing. Additionally, the partner learns more accurately the type of touch that is most pleasing. This was especially helpful to Joel. To get away from any feeling of the spouse as spectator, it is helpful if he or she lies or sits closely, lightly placing a hand over his or her spouse's.

When good physical and verbal sexual communication has been established, the couple may leisurely reintroduce intercourse with no expectations. The desire that appeared to be missing is recognized and celebrated once again, and each partner has confidence that he or she knows what is pleasurable to the spouse.

Lack of Desire

Sensate focus is only one technique in overcoming lack of desire. Other counseling techniques may include various activities that reflect the complexity of the problem. Barbara had to be made aware of her personal feelings about sex and not just how she responded to sex.

Insights were used to provide clues to the source of the problem. She had mistakenly assumed that being a good Christian wife sexually meant suffering in silence. When this was pointed out and a more adequate understanding of God's message was revealed, she was able to share more openly what she really needed.

Distorted ideas and wrong assumptions can be changed by reinforcing correct ones. Sometimes this may take the form of affirmations: "God made me capable of pleasurable sexual expression"; "My husband married me because I'm the one he wants to be with"; "I'm pretty."

Barbara and Joel's total marriage was enriched by the new understanding which they experienced within their sexual relationship. I'm sometimes asked, "If there are marriage and sexual problems, which do you fix first?" With the exception of seriously disturbed marriages and individuals who need considerable therapeutic intervention because of their own problems, marriages are often improved without any intervention. A total relationship can be considered a circle, containing both the physical and emotional aspects. Improved communication, the goal of marriage counseling, makes sex better. More compatible sexual functioning tends to improve other marital communication.

Difficulty with Orgasm

Lucinda was literally dragged into counseling by her husband, Lonnie. The words poured out as he expressed his frustration with his inability to "make" his wife orgasmic. He concluded that their marriage could be saved if Lucinda could just get "fixed." He knew the problem was hers because other partners from his wild bachelor days were always responsive and declared him a fine lover.

Lonnie is a perfect example to remind us that sexual problems are always relationship problems, even if a symptom manifests itself in only one partner. Lonnie had a lot to learn. Like many men, he felt he could "make" a woman orgasmic.

I decided not to point out to Lonnie that women who are involved in sexual liaisons are often notorious in their efforts to make a man feel he is a wonderful lover. In reality, sexual responsiveness, especially with intercourse, is quite difficult for most women, but easy to fake. I did work to help him see that past relationships have no bearing on a current one. Each new partnership has its unique nature, comfort level, and intensity.

Lucinda and Lonnie both needed to redefine sex to encompass a much fuller interpretation. Sex is not mere intercourse or intercourse with mutual orgasm; sex is whatever brings a couple closer, reduces tension, and provides pleasure. On any given day this may mean that the most fulfilling sexual act is a long and mutual hug, a laugh-filled afternoon where everything seems to go wrong sexually, or simply lying nude next to each other. Having a preset idea of the way sex should always be guarantees disappointment.

This is easier to understand when we think of food analogies. No matter how much you love lobster and chocolate truffles, if your diet consisted of them daily, you would eventually find them tiresome. Just as with your hunger appetite, in order to feel satisfied your sexual appetite must be in tune with what you are hungry for. The variety not only keeps sex interesting, but since it is what you want, you feel satisfied. Most of us are so performance-oriented that releasing sex from a checklist of preconceived behaviors is difficult.

Lucinda's background was different from her husband's. Her strict upbringing discouraged her from any self-exploration. Although she had been married a year, she was unfamiliar with her genitals and reluctant to touch them. Further questioning revealed that she probably had experienced orgasm but failed to recognize it. This is not unusual, for the media portrayal of orgasm is always highly exaggerated—leaving one incapable of work for the rest of the day and with neighbors wondering what all the noise was about!

Those women who determine to take responsibility to become orgasmic find that, with few exceptions, they are able to do so. Often women simply aren't aware of the amount of learning required in order to become sexually responsive. Self-help programs are very successful in helping a woman explore any psychological and/or physical blocks to expressing her sexual responsiveness.

Such programs are frequently avoided by Christian women because the quickest and most effective ones require masturbation. The goal, however, is not self-centered if the women is seeking to improve the sexual relationship between her and her spouse.

All orgasms are physiologically the same whether they are caused by manual manipulation or intercourse. There are many patterns to female orgasm. Additionally, while the clitoris is the site of the most intense feelings in most women, others enjoy the sensations from the outer third of the vagina (orgasmic platform) or enjoy stimulation of particularly sensitive areas within the vagina itself.

I recommend *Becoming Orgasmic: A Sexual Growth Program for Women*, by Julia Heiman, Leslie LoPiccolo, and Jospeh LoPiccolo because it has been well-accepted and is easy to use. At the end of seven to ten weeks, 90 percent of the women following the program experience orgasm in some way, 80 percent with their partner, and 40 percent solely with intercourse and no manual stimulation. These statistics are quite good, for on the average only 30 percent of all women can regularly have orgasm with intercourse and no other stimulation. The program works equally well with or without a therapist guide.

Like sensate focus, the program begins with psychological self-awareness and involves exploration of the body through observing and touch. The importance of relaxation is emphasized. As the woman becomes aware of her capacity for response, she is asked to role-play an exaggerated orgasm experience. Often this is a freeing precursor to the real thing.

Although the book does not suggest it, the husband's involvement in the same exercises that his wife is practicing is a good idea. By participating, he becomes part of the process of improvement. His willingness to explore his body gives her permission to enjoy her body and sensitizes him to the fears, inhibitions, and difficulties she is facing.

This proved to be very helpful for Lonnie. Once his misinformation was corrected and he identified with Lucinda, he became a sensitive and patient lover. One other point had to be cleared up, however. Experiencing a mutual orgasm was still an important goal to Lonnie. He was reminded that since sex is a natural function, insisting that their orgasms coincide perfectly was equivalent to demanding that they urinate at precisely the same moment—something obviously rather tedious and silly. Simultaneous orgasm through intercourse should be viewed as a nice serendipity when it happens, but not as the goal of each sexual encounter.

The Importance of Trust

Being able to sexually respond is highly related to the ability to trust in a relationship. It was with good reason that God declared that men and women were to "cleave" to each other. Anyone who has counseled following an affair by one or both marriage partners knows how difficult it is for the couple to reestablish trust. Sexual counselors understand the impossibility of a person "letting go" when trust needs aren't met.

Being unfaithful is not the only way a person is untrustworthy. Trust is violated when a man cannot be depended upon as a reliable provider. The most common occurrence, however, is by failure to be there emotionally. A TV talk show recently interviewed couples whose relationships were ostensibly in trouble because of the weight gain of one of the partners. As the show progressed it was clear that underneath all the venomous comments and conditional love expressed was a breach of trust.

We have previously discussed the necessity of trusting enough to be dependent. Couples who can risk being vulnerable are the ones most likely to experience good sexual functioning.

Vaginismus

Vaginismus, when it occurs, can be very disruptive of a couple's relationship. Technically it involves a reflexive and involuntary clamping down of the muscles surrounding the vaginal opening. The reaction may be severe enough to prevent intercourse or a vaginal exam.

Because we are able to control many muscles in our bodies, the assumption is made that a woman should be able to relax and allow penetration to occur. This is not always so. Often the condition is brought on by actual or imagined fear, but it is very real. Treatment involves mechanically retraining the muscles to relax when the vagina is approached. Treatment always includes the husband.

A doctor is able to demonstrate the reflex response to the husband and wife during an examination. The woman is instructed in the use of Kegel exercises in order to gain confidence in her ability to control the reaction. Kegel exercises are familiar to many women from a variety of sources. They may have been recommended by a doctor to a woman suffering from leakage of urine. Sometimes they are taught by an exercise instructor who points out that control over the perineal area heightens sexual feeling and responsiveness. Others are first introduced to Kegel exercises in their childbirth preparedness classes.

These exercises were suggested a number of years ago by the obstetrician-gynecologist A. H. Kegel for control of leaking urine in his patients. He discovered that the pubococcygeus muscle, which makes up the floor of the perineal area, can be strengthened by its systematic contraction over a period of time. The muscle is identified by stopping the flow of urine midstream or, in the case of men, lifting the penis. Two weeks of ten contractions six times a day will usually improve muscle tone as much as possible. Unlike other exercise, "Kegels" can be done inconspicuously in any attire, and seated or standing.

Progressively larger dilators are introduced to physically stretch the vaginal opening. When the woman's confidence and comfort allow it, the husband is encouraged to sensitively participate in their insertion. When the largest dilator can be inserted, intercourse is attempted with the female astride. The penis is different from a dilator, and great patience and encouragement is required.

Other aspects of intervention include the same history and sensate-focus format used in the treatment of orgasmic dysfunction. One-quarter of all cases of vaginismus are easily treated, while the rest are moderate to difficult to treat. Women who have suffered rape or incest have the hardest time overcoming the reflexic contraction. Frequently there is a history of restrictive attitudes toward sexuality in a woman's family history or a trauma involving the genitals. Vaginismus has even resulted from a physician's insensitive remark suggesting to his or her patient that her genitals are unsatisfactory in some way.

Back to Our Model

God knows us well. His marriage manual includes a sexual problem (Song 5:2-8) and its resolution (Song 5:9–6:13). His suggestions for cure involve the same process that we find in today's sex therapy.

What did the wife of the King complain about? It appears that Shulamith, like many of her modern-day counterparts, disliked being awakened late at night for sex. She countered Solomon's advances with excuses that sound vaguely familiar: "Solomon, can't you see I'm tired? Do you really expect me to wake up and be lively this time of night?" By the time she struggles awake, he is gone, wounded pride and all. Her conscience is piqued and she is moved to remember what he means to her and how appealing he is. "O Solomon, I know that hundreds of women would be delighted to be with you, but you have chosen me. You are so handsome and virile. How could I have been so foolish!"

Shulamith takes responsibility for the fact that she has taken her husband for granted, and she sets out to correct this wrong by approaching him in the way that he finds appealing—a physical, sensuous dance. She does not dwell on his shortcomings but on her own.

Solomon does not get into the act of blaming, either. We assume that he rethinks the wisdom of continually approaching his wife at times of her lowest energy because he willingly takes her on minivacations to places she finds revitalizing and relaxing. He also refuses to make her feel guilty, but instead acts all the more romantic by giving her a gift, verbalizing how special she is, and waiting for her to reach out to him. Solomon didn't pout or institute the silent treatment.

How does this parallel our modern-day approach? Both partners accepted responsibility for aspects of the problem which they were capable of changing. There was no blaming. The problem was not allowed to go on indefinitely. A concern to set things right involved an effort at improved communication plus focusing on positive traits and the special needs and desires of the other person. Shulamith focused her thoughts on the erotic, insuring her desire and responsiveness; Solomon remembered to be romantic. A review of the literature of Masters and Johnson and of other sexual counselors could hardly improve on those considerations.

One thing not emphasized in many therapeutic formats is an attitude of commitment to the marriage that emphasizes finding solutions rather than bailing out. Turning to God for His supernatural help enables Christians to stretch and change in ways that appear humanly impossible. Most important is the simple but powerful act of acknowledging that God is rightfully in our bedrooms. He wants us to experience sexual pleasure, and He can be depended upon to come to our aid when things aren't going right.

We need to pray for God's blessing over each sexual experience, and ask for His guidance and wisdom. An appropriate prayer might be, "O Mighty Counselor, I love my husband, but I am having difficulty focusing tonight. Please help me to be the responsive wife I was made to be."

Taking Responsibility

Enjoyable sexual relations do not happen automatically. A good sexual relationship will not necessarily hold a marriage together, but it is an important ingredient in the glue that bonds a husband and wife. A poor relationship weakens the marital bond. It also affects the self-image of both partners. God's design is that we find physical pleasure in each other. But sex itself is not just a physical act that one learns to perform well; it is communication, intimacy, and pleasure.

The most important thing we can learn from successful long-term marriages is to give sex its proper priority in order that it may be rich and fulfilling both for us personally and for our family. Closely tied to sexual functioning is a good self-image. Introspection may be a necessary part of taking responsibility for sexual functioning.

Fulfilled sexuality requires the courage to confess that our relationship does not measure up to what the Lord wants for us and the willingness to undergo the neccesary changes and/or treatment. This may include committing to a program that works quickly and enriches a relationship through increased communication and heightened responsiveness. At the very least it requires willing movement from the status quo.

"Rejoice in the [husband] of your youth" (Proverbs 5:18).

Chapter Nine

The Complete Woman and Her Most Common Gynecological Concerns

In the thirty-ninth year of his reign Asa was afflicted with
a disease in his feet. Though his disease was severe, even
in his illness he did not seek help from the Lord, but only
from the physicians.

—*2 Chronicles 16:12*

Unfortunately we live in a fallen world. Our bodies, as incredibly designed as they are, sometimes cause us grief and concern. In this chapter we will look at a variety of conditions that women normally face throughout their lifetime. Most of these conditions are not life-threatening, but sometimes they may prevent women from living a healthy, active life. Occasionally one of the conditions must be considered a serious health problem. Our discussion will be limited to the most common manifestation of female health problems.

In any Ob-Gyn practice, questions and problems arise daily. Let's categorize these under the following headings: disorders of menstruation, premenstrual syndrome, urinary tract infections, vaginal infections, Pap smears, contraception, sexually transmitted diseases, and substance-abuse.

Disorders of Menstruation

Diane was a perky college freshman. Her periods had always been regular, so when they became erratic she became concerned. An examination revealed no physical pathology. Diane was a Christian and denied any sexual activity, so there was no possibility of pregnancy.

There were several other factors in her lifestyle that clearly could affect her periods. She was new on campus and worried about being accepted. Her scholastic load was heavy, requiring a great deal of study.

Lately, in an effort to relieve stress and keep her weight down, she had begun to jog with some men and women in her dorm who were long-distance runners. Any and all of the above changes in her lifestyle could alter her menstrual pattern. The combination made me confident that no further testing was needed at this time.

More commonly a woman comes in whose history reveals a continuous pattern of dieting and whose lifestyle involves juggling 32 hats in her role as mom, wife, and worker. Any major change in lifestyle which encompasses more stress, erratic weight gain or loss, and vigorous exercise or travel may produce menstrual irregularities. These should be considered first, before more drastic treatment is decided upon.

Sometimes for reasons not obvious, a woman will have a change in menstrual pattern. I sometimes refer to this as "abnormally normal." This seeming contradiction in terms does indeed describe what is happening, for in most cases the problem rights itself with time.

Irregular periods are sometimes accompanied by irregular bleeding patterns. Menorrhagia (excessive menstrual flow) becomes a problem when the flow occurs as often as every two weeks and/or is characterized by prolonged bleeding with clots.

Mrs. Fernandez started her menstrual flow right on schedule. After three days it became very heavy, with occasional clots. She had a busy week. Her youngest child was looking forward to a birthday party, her boy had extra soccer practice, and her husband, a CPA, was in his usual pretax panic. She simply had no time to think about herself. After two weeks of continually changing pads she was clearly drained. She fainted at her daughter's party.

Examination revealed that she was still hemorrhaging and was severely anemic. The bleeding was controlled by a D & C, iron pills were prescribed to cure the anemia, and rest was insisted upon. In a way she was lucky; had she lost blood more slowly, her anemia might have gone undetected, since the body compensates for the loss.

Mrs. Fernandez might never have such a problem again. But an investigation was warranted to determine the probable cause. Possibly her obesity and stress triggered a hormonal imbalance. A pathologist would be able to confirm this because he would see tissue changes that indicate whether there has been an "overgrowth" of the uterine lining (hyperplasia). Or perhaps there is evidence of no ovulation (anovulation), of fibroids, or of an infection of the lining of the uterus (endometritis).

If no cause is determined, such bleeding is called dysfunctional uterine bleeding (DUB). The course chosen by the physician and patient may vary depending upon the patient's age, desire for children, and severity, and upon such external factors as missed work and family responsibilities. A decision may be made to observe and await self-regulation.

The chance of cancer is less likely under the age of 40, so hormones may be given without first doing an endometrial biopsy. After age 40 the need for a biopsy will be determined by the history and the physician's clinical judgment. An endometrial biopsy (an office sampling of the lining of the uterus) may be decided upon. A Pap smear merely samples the cervical cells and therefore rarely gives evidence of uterine cancer.

A minor surgical procedure called a D & C (Dilation and Curettage) may be called for. The D & C procedure controls excess bleeding because it removes the overgrown tissue in the uterine cavity. In most cases the new replacement tissue grows back in a normal pattern. Unlike the endometrial biopsy, which samples one small area of the uterus, the D & C removes all the tissue, thus allowing complete evaluation. It is both diagnostic and usually curative.

In summary, there are four ways to treat heavy periods. The first is to take oral iron tablets and wait to see if the hormonal imbalance will correct itself. If the heavy flow continues, one could try oral progesterone for ten days each month, for three cycles. Finally, birth control pills can be prescribed if the woman is under 40 and does not smoke, or else a D & C may be called for.

Occasionally the problem with menstruation is the lack of it. This is called amenorrhea. In this chapter we are concerned with women who have had regular periods but have ceased menstruation for at least six months. It is always wise to first rule out pregnancy in a child-bearing-aged woman.

In a young woman the most common cause for a missed period is pregnancy. I am always amazed at the number of people who find it necessary to deny this possibility even to their doctor. Once it is determined a pregnancy does not exist, other causes are considered.

More likely, amenorrhea in a mature woman results from stress. A serious physical illness, a major accident, an emotional trauma, certain tranquilizers and other medications, persistent corpus luteum cysts, and extreme obesity can all cause missed periods. Birth-control-pill users may experience increasingly light periods that stop altogether because of the ovarian suppression. Competitive women athletes frequently find their periods interrupted. This can be explained by a combination of the emotional stress of competition, nutritional factors, and weight loss that causes the body fat to fall below 15 percent. Psychologically, an intense fear or hope of pregnancy may also be a factor in developing amenorrhea.

Since a pituitary tumor can cause secondary amenorrhea and in many women galactorrhea (a whitish discharge from the nipple), the presence of such a tumor can be verified by pituitary hormone levels, a CAT scan, or a magnetic resonance machine. Whether benign or malignant, such tumors can cause serious consequences. Treatment is by tumor cell destruction via external irradiation, surgical removal, or (if the tumors are very small and benign) hormonal suppression.

Some women have pain and slight spotting around the time of ovulation. This is called Mittelschmerz. More troublesome pain usually occurs prior to and during menstruation. This is known as dysmenorrhea. As stated in an earlier chapter, antiprostaglandins can be very helpful for both types of pain.

Premenstrual Syndrome (PMS)

Several years ago premenstrual syndrome became the "in" disease, replacing hypoglycemia. PMS results in such a mixture of symptoms and degrees of distress that an adequate definition of it is almost impossible. Basically it is characterized by distressing physical, psychological, and behavioral symptoms that are not caused by organic disease but which regularly recur during the same phase of the menstrual/ovarian cycle (and which disappear or significantly regress during the remainder of the cycle). For a while nearly every magazine and news show featured a PMS segment. "Experts" and PMS clinics sprang up like spring daffodils. The fact that women who suffered from PMS got off for murders and assaults made good copy.

The cause of this syndrome is still elusive. Today five observations can be made about PMS.

1. PMS is not a disease found before puberty, during pregnancy, or after menopause. It is related to cyclic ovarian function.

2. As long as there is ovarian function, a woman can suffer symptoms of PMS, even if she has had a hysterectomy.

3. Symptoms appear before bleeding begins.

4. As yet, all studies involving chemical and psychological

research have failed to find a specific cause of PMS.

5. There is considerable placebo effect.

The symptoms vary greatly in both severity and duration of distress from woman to woman. Some women experience them around the time of ovulation, but in most women the symptoms occur seven to ten days before the period starts. Keeping an accurate, written record of symptoms and the menstrual cycle is critical in helping the physician determine the diagnosis and treatment plan.

The most common complaints are breast tenderness, swelling, abdominal bloating, weight gain, and headache. The most distressful symptoms are usually psychological in nature and include depression, anxiety, tension, and tiredness. A total list of every conceivable sign is probably an impossible task. You may recognize that these indicators are commonly associated with monthly periods, and most women experience them to some degree. The difference in PMS is that they result in a woman being unable to function in her job, marriage, or other aspect of everyday life. Severity is the distinguishing factor. Such behaviors as suicide attempts, criminal acts, inability to think clearly, and accident proneness get the most publicity and are the most controversial because they involve isolated events.

Although there is no one magical treatment for the overall syndrome (beware of clinics or clinicians that offer one), relief can be found for specific aspects of the disease. In mild cases education, reassurance, and psychological support may be all that are necessary. More moderate cases involve a variety of interventions. Birth control pills, for example, work in 50 percent of the cases, probably because of the suppression of ovulation. Sometimes, however, this treatment is not helpful and actually makes things worse.

The medication Danazol is sometimes beneficial, but its side effects can be frustrating. They include weight gain and increased body hair (which in most women will reverse when the treatment stops). Water pills (diuretics) help to decrease general body swelling, which appears to be helpful. Antiprostaglandins, such as Advil, Motrin, or Ponstel, help with cramping and ovulation pain. Occasionally male or female hormone treatments give relief. One of the most recent studies found that subcutaneous estrogen or estrogen discs combined with progesterone for withdrawal bleeding provided relief for some women.

Nutritional factors are within the reach of every woman. Controlled studies are hard to come by, but reduction of sugar in the diet and elimination of caffeine and alcohol are worth trying. A balanced diet (some researchers suggest six small meals which include lots of protein and complex carbohydrates) maintains a relatively constant level of blood sugar and has helped many women. Vitamins B$_6$ and A have been a remedy in enough women to warrant a trial.

Psychological treatments include desensitization (to reduce anxiety in anticipation of the period). A greater sense of well-being is achieved through regular exercise that is not so excessive as to disrupt the monthly cycle.

There is no known cause of PMS, even though its biological, psychological, social, and genetic components have been carefully studied. Some studies indicate as high as 80 percent improvement after the patient believes that something was done (the placebo effect). The problem is complex because this result fails to stand up over long periods of time. At this point the only conclusion that can be drawn is that women who suffer from PMS are unusually sensitive to the normal, cyclical changes of their bodies and experience exaggerated symptoms.

Urinary Tract Infections

Soon after we married, my wife was teaching her high school class when she was overwhelmed with the need to urinate. She barely managed to dismiss the kids, who were truly confused at being shoved out the door prior to the bell. Within seconds she lost bladder control. Fortunately, a lab coat was nearby and she made her way to the women's lounge. Her experience is more dramatic than most but is a common occurrence among newlyweds. "Honeymoon cystitis" can actually occur whenever there has been frequent and perhaps energetic intercourse or a new partner.

Bacteria from the rectal area can spread and enter the urethra, causing an ascending infection to the bladder and possibly the kidneys. Women with moderate to severe pelvic relaxation do not completely empty the bladder, thus leaving a stagnant pool of urine, ideal for bacterial growth.

The common symptoms can be experienced quickly. They include a strong urge to urinate (urgency), painful urination (dysuria), frequent urination, and loss of bladder control (incontinence). The diagnosis is made by a laboratory analysis of the urine. A culture may be needed if the infection is recurrent or does not respond to the antibiotic given within 24 to 48 hours. If a woman has recurrent infections (more than three within a year), a urological consultation is recommended. Ignoring the problem could lead to permanent kidney damage.

Some helpful hints to prevent urinary infections include the following: drinking lots of fluids (including those with high vitamin C content, which make the urine acidic), good hygiene, cotton undergarments, and varying sexual positions to reduce urethral irritation.

If burning with urination, urgency, and increased frequency persist but no cause can be demonstrated, then one must consider the possibility of "urethral syndrome." This can be caused by infection, trauma, allergy, or chemical irritants. Initial therapy involves antibiotics and/or removal of the offending source.

A number of therapeutic approaches may have to be experimented with, but the right combination provides relief for 60 to 70 percent of patients. Such approaches include vaginal estrogen, urethral dilation, paraurethral steroid injections, long-term, low-dose antibiotics, and urethral cryosurgery.

Vaginal Infections

The worst vaginal infection I ever encountered was that of a woman whose discharge and odor were so severe that one was aware of the problem across the room. She had no explanation of what might be wrong. The examination revealed a brass doorknob lodged within the vagina. This was probably the only time in my medical career when I was at a total loss for words! When she asked, "What did you find?" I was so stunned that I answered, "It must be the tip of your douche bag." Although I've seen this patient annually, she has never alluded to the "brass douche-bag tip" and neither have I.

Retained items are characterized by particularly foul-smelling discharges. Two items commonly retained are tampons and contraceptive sponges. Little girls have been known to insert pebbles, buttons, and beans into their vagina, just as they place them in their nose and ears.

The most frequently encountered vaginal infection is moniliasis, a yeast infection. It is characterized by a thick, cottage-cheese-like, white discharge and by itching. It is not uncommon for a healthy woman to have one or two yeast infections a year. However, if the infection never quite goes away with treatment, diabetes should be considered. Occasionally, repeated infections occur due to the normal flora of the rectum spreading to the vaginal area through sexual practices, or improperly wiping from the back forward. Oral medication is most effective in this case.

Infections are common after a woman has taken oral antibiotics, particularly tetracycline and penicillin. The usual treatment is a three- or seven-day use of vaginal suppositories or creams.

A nonspecific vaginitis is caused by any number of bacteria, although it is associated with Gardnerella vaginalis. The discharge is usually white to yellowish in color, is occasionally blood-streaked, and sometimes has an unpleasant fishlike odor. Most of the time the body effectively fights off this type of infection, but times of stress or changes in body health can make a woman more susceptible. She can also carry this organism in the vagina without having symptoms. Bacteria can be harbored under the. foreskin of an uncircumcised male with poor hygiene or who has a chronic bacterial prostatitis. Sometimes both partners must be treated, using sulfa vaginal creams or suppositories for the female and oral antibiotics for the male.

Trichomoniasis is a small protozoan that causes a frothy, greenish, occasionally itching discharge. Both partners must be treated in this case, for this is a sexually transmitted disease. It can cause great upset among long-married, faithful couples when it appears. It does not mean that one or the other partners has been unfaithful, but only that the disease has been harbored and kept under control by the person's own physiology. (Men usually have no symptoms.) Changes in vaginal chemistry caused by aging, medications, inadequate hygiene, and poor health allow the disease to take hold. Treatment is by oral medication taken by both partners.

Until recently these were the most common problems. Today there are three more infections that are a cause of greater concern. They are herpes, condyloma acuminata, and chlamydia. Although these are common vaginal complaints, our discussion of them will take place later in this chapter under the heading Sexually Transmitted Diseases.

It is important to mention agents that irritate the vulva or vaginal lining and make the tissues more susceptible to infection. These include such things as certain soaps and perfumes, dyed or perfumed toilet paper, scented tampons, feminine hygiene sprays, bubble baths (especially in young girls), and vaginal contraceptive suppositories, creams, or gels. Recently Procter and Gamble sent a medical memo to Ob-Gyn physicians announcing the elimination of perfumes and dyes from their products.

The risk of getting these diseases can be minimized by a number of good health practices: good vaginal hygiene, wearing cotton panties or pantyhose with a cotton crotch, frequent changing of tampons or pads, avoiding excessive douching (more than once a week), and avoiding any products that cause irritation.

The Pap Smear

Forty years ago cervical cancer was a leading cause of death from malignant disease in American women. During the 1920's a Dr. George Papanicolaou discovered that cancer cells are shed from the cervix into the vaginal fluid. By taking a sample of this fluid, abnormal cells could be observed. This procedure is called a "Pap smear."

Since the 1950's this test has become a routine part of gynecological examinations. Because of this, the death rate from cervical cancer has decreased over 50 percent. A women is more prone to cervical cancer if she begins sexual activity before age 20, has three or more sexual partners, and has pregnancies that are close together.

A Pap smear is basically painless. Its accuracy depends on how meticulously the specimen is obtained and how well-trained the screener and/or pathologist is. An abnormal test may show an inflammatory change, dysplasia, or malignancy. Inflammatory changes can result from any number of infections. They are treated, and the Pap smear is repeated in three months. This type of problem is classified as a Class II Pap smear. If the changes persist, a colposcopy is done. (A colposcopy is a microscopic examination of the cervix.) Tissue is removed to determine the degree and extent of the disease.

A Class III Pap smear is so defined because of the presence of dysplasia. Dysplasia represents a precancerous lesion which is categorized as mild, moderate, or severe. Mild dysplasia may be treated like a Class II Pap smear, although most Ob-Gyns would do a colposcopy. Moderate or severe dysplasia should have a colposcopy followed by appropriate treatment such as cryosurgery, cone biopsy, laser surgery, or cauterization. These methods destroy or remove the dysplastic tissue. They are office procedures except for the cone biopsy. All types of dysplasia are 99 percent curable with conscientious follow-up.

Carcinoma in situ, cancer on the surface of the cervix, is classified as Class IV. The option exists to remove the uterus or simply excise or destroy the affected tissue. It is important that childbearing women understand that either choice is 99 percent effective and that after six months to a year a pregnancy may be attempted.

Mrs. Broderick seemed in peak condition. She was embarrassed to admit that she had neglected her "annual" exam for 15 years. A Pap smear revealed probable invasive cancer. A cone biopsy confirmed this, and she was dead in six months. Had she come in sooner, her cancer would have been curable. Class V Pap smears indicate that invasive cancer is likely. An early invasive cancer, when the tumor is still confined to the cervix, has a 75 to 80 percent cure rate.

With minimal invasion a hysterectomy may be all that is needed. More widespread invasion within the cervix can require radical pelvic surgery and/or radiotherapy. The survival rate drops dramatically as the tumor spreads to adjacent or distant tissues.

An additional test for cervical cancer will soon be available for general use. Cervicography is a painless, inexpensive procedure that, like the Pap smear, can detect cancerous cells. In combination with the Pap smear, it will give a highly accurate diagnosis and permanent record. Your doctor may use a second system of classification of Pap smears: CIN I, II, III.

Contraception

Teenagers are only mildly concerned with sexually transmitted diseases; they fear AIDS only because they might be labeled homosexual. The idea that they can die or suffer serious consequences other than a possible pregnancy is not high on their list of concerns. The concerted effort to make them aware of such problems has not been highly effective. Even if they fear pregnancy, their knowledge of prevention is deplorable. A vast number of teenagers still think that saran wrap is an effective condom. Coke douches are touted as adequate birth control. Many teenage girls think that if they stand up, don't remove all their clothes, and/or don't have an orgasm they won't get pregnant.

I am sometimes asked if I automatically advise birth control for young girls who have decided to be sexually active. I am always pleased when a teenager goes to her mother or physician before making this decision. It gives them an opportunity to help the girl think through her decision. If she cannot be dissuaded, birth control pills will not affect her future cycles or fertility. They are by far the safest and most effective birth control method available to her.

In fact they comprise the safest method for any nonsmoking woman under 35 years of age who has normal blood pressure, is not obese, has normal blood cholesterol, and is not diabetic. Most side effects are temporary and minor in nature. Occasionally there are serious risks, such as circulatory disorders, liver tumors, and gallbladder disease. This is why getting pills requires routine medical follow-up and a prescription from a physician.

The major advantage of pills is their 98 to 99 percent effectiveness and their convenience. But other methods may also be very effective when used properly. For example, the diaphragm has been shown to be 86 to 97 percent effective. The fitting diaphragms which we use in the office all have holes cut in the center. A very worried patient returned to my office with her recently purchased diaphragm, concerned that hers lacked the hole. We assured her that hers was preferable if she was not interested in becoming pregnant!

Diaphragms must be fitted by a doctor and are most effective when used with a spermicide. They must not be inserted more than six to 12 hours before intercourse. A new application of spermicide is needed before each act of intercourse in order to achieve maximum protection. If cared for properly, diaphragms can last three to five years. After childbirth or a major weight loss or gain, a refitting is in order.

One of the most recent developments in contraception is the sponge. It is prefilled with spermicide and acts as a barrier against sperm. It is effective for 24 hours but must be kept in place for six hours after intercourse. Sponges are 85 percent effective. The ease of purchase without consultation with a physician is offset somewhat by allergic reactions, toxic shock, and the occasional inability to remove the device, necessitating a visit to the doctor.

Today condoms are probably as important in disease prevention as they are in birth control. They should be put on before any contact with the vagina and removed soon after intercourse to prevent sperm from escaping. Without spermicide they are 82 to 95 percent effective.

Vaginal spermicides in the form of creams, jellies, and foams can be 77 to 97 percent effective. Foam is the most effective of these. It is inserted in the vagina with an applicator, producing both a physical and a chemical barrier. Application is made 15 minutes before intercourse.

The rhythm method is the most natural of all birth control methods and the only one approved by the Roman Catholic church. It is 65 to 85 percent effective. Success depends on the prediction of ovulation and on abstinence from sex during the fertile period. This may be calculated from a calendar, body temperature, or cervical mucus changes (vaginal discharge). New timing technics, although sometimes expensive, can increase the safe times for intercourse.

No method of contraception is 100 percent effective, and each has its advantages and disadvantages. No matter which method is chosen, maximum protection occurs only if instructions are followed carefully and the doctor is consulted regularly to insure that the method of contraception remains effective and the woman remains healthy.

Sexually Transmitted Diseases (STD's)

What many people would consider a modern mother brought in her daughter, dressed in her cheerleading outfit and all of 14 years old, for birth control pills. The mother expressed concern that her daughter practice "safe sex," but she meant sex in which the chance of pregnancy was reduced. She had no concept of the other risks she was allowing her child to be exposed to.

Today pregnancy might ironically be one of the least health-threatening aspects of promiscuous sex. Chronic pelvic pain, sterility, genital cancer, birth defects, and fetal and maternal death are very likely to be the consequences for indiscriminate sex. The earlier sexual activity begins and the greater the number of partners, the more chance of susceptibility. Conversely, a man who is sexually active beginning in his early teens (with multiple partners) places a chaste woman partner at high risk for cervical cancer and pelvic inflammatory diseases, and may risk his own fertility. It is estimated that 33,000 people a day acquire some type of STD.

Even with our increased awareness of the problem, diagnosis of STD's is often missed because so many people lack clear signs of infection. Herpes, for example, is often passed to another person when one partner appears to be symptom-free but is still contagious. The Centers for Disease Control reports that 16 percent of the adult population has herpes. Only about 25 percent of affected people realize that they have herpes, leaving 75 percent to transmit herpes to other people unknowingly.

Herpes Type II (genital) virus causes one or more fluid-filled lesions that rupture, leaving a severely painful ulcerated area. Herpes Type I (oral) virus can infect the genital area through oral sex. Herpes Type II is highly associated with cervical cancer.

Patients who come in with herpes are some of the most miserable I see. I felt extremely sorry for one young lady who accepted a date for her twenty-first birthday with an older male "gentleman." He told her that his active cold sore could not be transmitted to the genitals. Twelve hours later she was covered with lesions on her thighs, lower back, buttocks, and perineal area. Because she was unable to urinate due to pain and swelling, a catheter was necessary for two weeks.

At the moment there is no cure for herpes. Fifty percent of first infections may clear and never recur because the body builds up immunity. The other unlucky 50 percent can anticipate a lifelong struggle. A new drug, Zovirax, shortens the healing process. The ramifications of herpes are immense. One's sexual activity must be planned around noninfectious times, and new partners must be informed.

Herpes presents a particular threat to newborns, who can be mentally retarded or can die. Some researchers estimate that at least half of the mothers who transmit herpes to their babies at the time of delivery have no history of genital herpes. Where herpes is known to exist, doctors take weekly vaginal cultures during the last month of pregnancy. If a positive culture or an active lesion appears, a cesarean section must be done, for if vaginal delivery occurs, herpetic meningitis may cause rapid death of the fetus.

The real damage with herpes may very well be the psychological impact. People who are infected often feel unclean. There is great resentment toward the partner who is responsible for the infection. Many people with herpes suffer depression and find that they need the support of persons facing similar situations.

Currently the number one STD is chlamydia, and yet at the moment there is no large-scale prevention or control program for this disease. Only half of the states require reporting and follow-up of chlamydia even though such measures effectively decrease its incidence. It is estimated that 20 to 40 percent of the American population has chlamydia, even though most infected persons don't know it. Indeed, four out of five women have no idea they are infected.

Chlamydia is a bacteria that can cause severe damage to the upper genital tract but affects the vagina as well. Half of the million or more cases of pelvic inflammatory diseases are caused by chlamydia. Symptoms seen in men are burning during urination and penile discharge. Women complain of vaginal itching, chronic abdominal pain, vaginal discharge, and bleeding between menstrual periods.

Some studies suggest that men may have problems with infertility as a result of the infection. Thousands of women are rendered infertile annually. Most tragically, babies can die or develop serious infections of the eyes, ears, and lungs. Such a record of suffering is deplorable, since it is fully preventable.

Diagnosis is made by the use of a direct fluorescent antibody smear, which, though not as accurate as a tissue culture, is more cost-effective. The bacterium is sensitive to tetracyline, doxycycline, or erythromycin (for those allergic to tetracyclines).

Also of great concern is the rapidly increasing incidence of genital warts (condyloma acuminata). Again, most people are unaware of these warts. Very little is understood about the virus that causes the warts. However, there is a high association with genital cancer. Warts that can't be seen are actually more common than obvious ones. Since the recurrence rate is so high, it is recommended that the partners of females with this disease be regularly screened. Women with genital warts should have a Pap smear every six months, which may indicate the presence of warts as well as any malignancy. Treatment is through chemical agents, freezing (cryosurgery), electrocautery (electrical burning), or laser therapy (which appears to be the most effective). Because of the increased hormone levels seen in pregnancy, these lesions can grow rapidly. Prompt treatment is recommended.

Although these relatively new STD's are of great concern, long-existent types are still with us. Syphilis was declining, but in 1985 there was an increase in births of syphilitic babies. Such infants can be blind, deaf, or crippled by bone disease. In the same year, for the first time in ten years, gonorrhea increased.

Gonorrhea is most prevalent in the sexually active 20-to-24-year-old group. Men are "fortunate" in that the symptom of a burning discharge indicates that they have the infection. Women, on the other hand, usually remain symptom-free until the disease has progressed significantly. It may remain localized but can spread to the upper genital tract by an ascending route or through the bloodstream.

The female can suffer from back pain, arthritis, urination problems, sterility, and blindness to her newborn. Treatment is usually penicillin or tetracycline. Unfortunately, strains of the disease are mutating and becoming resistant to both these medications. Last year 9000 cases of penicillin-resistant gonorrhea occurred in Florida and New York.

Chancroids had all but disappeared until the 1980's. The disease, an open sore usually appearing on the genitals, is again on the rise at the rate of 1000 cases reported yearly. Ninety percent are found in New York, California, Florida, and Georgia. Chancroids have become resistant to previous antibiotic treatments. Today, erythromycin is the drug of choice.

It is not unusual to diagnose more than one STD in the same

person. The highest number of STD's are found among sexually active young people with multiple partners. A number of these diseases can result in the development of pelvic inflammatory disease (PID). A women increases her chance of PID threefold when she has more than four sexual partners. Although PID can be acquired through a number of diseases, in the past the most common cause of the first episode was untreated gonorrhea. Other causes include the spread of bacteria, viruses, and fungi from untreated vaginitis/cervicitis; prostatitis in the male; and infections resulting from complicated deliveries or abortions.

PID is not a single disease. It is a number of infections involving the uterus, tubes, ovaries, and/or lining of the abdominal cavity. A woman may experience a sudden onset or have slowly developing symptoms. She may have generalized pelvic pain, painful menstruation and intercourse, irregular bleeding, a profuse vaginal discharge, and general fatigue with or without chills and fever. Problems tend to escalate after the menstrual period because bacteria spread upward and are nourished by the menstrual flow.

Left untreated, PID can cause infertility by producing scar tissue that may obstruct the tubes. Abscesses can occur in the tubes and ovaries which may lead to life-threatening situations. One in seven women develops infertility after PID. After three attacks 75 percent of these women can't conceive and have a sixfold increase in the risk of an ectopic (tubal) pregnancy. Treatment should never be delayed and should be aggressive. (There is a tendency to stop medication after the symptoms disappear.) It is vital to continue the full course of treatment in order to prevent smoldering infection and progressive damage.

PID is responsive to broad-spectrum antibiotics, complete bed rest for one week, and no sexual intercourse for two weeks. If symptoms get out of control and medications no longer give relief, surgery may be the only alternative.

Acquired Immune Deficiency Syndrome (AIDS)

In 1494 bathhouses and brothels in parts of Europe were closed. Prostitutes were told that if they did not quit their profession, they would be branded on the cheek. Special hospitals were built and travelers who were suspected of having the disease were denied entry into many cities. Syphilis was on the rampage. Judging by the recent media reports, history may repeat itself.

The Acquired Immune Deficiency Syndrome, known as AIDS,

has passed from a moral problem to a public health hazard. We are likely to face a situation unlike any we have faced in our near past as AIDS moves into the mainstream population.

HIV was first recognized in the United States in 1981. Each year it has doubled the number of victims. The AIDS virus destroys the immune system of the body, allowing even the most benign infections to become life-threatening. At first the high-risk groups were homosexuals, IV drug-users, and persons who received blood transfusions. But AIDS is now rapidly becoming more prevalent in the general population through bisexual males and prostitutes. In Africa the disease has always been a heterosexual one.

Because of the life-threatening nature of AIDS, funds have been diverted away from other STD research to seek a cure for this disease. It is interesting to note that syphilis has been around for decades with no preventive vaccine. Chances are that drugs to prolong the life of the victim will be developed long before a cure or vaccine is found.

The disease may show itself from six months to five years after exposure. Fifty percent of all AIDS patients die within two years and 85 percent are dead within three years. There are only two counties in the United States known to trace the sexual contacts of AIDS patients. It has been pointed out that if AIDS were cured today, over a million Americans would still die.

Symptoms of AIDS are tiredness, fever, loss of appetite, diarrhea, night sweats, and swollen glands. Diagnosis is made by recognizing certain types of infections characteristic of AIDS patients, by blood antibody tests, and/or by evaluating white blood cell damage. There is no known cure.

Sexually active people are being told to practice "safe sex." This means using condoms and refraining from promiscuous behavior. Although condoms should always be used in other than monogamous relationships known to be infection-free, they do not guarantee "safe" sex. A recent political cartoon illustrated this point. The young man approached his grandfather and asked, "What did you use for 'safe sex' in your day, Grandpa?" The reply was, "A wedding band."

Soon we are going to be called upon to suggest solutions which are not based on hysteria, which involve common sense and compassion, and which nevertheless protect the public. Education to eliminate the behaviors that contribute to the problem is our most effective weapon at the present time.

Substance-Abuse

Smoking and use of drugs, including alcohol, have more far-reaching and devastating effects on a woman's health than any other factors in her life. Lung cancer is the number one killer of women in the United States, and smoking accounts for 30 percent of all cancer deaths. Smoking is not just the concern of the person who smokes, either. If one person in the home smokes, there is a 60 percent increase in all cancers in their children and a 50 percent increase among adults.

An individual who smokes has a 70 percent higher death rate from heart attacks. Sudden death from heart attacks is increased twofold to fourfold. The combination of birth control pills and smoking increases the risk of heart attack ten times.

Other diseases, such as chronic bronchitis, emphysema, and arteriosclerotic heart disease, are related to smoking. I can always pick out the lifelong smokers in my practice by their leathery, dry skin. After years of blowing smoke in their face, the damage is evident. Unlike wine, aging before our time is not desirable!

The good news is that when a person stops smoking the risk of heart attack diminishes immediately. After ten years the rate is the same as for a nonsmoker. "Crutches" (such as nicotine gum, support groups, or any other method that helps break the habit) are appropriate to use. The important thing is to stop placing yourself and your family at risk. Sixty-four percent of all medical doctors who smoked have quit. The result is that there is now a lower death rate among physicians than in the general population.

Smoking is only half the problem, however. Of the ten million problem drinkers in America, one-third are women. Since the early 1960's, for every male who begins to drink there are two females. This is particularly disturbing because a woman's body does not absorb or tolerate alcohol the same way a man's does. Hormonal fluctuations can make a woman more susceptible to alcohol at certain times. Being pregnant or on birth control pills may, therefore, increase the toxic effect of alcohol.

Just recently the New England Journal of Medicine reported that even three drinks a week increases a woman's risk of breast cancer. The risk is clearly related to the amount of alcohol consumed (nine drinks increases the chance 60%). Younger women have the greatest vulnerability.

Sixty percent of all women drink, half of these at least once a week or more. The line between use and abuse is hard to draw. It has been pointed out that women sometimes think they don't have a problem because their first drink may not be until evening, but this ignores the fact that they started the day with a Valium tablet, the woman's version of the morning "pick-me-up."

There is no single profile for an alcoholic. Substance-abuse may take a few months or many years to develop, but the most vulnerable women are: young women, women who have never married, and women who are divorced, separated, unemployed, or holding a part-time job. Commonalities include stress, poor self-image, and increased opportunity.

Using alcohol as a stress-reliever is a poor way to cope with life's problems. Whether or not you have an alcohol problem is not dependent on a pattern or length of involvement but on how important alcohol has become to you and how seriously it affects your life.

Medically, alcohol is an addictive, anesthetic drug. Its empty calories contribute to poor nutrition. It damages the heart, liver, brain, and digestive tract. It makes a person more susceptible to pancreatitis and pneumonia. Since it affects a person's perception of muscle control, it is highly associated with accidents of all types.

It is increasingly common to find substance-abuse related to a combination of alcohol and other drugs, particularly prescription ones. Be thankful when your physician is reluctant to refill medication without careful consideration!

Taking Responsibility

Most of us do not live in a consciously sinful way, but many of us live apathetically. Our task is one of stewardship, and stewardship of our bodies requires a commitment to help them function not only as they should but with ever-increasing improvement and enrichment. The payoff for a life of active stewardship is the joy of right living and the reward of a full life.

Being a good steward of our health can be a big order, and no one promises that it is easy!

"I know your deeds, that you are neither cold nor hot. I wish you were either one or the other! So because you are lukewarm—neither hot nor cold—I am about to spit you out of my mouth" (Revelation 3:15,16).

Chapter Ten

The Complete Woman and Special Health Concerns

He who listens to a life-giving rebuke
will be at home among the wise.

—*Proverbs 15:31*

In the last chapter we concerned ourselves with health issues that even healthy women may face at some time during their lives. In this chapter we will consider illnesses and happenings that occur less frequently and may require extra diligence, care, and attention.

Benign Tumors

Mrs. Robinson's husband was on the phone. I had seen her for her annual checkup that morning. "What did you tell her?" he demanded. "She's hysterical and I can only make out the words 'tumor and death.' " Mrs. Robinson had a noncancerous tumor, a Gartner's duct cyst. She had made a common assumption: The word "tumor" automatically meant "cancer" to her. A tumor is any growth or swelling; it may be malignant or benign. She clearly had nothing to fear.

Benign tumors are rarely a cause for alarm. Most are simply followed routinely. If they enlarge to a point where they bleed or cause painful intercourse or chronic discomfort, something needs to be done. If it is a cystic tumor, drainage may be all that is required; a solid tumor may need surgical removal.

Working from the outside of the vulva inward, the neck of the Bartholin's gland may become obstructed, forming either a cyst or, if it is infected, an abscess. Besides the above measures, antibiotics may sometimes provide a cure. Although it is rare, these Bartholin's cysts may become malignant.

Gartner's duct cysts, like Mrs. Robinson's, occur in the lateral

140

vaginal wall. Most of the time they are simply observed. Vaginal polyps are tissue growths clumped together within the vagina. These surface tumors may bleed if bruised with intercourse, tampons, or diaphragm use. If they must be removed, the procedure can usually be completed in the doctor's office.

These same tumors can occur on the cervix and are then referred to as cervical polyps. Often they are the result of infection. Treatment consists of clearing the infection or surgical removal. In rare cases these can become cancerous, so careful monitoring must be done if they are not removed.

Most women have experienced the discomfort associated with a functional ovarian cyst. Although such cysts are common within the ovary, problems occur when the egg is not released and excess fluid is produced. The pain is caused by the enlarging ovarian cyst stretching the ovarian capsule and irritating the nerve fibers within. Most of these cysts regress spontaneously after one or two menstrual cycles.

We have discussed persistent corpus luteum cysts in other chapters, but they are worth mentioning again since they are a frequent occurrence. These cysts develop when the egg is released but the cyst does not degenerate on schedule. If there is a two- to three-week delay in menstruation and a mass can be felt, this raises the suspicion of an ectopic pregnancy. A pregnancy test or a sonogram may be necessary to confirm such a diagnosis.

Benign Breast Disease

"Mrs. Garcia, how long have you had this mass in your breast?" I asked.

"What mass?" she answered.

After pointing out what I was referring to, Mrs. Garcia admitted to having been aware of this enlarging mass for months. When it comes to breast cancer, many women wait too long before acknowledging the possibility.

In Mrs. Garcia's case, she had chronic cystic mastitis which had advanced to a large cyst. This is the most common benign breast disease. It appears that women who are susceptible have breast glands that are more sensitive to hormone levels and chemicals. Fortunately, most of such women can be helped by eliminating caffeine and methylzanthines from their diet. The primary sources of these chemicals are coffee, tea, chocolate, and cola drinks. Within one month they will notice a marked improvement in the amount of nodules, pain, and aching previously felt.

My wife has had a subcutaneous mastectomy. When she is not careful about the amount of caffeine she consumes, even with very little breast tissue remaining, she finds herself in considerable discomfort. Medications are available for severe cases. Birth control pills and hormone replacement given to menopausal women can aggravate the condition.

When the small cysts join and form a mass of multiple small cysts or one large cyst, needle aspiration may be performed by a general surgeon. This causes the collapse of the cyst. If it does not reoccur, the chance of malignancy is slight. Some surgeons may choose to biopsy immediately while others may opt for a mammogram or sonogram first.

Fibroadenomas are solid tissue masses that can appear as early as adolescence. Unlike the cysts, they are not painful to the touch and therefore many women fear they are malignant. To eliminate the worry, such masses are usually removed. They rarely reoccur.

A discharge from the nipple (galactorrhea) can be a sign of either cancer or benign disease and should always be evaluated. A clear-to-whitish discharge may result from breast duct ectasia (dilation) or from taking antidepressant or antihypertensive drugs. A dark, blood-tinged discharge may be due to a benign intraductal papilloma (a wartlike growth inside the breast ducts) but may also indicate a malignancy.

Breast disease comes under numerous names and has many treatments. For example, chronic cystic mastitis may also be known as fibrocystic disease. Physicians will vary in their approach to treatment. Ob-Gyns diagnose but rarely treat breast disease.

Because breast tissue is affected by hormones, checking one's breasts must be done on a regular schedule, preferably five to seven days after the beginning of menstruation. The procedure for a proper exam can be found in Appendix A. The American Cancer Society recommends a baseline mammogram between the ages of 35 and 50 and routine mammograms after age 50.

Like any other part of the body, the breast can be injured and become infected. Antibiotics are the obvious treatment for infection. Trauma usually requires no special attention. An injury to the breast does not cause cancer but can cause internal scarring in the fatty tissue later on, which may mimic malignant growths. To be on the safe side, these growths should be biopsied.

Pelvic Diseases

A patient was referred to me by her family doctor because he felt a tumor. As I proceeded with the history, I asked if her doctor had mentioned the type of tumor she had. "Oh, yes," she replied; "he says I have a bad case of 'fireballs.' " Needless to say, I was somewhat confused and wondered if I had overlooked something in the latest journal. After examination, I realized that the "fireballs" were "fibroids."

Fibroid tumors (myomas) are usually benign round growths of the uterine muscle. It is estimated that 20 percent of women over the age of 30 have fibroids. They can be found in the uterine cavity, in the muscle wall, or hanging from a small attachment from the outer surface of the uterus. Diagnosis of fibroids does not mean that one must immediately undergo surgery. As long as they are not enlarging rapidly, or are not symptomatic, there is little likelihood of malignancy. Four percent of the time they may progress to a cancerous state called leiomyosarcoma, which is often a very difficult malignancy to cure.

Three things can happen to the fibroids: They can regress in size, they can remain the same, or they can enlarge. In pregnancy and sometimes in menopause, hormones can escalate the growth of fibroids. Removal facilitates the possibility of a vaginal delivery by eliminating the chance of the fibroid obstructing the birth canal. A new medical treatment (Lupron) is being studied that shrinks fibroid tumors up to 50 percent, thus negating the need for surgery.

One of the most common pelvic diseases seen among young, middle-class women in the United States is endometriosis. The most prevalent theory for the cause of endometriosis is based on the idea that endometrial tissue, at the time of menstruation, flows backward through the Fallopian tubes and implants in various areas of the pelvis. The hallmark symptoms of this disease are infertility and painful menstruation (dysmenorrhea) and intercourse (dyspareunia). These symptoms usually worsen around menstruation because the displaced tissue is still responsive to hormone stimulation, thereby growing and bleeding as if it were in the lining of the uterus. This internal pelvic bleeding causes irritation and pain and may lead to severe scarring.

The discomfort related to endometriosis varies considerably. For example, during Mrs. Bluestein's annual checkup a large pelvic mass was felt. Because she was 48 years old, the possibility of ovarian cancer had to be considered. She had no symptoms or complaints, but I was worried due to the size and firmness of the mass. Surgery revealed a large endometrioma, which was confirmed by the pathologist. Endometriomas are formed when blood accumulates monthly into endometrial cysts located on the ovaries.

By contrast, Mrs. O'Grady came in because of failure to conceive after 14 months of unprotected intercourse. Her history revealed the three typical complaints of endometriosis. Laparoscopy indicated one tiny area of endometriosis on the surface of the right ovary.

Diagnosis can be confirmed, in some cases, by feeling tender nodules at the top of the vagina during the pelvic exam. Occasionally these nodules can be biopsed vaginally for tissue confirmation. But most often the doctor will recommend a laparoscopy for visual and/or tissue verification. (The laparoscope is a thin tube with fiber-optic lighting that allows the doctor to see within the pelvis.)

At Stanford University Infertility Clinic, studies have revealed a great number of women who have no symptoms of endometriosis except infertility. Indeed, it is felt that endometriosis is the cause of infertility in one-third of all women who have it. No one really understands this relationship. Researchers surmise that endometriosis causes the tube to be distorted or destroyed by scarring, or that it causes the egg to pass rapidly through the tube, thus reaching the lining of the uterus too soon. Other theories suggest that the disease decreases sperm mobility.

Endometriosis may be treated with hormones or with conservative or radical surgery. High doses of female hormones, progesterone, or progesterone-estrogen combinations are given to prevent periods for six months to a year, thus the endometrial implants are suppressed as well. This relieves the symptoms in most cases and improves the chance of conception, especially within the first six months after treatment. A synthetic hormone, danazol (Danocrine), suppresses menstrual and endometrial implant bleeding by shutting down the supply of hormones from the pituitary gland. There are a number of frustrating side effects with danazol, including the increase of body and facial hair, weight gain, hot flashes, and some reported cases of clitoral enlargement and deepening of the voice.

Conservative surgery as a means of treatment prefers the use of electrocautery or laser to destroy all visible endometrium implants. This is done in younger women who desire to maintain their fertility. If the woman does not wish more children, the ultimate cure is radical surgery, which means a total abdominal hysterectomy with possible removal of the tubes and ovaries. In these instances hormonal replacement is necessary.

Varicose Veins of the Pelvis

The presence of varicosities within the pelvis is called pelvic congestion syndrome. A typical patient complains of a chronic dull, aching pelvic pain, pelvic pressure, and discomfort with intercourse. Orgasm intensifies the symptoms. Diagnosis is usually made through elimination of all other possibilities.

Normally the pelvic blood vessels double in size during pregnancy. Occasionally these vessels remain engorged and dilated. During surgery they appear like the varicosities of the legs. They don't spontaneously disappear, and thus surgical treatment is necessary if symptoms warrant it.

Vulvar Vestibulitis Syndrome

Vulvar vestibulitis is an unusual and puzzling problem that causes severe pain when intercourse is attempted, with tampon placement, and upon wearing tight-fitting slacks or jeans. Horseback or bicycle riding or any stimulus that results in pressure on the vulvar vestibule is intolerable. Although this disease was commonly written about in the past, it has only recently resurfaced. Its cause is unknown and at this point treatment is discouraging. Surgical removal of the vestibule and treatment with Zovirax provides relief for some patients but is not always permanent.

Diethylstilbestrol (DES)

During the 1940's until 1953, pregnant women who were threatening to miscarry were given DES. This involved millions of women. Years later it was discovered that such treatment escalated the incidence of vaginal adenosis and clear cell carcinoma of the vagina in the daughters of the exposed mothers. Seventy-eight to 90 percent of these children developed one of these complications, compared to 2 percent of persons in controlled studies. Even sons have been shown to have an increase in testicular problems and poor sperm quality.

Besides cancer, a number of other problems are possible. It is important that any sons or daughters that have been exposed to DES be given this information so they can take the extra precautions necessary to prevent life-threatening complications.

Infertility

When a couple has seriously concluded that they are ready for the mixture of responsibility and joy that is parenthood, it is helpful for them to understand the timing and techniques that will enhance their probability of achieving fertilization.

If a woman has the average 28-to-32-day cycle, her most fertile days will begin 12 days from the first signs of menstruation. Intercourse should occur every other day—days 12, 14, 16, 18, and 20. A basal body temperature chart is helpful in depicting the most probable days. A woman's basal body temperature will rise approximately one-half degree when ovulation occurs. Recently new products have appeared on the market that simplify identifying the time of ovulation by chemically testing cervical mucus.

The possibility of pregnancy can also be increased by positioning the woman's hips on a pillow and remaining in that position after intercourse for at least 45 minutes. No lubrication, saliva, or other products should be used, as they can immobilize or destroy the sperm. Thrusting should be stopped as soon as ejaculation occurs to prevent sperm from being brought out of the vagina.

Eighty-two percent of couples who want to have children find that pregnancy occurs within six months. Within nine months 88 percent (and after one year 92 percent) follow suit. The remaining 8 percent have problems with fertility and should begin a fertility workup.

Even with current technological advances (creating new procedures that seemed unimaginable a short time ago), infertility is outstripping the solutions. The major factor for this phenomenon is the epidemic of sexually transmitted diseases. Environmental conditions also contribute to the problem. Some studies indicate that as many as 15 percent of all American couples must deal with not having a child when they wish to.

A couple is defined as having an infertility problem if they have had regular, unprotected intercourse for one year without pregnancy. Evaluation might reveal an obvious cause or a "negative workup," meaning that no clear reason for the infertility is found. If a couple never conceives, they are said to be sterile.

A lovely Christian couple visited my office recently to show off their three beautiful children. It was a pleasure for me to take a moment to share in their pride and joy because eight years earlier the possibility of having a family was a frustrating, impossible dream. The Naves were college graduates who desperately wanted children. They had been married four years and were experiencing pressure from friends and family to have a baby.

The source of their problem was easy to uncover. Although they loved each other dearly, they had not been able to consummate their marriage. Vaginismus was the diagnosis. It resulted chiefly from her traumatic experience as a child with a doctor (involving catheter insertion for a kidney evaluation). Sexual counseling, her determination, and a very loving and patient husband enabled them to overcome this hurdle. A pregnancy occurred six months later.

Usually the cause for infertility is damage due to pelvic inflammatory disease (PID). Sometimes it is problems with ovulation, corpus luteum deficiencies, endometriosis, and sperm antibodies. Men account for up to 50 percent of problems of fertility. A semen analysis reveals the number of sperm, their mobility, and the percentage of abnormal sperm (among other findings).

An infertility assessment should never be undertaken unless each partner is willing to accept responsibility for a complete evaluation of all possibilities. It is not uncommon to have a multifaceted set of causes for infertility. Going through the complete evaluation need only be done once and can be a comfort, since those who do it can then know that they did everything possible to correct the problem.

A husband's refusal to have a semen analysis could result in the woman enduring expensive and at times uncomfortable procedures to no avail. Semen quality is readily affected by legal and illegal drug use, alcohol, varicose veins of the testes, trauma to or infection of the testicles (such as mumps), and increased heat due to hot tubs or tight-fitting clothing. Unless there is total absence of sperm, there is hope for improving the sperm count and semen quality. Two samples are required for verification of the findings.

No infertility workup should be prolonged more than three to four months. It is helpful prior to visiting the doctor to have at least two months of recorded basal body temperatures (BBT). More than its use in timing intercourse, these charts are invaluable in determining the appropriate timing of each test.

Tests for Infertility

There are six procedures which comprise a general infertility workup. Occasionally the results will require a subspecialist who deals with the most complex aspects of infertility.

1. Semen analysis.

2. Endometrial biopsy. This is a sampling of the endometrial lining that is done at approximately day 24 to 27 of a 28-to-32-day cycle. This will reveal ovulation or anovulation, corpus luteum deficiency, and/or endometrial infections.

3. Sims-Huhner Test. One hour after intercourse a sample is obtained from the endocervical canal and evaluated microscopically. Live, active, progressing sperm means that the sperm are advancing up the reproductive tract without hindrance and that the antibody factor that could destroy sperm is not present. This test is accurate only if performed around ovulation.

4. Hysterosalpingogram (HSG). This procedure is done in the X-ray department. Dye is injected directly into the uterine cavity, revealing possible fibroids, septal defects, or other congenital anomalies. If dye goes directly into and through the tubes and shows no abnormalities, it can be concluded that the egg and sperm can also pass unhindered. Occasionally HSG is therapeutic because the pressure of the injected dye "blows open" the closed tube.

5. Laparoscopy. A laparoscope enables the physician to directly visualize the pelvic cavity. Direct evidence of ovulation in the form of the corpus luteum can be seen, endometriosis can be verified, and the extent of PID damage can be assessed. Congenital deformities such as Salpingitis Isthmica Nodosa (severe nodularity to the tubes) can be observed. Finally, dye can be injected to visually verify open tubes.

6. Hysteroscopy. A hysteroscope is an instrument used to view the lining of the uterine cavity for abnormalities or problems that may lead to infertility.

Psychological Considerations of Infertility

For many women, having a child has been an expectation since childhood. Not being able to conceive is seen by them as a strike against their femininity, sexual adequacy, and self-worth. The strong feelings that well up when a couple experiences infertility are not unreasonable, since the desire to parent is a normal phase of adult development.

Frequently a couple's sexual adjustment will suffer as a result of infertility. Childbearing and sex are separate issues, and couples understand this intellectually, but on the feeling level they can't get over viewing themselves as defective or damaged. The heavy focus on the procreative aspects of sex tends to contribute to an attitude of "If sex is to produce a baby, and our sex doesn't, why bother?"

Both men and women may turn to affairs to bolster their flagging egos. Males may experience impotence, especially after abnormal semen analysis. Spontaneity is lost as sex becomes an act to perform on demand rather than as a response to one's natural appetite.

The drive to reproduce is so compelling that some couples will do almost anything to achieve this goal. On the advice of their psychologist, a young couple, both suffering from cerebral palsy, decided to have a child. Due to the progression of their disease, sexual intercourse was impossible. Ingeniously, they created their own version of artificial insemination. The male masturbated, ejaculated into a jar, and used a straw to blow the sperm into the vagina. Miraculously, conception occurred.

The pregnancy progressed normally and signals were devised to alert the obstetrical department that labor had begun. The woman was unable to speak clearly and certainly could not drive. The delivery was a nightmare. After 25 hours of slow progress, the decision was made to perform a cesarean section. A healthy baby girl was delivered, but three days later the mother's wound opened and her bowel protruded. A week-and-a-half after that, while practicing her infant care, she dropped the baby. She and her husband wisely determined to place the baby for adoption.

People accept the fact that they may not ever become president of the company or ever look like a movie star, but they all believe they can become a parent. When this doesn't happen, dreams are shattered and great deprivation is felt. Such anger, while normal, does not have to be destructive. Feelings of self-criticism must be countered with self-acceptance, and this takes time, patience, and immense support. Open discussion with trusted and close friends helps to eliminate feelings of alienation and isolation. Physical and emotional limits constantly change, and accepting this fact is a way of nurturing oneself. Ultimately the task may come to "letting go" as opposed to "giving up." The challenge is to turn resistance and energy-draining resentment into acceptance and self-respect.

Artificial Insemination

In 29 states of our country the husband is accepted as the legal father of any baby born within the marriage, whether he provided the sperm or not. Today modern sperm banks provide sperm that has been properly screened and whose donor's history is known. Those clinics are recommended which respect anonymity but keep adequate records in case a hereditary history is necessary. As with most things in life, the more one practices a procedure, the more adept he becomes at it. Therefore in most cases the services of an infertility subspecialist should be enlisted.

Surrogate mothering, apart from the moral questions one might have, is not yet legally safe. At the present time there is no law that supports the fact that the mother who raises the child is legally the mother.

In Vitro Fertilization (IVF)

The In Vitro fertilization procedure involves the use of ultrasound and surgical equipment to locate and remove a mature egg from a woman's ovary. The egg is then placed in a special solution and the husband's sperm is added. Fertilization takes place within the test tube. At the appropriate time the fertilized egg is transferred to the uterine cavity by way of the vagina. Less than a decade old, IVF is now available in every state.

Couples choosing to participate in this type of therapy must understand that IVF is very stressful and is successful less than 20 percent of the time. During the first two weeks of treatment the medical procedure requires long and daily visits for both husband and wife. There are many psychological and physical discomforts associated with the therapy. The hormones used (menotropins), when given daily, can cause the female to feel sick, to be very moody, and at times to feel anxious. Couple-support groups are beneficial for husbands and wives who choose to go this extra mile.

The questions that these technologies raise are flooding the legal and theological professions. To whom does a baby belong when there is a genetic mother, a gestational mother, and a rearing mother? Paternity and maternity are becoming increasingly difficult to define. The most perplexing problem is frozen embryos. To whom do these belong? Couples wishing more information may contact a national organization for couples with infertility problems: RESOLVE, INC., P.O. Box 474, Belmont, MA 02178.

Miscarriage, Stillbirth, and Therapeutic Abortions

Mrs. Broadbanks had had a sleepless night. Her pleading eyes sought to ferret out any message of hope I could give her. But the sonogram had revealed the worst; the pregnancy was over. Her options were to wait and see if the products of conception would be passed spontaneously or would require a D & C. Like most women in her situation, she decided on the surgery.

My job was not over after the surgical procedure; Mrs. Broadbanks had to be reassured that she had done nothing to cause the miscarriage. Guilt is a very common response in such cases; some people decide that their loss is a punishment. Yet the vast majority of early miscarriages are caused by genetic or chromosomal defects entirely out of a woman's control. The remainder are related to diseases and other health factors. (When a health factor is the cause, sometimes it can be successfully dealt with in future pregnancies.)

No matter how early the baby is lost, there is always sincere grief and a sense of loss. Along with the baby, hopes and dreams also die. Husbands need to be reminded that the effect on the woman can be as intense as the death of a full-term child. Allowing time to grieve is important, since our society offers no ritualized ceremony for this type of loss.

After two to three complete menstrual cycles the couple is free to try again. Seventy-five percent of such couples will find themselves expecting again within nine months. After two or three spontaneous miscarriages a women is labeled a "habitual aborter." At this point a medical workup is in order.

Fetal death prior to delivery is known as a stillborn birth. Demise after delivery is a neonatal death. In most cases the cause of death can be determined. Some causes may be correctable, while others are true random occurrences (ones that may never happen again). Recovery is much more complete and rapid when the parents agree to see and hold their child. Giving the child a name and having a service of some type is beneficial in helping the couple proceed through the grieving process.

Spiritual Considerations

In Genesis chapters 1 and 2 man and woman are given the capacity to generate life, and in fact are told to do so. Even as they are to be stewards of the earth, so they are to be stewards of this life-giving capability as well.

"Life" involves both our physical bodies and our spiritual natures: "You created my inmost being; you knit me together in my mother's womb" (Psalm 138:13). The Hebrew term for "innermost being" has the same meaning as our modern term "heart" when we use it to refer to the emotional and spiritual side of mankind's nature. John the Baptist leaped in his mother's womb (Luke 1:39-45) at the recognition of being in Christ's unborn presence, indicating the spiritual sensitivity of even the unborn child.

An aborted baby is far more than a "clump of cells." God created a plan and a purpose for each person even before conception. Truly, no one is an accident. We are told in Jeremiah 1:5, "Before I formed you in the womb I knew you, before you were born I set you apart."

That those children whose lives were so brief are now in heaven is generally accepted. Angels in heaven have interceded for them, and God is a righteous God (Matthew 18:10; Genesis 18:23-25). How is this a comfort? By the knowledge that the pain and suffering which the parents endure is not in vain, for an eternal life has been brought into being. For those whose child was stillborn, they will have an opportunity to get to know their child someday.

Further information on this subject is available in Jack Hayford's small book titled *Early Flight*. It can be obtained by writing to Haven of Rest Ministries, P.O. Box 2031, Hollywood, California 90078.

Understanding Pregnancy Loss

My routine history-taking includes the questions "How many times have you been pregnant?" and "How many children do you have?" Without fail those women who have had a therapeutic abortion inevitably drop their eyes and lower their voice as they share this fact.

When a woman replies with something like four pregnancies and three children, I have learned not to ask about the one pregnancy by using the term "abortion." Abortion is a correct medical term for a pregnancy loss, but it has become highly associated with deliberate pregnancy termination, called therapeutic abortion. The majority of women do not make such a decision lightly.

Considerations that should be kept in mind when deciding whether to continue the pregnancy or to terminate it include a realistic under-standing that the developing embryo is a person and that there are medical risks in abortions. Potential problems with a therapeutic abortion include uterine perforation with the D & C instruments, injury to the cervix, hemorrhage, and infection which may be serious enough to affect future fertility.

A Christian's primary responsibility is not to judge a woman's decision to end a pregnancy, but rather to insure that all women understand the facts and that they have other options. This means a commitment to making those options available through adoption or homes or support systems for pregnant women. The church has a clear role to teach the value of human life and to witness Christianity at work by showing love and compassion to people who are hurting.

Most women are more comfortable referring to unplanned loss of pregnancy as a miscarriage. Twenty percent of all women will miscarry. The five classifications of spontaneous abortion or miscarriage are as follows:

1. Threatened. Around 25 percent of all pregnancies will have some bleeding, usually related to implantation of the embryo into the uterine wall. It is most common between six and ten weeks. The bleeding is often light, with or without minimal cramping. The amount of blood has little relationship to the outcome of the pregnancy. The primary treatment is bed rest and no sex until the bleeding stops.

2. Inevitable. A miscarriage is inevitable when bleeding becomes profuse, cramping becomes intense, and the cervix opens up. There is no treatment; it is simply a matter of time until the products of conception are expelled.

3. Complete. Complete abortions usually occur prior to the eighth week of gestation. No further medical intervention is necessary because all tissue is spontaneously passed.

4. Incomplete. When portions of fetal tissue remain in the uterus, the cervix is open, and bleeding is profuse, the abortion is called incomplete. In most cases a D & C is required to complete the removal of the remaining tissue.

5. Missed abortions. When the fetus dies and remains in the uterus, and pregnancy symptoms disappear, a missed abortion has occurred. In many cases, if given enough time, the body will expel the pregnancy. After four to six weeks medical intervention is advised to prevent severe bleeding problems. Most women prefer medical intervention when the diagnosis of a fetal demise is without question.

Women under 20 and over 35, especially if they have had a previous miscarriage, are at the highest risk. Besides developmental abnormalities and chromosomal problems, there are numerous other causes for the above five problems. An incompetent cervix (caused by a congenital weakness of the cervix) cannot sustain the pressure and growth of the enlarging fetus, causing premature opening of the cervix. In some cases this can be successfully treated by suturing the cervix after the fourth month.

Some women have anatomical abnormalities which may cause repeated abortions. These include septums in the uterine cavity, fibroids, and a "double" uterus. Infectious diseases (and in rare cases extreme physical trauma) account for a number of miscarriages. Evaluation may reveal less prevalent reasons.

The two most common questions asked after miscarriage and stillbirth are "What could I have done differently?" and "Why me?" There is no easy or absolute answer. It is wise to wait three months before attempting another pregnancy. This gives the body time to heal and the mother an opportunity to prepare for the new pregnancy.

Taking Responsibility

"Why me?" is a question that is asked by many women who face any of the medical concerns discussed in this chapter. There is no simple answer. Intelligent care requires the input and cooperation of both doctor and patient. Taking responsibility is synonymous with diligence and conscientious health maintenance.

"Consider it pure joy, my brothers, whenever you face trials of many kinds, because you know that the testing of your faith develops perseverance. Perseverance must finish its work so that you may be mature and complete, not lacking anything" (James 1:2-4).

Chapter Eleven

The Complete Woman and Surgery

Take away this cup. . . .

—Mark 14:36 TLB

Surgery is a last-resort procedure. It is never embarked upon lightly, but always with the expectation that such an extreme procedure will bring about new hope. Rarely does surgery need to be decided upon in the spur of the moment. Normally it should not even be discussed until a logical and prayerfully considered alternative treatment plan has been implemented without success. The choice of a surgical cure for an illness is traumatic: The risk factors and the sense of violation to one's body makes the decision to proceed difficult and painstaking. Few things result in a greater sense of powerlessness then placing one's life in the hands of another person.

Some of the material you are about to read is not easy to hear. Such dire warnings often appear unwarranted as modern medicine continues to improve both the anesthesia monitoring and surgical techniques. However, a physician must legally and morally inform you of the positive and negative consequences of surgery even though most complications never occur. Today sophisticated technology often reduces the need for extensive procedures.

Cut and Cure or Cut and Complicate?

There is no medical reason for making a decision regarding elective surgery when the alternatives are first presented. Time should be taken to seek God's wisdom and to discuss with family and friends (or others who have experienced the same type of surgery) the procedures and any options that exist. Gather up the facts and feel no hesitancy about seeking a second opinion.

Recovery is smoother and more rapid when a patient has a realistic

concept of exactly what will transpire and how she will most likely
adjust to the surgery. Be clear on preadmission preparation, the hospital
regime, and the home-care and recovery period. Most patients accept
the time required for full recovery, but sometimes mothers of young
children find themselves overdoing.

More than in any other area of medicine, good rapport and complete confidence in your doctor's skills have a positive effect on the
outcome of your surgery. If you are uncomfortable and/or feel at odds
with your physician, it is probably best not to proceed with him or her.

Office Surgery

Of late, more and more surgical procedures are being done in the
office or in an outpatient surgical center. Not only does this help to
control the rising cost of medicine, but new equipment and techniques
enable procedures to be done that weren't possible a short time ago.
Office surgery is usually short and requires very little recovery time.

Many procedures are performed to obtain tissue needed for diagnostic and treatment purpose. In the area of the vulva, vagina, and
cervix, the colposcopy microscope is invaluable in identifying and di-
recting the physician to the exact location of the problem. Depending
on the size and location of the lesion, various instruments are used to
obtain the specimen. This is sent to the pathologist, who returns his
analysis to the attending physician. The findings are used to decide the
most appropriate treatment plan.

Specifically, this office technique would be chosen for the following problems: polyps, papillomas (wartlike growths), lipomas (fatty
tumors), condylomas, Bartholin cysts or abscesses, Nabothian cysts
(obstructed secretion glands of the cervix), cervical dysplasia, infertility, and molluscum contagiosum (soft, rounded skin tumors).

Outpatient Surgery

Outpatient facilities may be within the hospital or freestanding.
Outpatient surgery means that surgery and anesthetic recovery are completed within the same day. If an unforeseen complication occurs, transfer to a hospital is preplanned and thus easily accomplished. The belief
that many procedures can be done on a one-day basis is gaining cred-
ibility. In the future it is likely hysterectomies, for example, will be
done in an outpatient facility. Postoperative recovery will take place in

an adjoining recovery facility apart from the hospital. The stays will be shorter and less costly.

Dilation and Curettage

One of the most common outpatient procedures that women face is dilation and curettage or D & C. This is a minor procedure with very few complications. No surgical incisions are necessary and recovery time is short.

The doctor dilates the cervix with a smooth dilator, allowing access to the uterine cavity. He then uses a second instrument, a curette, to remove the lining of the uterus. Most D & C's are done under general anesthesia, although local anesthesia may be selected.

The most frequent problems which require a D & C are menstrual irregularities, growths, cancer, miscarriage, and abortion. Complications include perforation of the uterine wall with the instrument, hemorrhage, or infection.

Conization

A conization is sometimes added to a D & C when cervical cancer is suspected. The malignancy's extent and severity can be verified if it is present. With a scalpel a core is removed from the cervix. The surgical site is repaired by suturing the edges back into place. The "cone," which is shaped like an ice cream cone, is sent to the pathologist for final diagnosis. This one procedure can cure cervical cancer if there is no invasion. Future childbearing is not in jeopardy. The complications are basically the same as with a regular D & C. Some controversy exists over whether this procedure causes other problems that are not immediately obvious.

Laparoscopy

Diagnosis and causes of chronic pelvic pain and infertility are made with the use of a laparoscope. With the direct visualization afforded by this lighted tube the physician is able to see internally without major incisions. Because carbon dioxide gas is pumped into the abdominal cavity to enhance viewing, patients often complain postoperatively of shoulder pain. This lasts one or two days until all the gas is absorbed.

Although this is sometimes referred to as "Band-Aid" surgery, many women are unprepared for the amount of discomfort involved. Doctors may not see the patient again for three to four weeks, long after such complaints have been forgotten. As a result, they rarely get accurate feedback on the first few days of recovery.

Tubal Ligation

Mrs. Ducat came to her afternoon appointment slightly tipsy. She and her girlfriends had been out celebrating the "end of her womanhood." She was scheduled for a tubal ligation the next day. Like many women, she mistakenly assumed that having her tubes tied affected her body's production of hormones and that menopause was therefore imminent.

Other women have expressed concern that eggs will float throughout their bodies. This is not the case. Regular monthly ovulation still occurs, but the eggs are expelled into the abdominal cavity, where white blood cells eliminate them.

A tubal sterilization may be done in three different ways: by laparoscopy, by minilaparotomy, or by vaginal surgery. There are advantages and disadvantages to each method. For example, laparoscopy results in shoulder pain and visible incisions. The silastic rings or metal clamps placed around or across the tube have a slight risk of displacement. The advantage is its greater ease of reversibility.

The minilaparotomy has the disadvantage of a larger incision (two inches) in the mons pubis area. Obviously, there is more discomfort because of it. Its advantage is that the physician is able to tie, cut, and cauterize the tube, thereby insuring a better success rate of sterility. A specimen is sent to the laboratory to verify that the tissue removed was tubal.

A vaginal tubal ligation has several advantages if your doctor is trained in the procedure. There is no visible scar, the area of incision (the upper vagina) has very few nerve endings and therefore there is less discomfort, and the tube is also tied, cut, and cauterized.

With all tubals there is a failure rate. Although much progress has been made in tubal reversals, they are expensive and time-consuming, and the failure rate is still high. The procedure should always be considered permanent. The decision to have a tubal is not dependent on any one factor. Many doctors arbitrarily determine that they won't do tubals on young women, but many circumstances besides age can legitimately lead to a decision for permanent sterilization.

A future form of permanent sterilization may be done with the hysteroscope. This instrument is simply a laparoscope that is inserted through the vagina and cervix into the uterine cavity. The physician is thus able to evaluate abnormal findings of the uterine cavity. Present research involves procedures to introduce a silicone-like plug into the tubal opening. This would act as a barrier and prevent pregnancy.

Cauterization and Hymenotomy

Two fairly simple procedures that require outpatient surgery (because of the highly sensitive area involved) are removal of massive condylomas and the opening of a tight or imperforate hymen. Condylomas (warts) can grow to such size, especially during pregnancy, that they must be removed under general anesthesia. Procedures involving the hymen may be done to make intercourse possible, to enable a young woman to use tampons, or to create an opening for menstrual flow.

Breast Biopsy

The gynecologist will probably be the one to discover a woman's breast lump or mass. It is a long-standing tradition among physicians that any breast surgery required is referred to a general or plastic surgeon. Today it is less common for a diagnosis for cancer to be followed by an immediate mastectomy. An incision is made, and when possible the entire lump is removed and sent to a pathology lab.

Enterocoele—Bladder—Rectal Repair

A vaginal support system that has been weakened by any of a variety of causes can often be corrected through outpatient surgery. Some people are motivated to have this procedure in hopes that it will improve their sex life. Men or women who have sexual complaints about the size of a woman's vagina almost always have a problem in some other area of their relationship. Rarely is the size of the vagina the cause of dysfunction. Reconstructive repair of the perineal area is done to provide proper support for the bladder, rectum, and vagina. This is helpful in controlling urine leakage and in overcoming difficulty in expelling feces.

Surgeries Requiring Hospitalization

Today it would be very rare for any surgery to be "unnecessary." Presurgical approval is required by a great number of committees and organizations. Hospital tissue committees review all postoperative specimens. Although the most thorough workups and diagnoses are sometimes not verified through surgery, the decision that led to surgery has been carefully considered and monitored.

Gynecologists use two basic approaches to surgically correcting gynecological problems. He or she may choose the abdominal technique, called an exploratory laparotomy, or a vaginal technique. Giving the doctor permission to do an exploratory laparotomy means that he may perform abdominal surgery and surgically correct any abnormalities found. The vaginal technique is used in cases of pelvic relaxation and hysterectomies when the doctor knows exactly what the problem is.

Ovarian Cysts

An exploratory laparotomy could disclose an ovarian cyst that needs to be removed. If the cyst is suspicious-looking, a frozen section is rushed to the pathologist for confirmation. If malignancy is found, the physician will alter his plan of action and perform a total abdominal hysterectomy with removal of the tubes and ovaries.

If the cyst is benign and does not involve the entire ovary, a simple cystectomy may be done. Essentially, this involves dissecting and removing the cyst. If the ovary is consumed by the cyst, then an oophorectomy (removal of the ovary) is required. If one ovary is removed, the second usually compensates by increasing its hormone production. This should be a comfort for women who must have this procedure and who worry about future pregnancies and/or early menopause.

Salpingectomy

It may be determined that a salpingectomy (removal of a Fallopian tube) needs to be done. The most frequent reasons that such surgery would be required are ectopic pregnancy, endometriosis, or chronic pelvic inflammatory disease. Today, in the case of ectopic pregnancy, tubal preservation is of prime concern because of the availability of reconstructive microsurgery. Because of improved diagnostic tests, ectopic pregnancies are usually diagnosed before rupture. This also helps in consideration of future pregnancies.

Ectopic pregnancies have increased from 1 in 230 to 1 in 50 during the last ten years. This escalation is due to the use of intrauterine devices (which are now off the market), the mounting cases of pelvic inflammatory disease (PID), and the greater numbers of therapeutic abortions. Ectopic pregnancy is the leading cause of maternal death and should always be considered when a period has been missed and there is severe abdominal pain.

Abnormalities of the Uterus

Women who have septums or other abnormalities of the uterus may need them repaired before a healthy pregnancy can occur. In case of a septum, a metroplasty is done. This is accomplished by opening the uterus and removing the septum. The uterus is reconstructed to form one cavity. A cesarean section will be required, but a normal pregnancy is usually possible.

Do You Really Need a Hysterectomy?

Hysterectomy is one of the most common major surgical operations performed in the United States. Sixty-five percent of hysterectomies are done on women under 44 years of age. One-quarter of all American women will have their ovaries removed along with the uterus, thus creating surgical menopause.

As with any other type of surgery, the decision to have a hysterectomy should be well thought out and the expectations clear. People do occasionally die as a result of complications of surgery and anesthesia. Even when ovaries are left in place, some women sense temporary hormonal fluctuations which they may experience as "hot flashes," urinary problems, fatigue, headache, dizziness, and insomnia. There may even be a different sensation during sexual orgasm.

Technically, a hysterectomy is the removal of the uterus. Prior to 1960 some women had hysterectomies which removed the top (fundus) of the uterus, leaving the cervix in place. This procedure was referred to as a supracervical hysterectomy. Women who have had this procedure must continue to have routine Pap smears to rule out cervical cancer. (Even women who have had complete removal of the uterus are well-advised to continue having annual Paps to monitor changes in the vagina.)

A hysterectomy may be accomplished abdominally or vaginally. Originally, vaginal hysterectomies had a higher infection rate. Today, with the use of preoperative antibiotics, the incidence of infection has fallen from 16 percent to less than 1 percent. The advantage of the vaginal route is less discomfort and more rapid recovery. Because the women frequently feel well, it is difficult to convince them that they have had major surgery and need a proper recovery period.

If there are large pelvic masses or cancer the abdominal approach is preferable, since with this procedure it is easier to evaluate the entire abdominal cavity. However, this procedure is uncomfortable and a visible scar is unavoidable. In very obese women there is a higher risk of wound infection and separation with abdominal surgery.

Approximately one-half of all hysterectomies leave the tubes and ovaries in place. Removing the uterus, tubes, and the ovaries is called a total abdominal hysterectomy with bilateral salpingo-oophorectomy. If a woman is younger than 40, everything possible is done to leave the ovaries. Between ages 40 and 50 she should be made aware of the chance of ovarian cancer and may elect to have the ovaries removed. Functioning with her own hormones is obviously preferable, but regular and conscientious checkups must become part of her lifestyle. After 50 or 55 years of age it is recommended that ovaries be removed because of the particular virulence of ovarian cancer and the fact that its occurrence is more prevalent during this stage of life. Approximately 1 to 3 percent of all women develop ovarian cancer, with only a 20-percent five-year survival rate. Most women are not aware of any symptoms until their enlarging girth and pelvic pressure indicates that the disease has progressed extensively. Ovarian cancer is not commonly found in poor women with many children. It appears to be a disease of upper- and middle-strata women who have had one or no children.

The "Necessary Hysterectomy"

A hysterectomy is the treatment of choice for cancer of the uterus, ovaries, or vagina, for obstetrical hemorrhage, and for cancer that has spread from other areas of the body (metastatic cancer). If a woman is past her childbearing age and/or has very large fibroids, a hysterectomy is the preferred choice. It is used for dysfunctional uterine bleeding when all other treatments have failed.

With endometriosis whose symptoms are not responsive to hormonal suppression, the only cure is hysterectomy. In some cases, symptoms of endometriosis may be abated and radical surgery avoided by using conservative surgery. This means that all visible abdominal cavity endometriosis is destroyed by cautery or with the laser laparoscope. This is no cure, but it buys time for the younger women who may desire a future pregnancy. If possible, it is best to perform the surgery shortly before pregnancy is desired.

In the past ovaries were automatically removed with endometriosis. Today the decision to retain or remove the ovaries is a very individualized decision between doctor and patient. Age, family history, a woman's temperament regarding further surgery, and extent of the disease are all considerations. Your doctor may refer to removal of the uterus, tubes, and ovaries as a total abdominal hysterectomy and bilateral salpingo-oophorectomy (TAH-BSO) as a complete pelvic sweep or "radical surgery."

When pelvic inflammatory disease can no longer be controlled by antibiotics and pain medications, hysterectomy may be called for. Unless malignant, ovarian cysts do not require such radical surgery.

The "Unnecessary Hysterectomy"

There are some problems that are not life-threatening and thus "unnecessary" though they may interfere with the enjoyment and quality of life. When all other treatment modes have been exhausted, a hysterectomy may be decided upon. Severe menstrual cramps, chronic pelvic pain, pelvic congestion syndrome, adenomyosis, and pelvic relaxation all fall into this category.

Pelvic relaxation is caused by a variety of factors from bearing large babies to obesity or chronic coughing. Many women experience slight leakage of urine, especially with exercise, coughing, or sneezing, but others find the problem so serious that they must wear pads daily. Since leaking urine (urinary incontinence) may have many underlying causes, proper diagnosis is vital. The gynecologist and the urologist must work together to ensure that the correct treatment plan is decided upon.

"Quality of life" is individually defined. Mrs. Kunkel was referred to me by her internist, who had been following her for a "sagging" bladder (prolapsed bladder) that literally protruded outward through the vaginal opening.

Mrs. Kunkel had put up with this problem for 12 years. During her annual physicals she regularly refused gynecological correction.

164

She never complained about having to manually push her bladder back into the vagina. Her love of life was a well-kept rose garden. One day she was tending her roses wearing a loose-fitting dress and no underwear and found her bladder impaled on a rose thorn. While nothing else could motivate her to have surgery, the thought of being restricted in her gardening convinced her. Mrs. Kunkel was fortunate that she could still withstand surgery. The need to have her problem corrected could have occurred at a stage in her life when she was an unacceptable anesthetic and surgical risk because of poor health.

The ultimate prolapse occurs when the uterus, bladder, and rectum all protrude through the vaginal opening. In other words, the vaginal vault is turned inside out like a glove whose fingers are inverted upon removal of the hand. This surgery is called a vaginal hysterectomy with anterior (bladder), posterior (rectum), and enterocoele (bowel herniation into vagina) repair.

Making the Decision

In the past the decision against hysterectomy was sometimes made because a woman was considered too old to derive benefit from the procedure. Today women are living longer than ever before, and therefore the quality of their lives is a greater consideration. If a women's general health is good, and the discomfort without surgery is worsening, hysterectomy should rightfully be considered.

Whether "necessary" or "unnecessary," the decision to have a hysterectomy should follow a standardized plan. All facts and information about the surgery and the woman's particular problem, including benefits and risks, should be gathered, discussed, and fully understood. Getting a second opinion is wise and can eliminate many fears and insecurities. She should not hesitate to ask if the problem will go away after menopause. If so, the woman may elect to tolerate the discomfort. The final decision is not the physician's, husband's, or mother-in-law's, but the woman's alone. A healthy fear of surgery is normal, but there needs to be a comfort level in the face of impending surgery.

Sex and Hysterectomy

Mrs. Pennington came under my care late in her pregnancy. After failure to progress in labor, a C-section was performed. Much to everyone's surprise, this seemingly healthy young mother was found to have cancer of both ovaries. After consulting the husband, a complete hysterectomy with the removal of the tubes and ovaries was performed. This was indeed a shock to husband and wife.

It was necessary for her to undergo a year of chemotherapy, with complete success. Each year, however, she reported her husband's sexual avoidance. He was convinced he would get cancer if he resumed their sexual relations. She was unable to get him to go for counseling or to visit me. Nine years later she reports that divorce proceedings have begun.

Cancer surgery is very disruptive of sex for a variety of reasons. Often the patient is tired and complains of lack of vaginal sensations and/or pain. Sexual desire is affected by the illness and depression which the individual experiences.

Never hesitate to inquire about sexual functioning after the surgery so that your expectations will be realistic. Sometimes problems that were present but unrecognized come to the fore with the additional stress of hysterectomy. It is important to have a realistic understanding of the sexual and marital relationship before surgery. Twenty to forty percent of women are aware of uterine contractions with orgasm. Some may miss this and perceive their response as less desirable.

I try to encourage a positive attitude by suggesting to my patients how much more sexual they will feel without the pain, bleeding, or other problems that they have been plagued with. I remind them to tell their husbands to be well-rested for the "new woman" who no longer needs to worry about pregnancy or needs to bypass sex for a period.

Some woman mistakenly equate their femininity with their ability to have children. They then tend to become depressed and view themselves as mutilated, defeminized, and "desexed." The majority of women, however, find that there is no change in their sex life or that it improves.

Surgery for Mastectomy

Fourteen years ago, at the age of 30, my wife had a bilateral mastectomy. Our comparative youthfulness precluded much thought of the possibility of widespread malignancy, and my concerns and support of her were superficial. I thank God that I have grown beyond those days when I was unable to share honestly my fears, feelings, and misgivings.

Mary Ann's Story

It has been years since my mastectomy. The reconstructive surgery is excellent, and I could tell you I have never given it another thought, but that would not be true. If anything, this past year has been, in a very private and inexplicable way, a year of mourning for myself and two of my friends who are now with the Lord. Breast cancer strikes one of every ten women and is just slightly behind lung cancer as the leading cause of cancer death among women; its frequency is increasing. The secret of survival is *early detection*. Finding a lump early results in a 90 percent survival rate after five years.

When I was 28, a routine medical exam resulted in my quick referral to a surgeon, who admitted me the next day for a biopsy. A year later the process was repeated, and shortly after our transfer to the Philippine Islands, two more lumps were scheduled for removal. Slowly but surely what might be referred to as a "piecemeal" mastectomy was taking place, for since I was not overly "busty," the biopsies were removing what little breast tissue I had. What was worse was that each biopsy produced a different diagnosis, with a varying degree of alarm on my part. I was unwittingly learning the first rule of cancer treatment: A plan of action would require my active input and decision-making—the doctors did not have all the answers.

Months elapsed and another lump was ready to be biopsied. The decision was made to escalate what all parties agreed was inevitable: Both breasts would be completely removed. Depending on the outcome, the surgeon promised that after six months an evaluation into the possibility of reconstructive surgery could be made.

Such a decision could not have come at a better time. I had recently completed graduate school, and my self-image as a person and as a woman was the best it had been in years. My body was firm and otherwise healthy from tennis and exercise classes. I was ready. Although a personal God was not part of my belief system at the time, I thanked the "God of the universe" for allowing me the option of choosing a procedure that would enable me to live. Losing two rather small and considerably scarred-up breasts seemed a meager price to pay. My mistake was assuming that everyone would agree with my assessment.

The rejection I experienced in the form of pity—the belief that I had been diminished—was by far the worst pain I experienced. An adverse response to the wound (or denial played out around me) would have been easier to understand.

I knew I wasn't less of a person or a woman, but some of my friends didn't know this, and my husband wasn't sure. The efforts at comfort by the male doctors, our friends and peers, reduced me to my greatest despair with comments such as "I'm so sorry—I don't think I could handle it if it were my wife." As strength was regained, I wisely recognized that the problem was theirs.

It was not the practice, as it is now, to do reconstruction immediately after surgery. There was no counseling and no talk of prosthesis. For six months I devised outfits to conceal my flat chest. Surprisingly, the decision to have reconstructive surgery was almost as difficult as the original choice of surgery. If I really believed my self-worth rested in other than my breasts, why go through the surgery?

A sensitive medical friend suggested that my consideration ought to include my newly adopted daughter. "Why," he asked, "put her through the unnecessary trauma of a mom who is different? Kids have enough to deal with." I heard his wisdom, and it gave me the "permission" I needed. Having the prosthetic surgery turned out to be a wise decision for me too—not just for my daughter. Life has been easier in very practical ways because of it.

Facing the Choices

This year a lovely friend, superior court justice, outstanding lawyer, beauty queen, and loving mother and wife died of breast cancer in her forties. Her family's history included cancer in almost every member. As a woman and a friend, I wish she had been advised to have a "prophylactic mastectomy." With two of her immediate family members suffering from breast cancer before menopause, the odds for her contracting cancer were increased tenfold from average. A total bilateral mastectomy reduces the chance of breast cancer in the highest-risk group from 40–60 percent to 1 percent and a subcutaneous bilateral mastectomy to 2–5 percent, a figure less than for the general population.

The decision to prophylactically remove the breasts is a precaution that is hard for most women in our society. Our overemphasis on breasts and physical beauty leaves our values skewed. Even when a woman is diligent about checkups, 20 to 25 percent of affected women have nodal involvement by the time the first malignant lump is discovered. Clearly this operation should be presented as a viable option for certain women.

Lumpectomy or Mastectomy?

A lumpectomy combined with radiation therapy results in a higher survival rate than a mastectomy alone. Lumpectomy is done in hopes of preserving the breast. If the breast is small, several biopsies must be done, and if there is nipple involvement a lumpectomy is not the treatment of choice.

If an experienced radiation therapist cannot be found in your area, the wisdom of radiation therapy should be carefully considered. A poorly done radiation treatment can result in burning, shrinking, or hardening of the breast and can harm the skin and underlying organs. There are 2000 radiation therapists in the American Society for Radiology and Oncology, but only 400 of these are qualified to treat breasts. A woman may need to go to a large university setting for proper treatment. This can be expensive, and she must be temperamentally suited to the five to six weeks of daily treatment.

Once a lump is discovered, the doctor may advise a woman to have a mammogram before the biopsy in order to see if other lumps that may need biopsy are present. If a malignancy is diagnosed, there is no reason to decide on the mastectomy immediately. For years women were put to sleep not knowing the extent of the surgery that would be performed. This is very difficult psychologically. For me, it was one of the hardest aspects I had to face.

A week or two to gather facts and live with the decision is appropriate and called for. There are many questions that need answering. Is your doctor Board-certified and experienced in the procedures that he or she is proposing to do? If the procedure requires radiation, is there a qualified person available? Is the doctor concerned about cosmetic results? If reconstruction is important, is the doctor familiar with the procedures that might make this possible, or does another doctor need to be consulted? Do the chest muscles have to be removed?

Free treatment can be obtained at the National Cancer Institute in Bethesda, Maryland, if a person is willing to participate in ongoing studies to evaluate the effectiveness of different treatments. The Breast Cancer Advisory Center (P.O. Box 224, Kensington, MD 20895) will help find an experienced surgeon or radiologist in your area.

Living with the Results

My husband discovered a breast lump during Mrs. Brunsma's annual exam. She was furious. For two years she refused to return to him for treatment. Finally, after a successful mastectomy and time to adjust, she apologized. Our coping mechanisms are unique to us as individuals. My need to avoid viewing myself as "damaged" precluded any nurturing at the time of surgery. Now, years later, I find I am greatly moved when I hear of someone struggling with this disease. My husband's empathy, so difficult for him at age 30, now provides the comfort and solace I wouldn't have easily been able to accept earlier.

I have been inspired over the years by the quality of women I have met through the programs of the American Cancer Society. As speakers or participants they have taught me a great deal. Volunteering or participating in American Cancer Society programs provides healing to many people.

Surgery that requires "disfiguring" mastectomy obviously affects one's sex life. Frequently men are less bothered by it than the women themselves. Many women feel damaged and have difficulty accepting the idea that their husbands find them appealing.

A recent survey revealed that one-third of women with mastectomies had not resumed sexual relations after six months. Almost all used the female-astride position less frequently than before surgery. About 40 percent of the husbands had not viewed the scar even after three months.

Healthy adjustment of the male has much to do with his involvement in the decision-making about the surgery and the frequency of his hospital visits. Quick resumption of sexual activity and his willingness to view the site of surgery, perhaps even helping with bandage changes in the hospital, give positive indications of his acceptance.

Taking Responsibility

Surgery is a radical choice of treatment, but in most cases it is nevertheless a choice. Here the call to take responsibility is clear, since a passive stance is still a decision to let others do "what is best for you" or a decision to do nothing. The result can be unnecessary pain, worsening of the problem, and even death.

It is common among cancer patients to speak of precursors to the disease. Frequently there is a severe and stressful event preceding the onset by 18 months to two years in which feelings of helplessness were characteristic. We know that a positive mental attitude, one not reflecting a victim mentality, helps the immune system fight disease.

No one looks forward to surgery but one can look forward to the new quality of life that can be achieved by going through the pain.

"A cheerful heart is good medicine, but a crushed spirit dries up the bones" (Proverbs 17:22).

Chapter Twelve

The Complete Woman and Pregnancy

You will give birth to children.

—Genesis 3:16

My wife and I were married almost six years before our son was born. The patterns we had established as a couple were comfortable and unquestionably self-indulgent. We wanted a baby, difficulty in becoming pregnant according to our timetable had made that painfully clear.

Our news was greeted by friends and relatives with a curious schizophrenic mixture of happiness and dire warnings: "Now you've done it! Your life will never be the same." Exactly what was meant by such proclamations resulted in a tinge of nervousness and wonder at what we *had* done. Not one person said anything about the joy and enrichment which a child can bring to one's life.

That son is now on the verge of leaving home to begin life on his own. Although I understand more of the ambivalence that characterized those first reactions, I can truly say that life is richer and has greater depth and meaning because my son was born. He has been a great teacher.

A picture of all joy would be false, but one of all heartache equally so. The mixture of positive and negative that characterizes parenting begins before conception for some parents but shows itself clearly for all during the months of pregnancy. Becoming pregnant can be one of the most exciting events of a woman's life. Facing the physical discomfort, restructuring one's body image, and in the truest sense living one's life for another person can be major physical and emotional challenges.

Prepregnancy Preparation

Suzy had intercourse after the prom. It happened only once. The chance of getting pregnant seemed remote, but she appeared in my

171

office three months later unquestionably expecting. Mrs. Johnson, childless and married 15 years, was sure she had gallstones. Her nausea and vomiting persisted, and the pregnancy test was positive. Ann was still nursing her three-month-old. She couldn't be pregnant, she thought, since she hadn't even had a period since the baby was born, but she was.

All these women were beginning an unexpected pregnancy. By doing so they had already missed what is now determined to be a critical time of pregnancy—prepregnancy preparation. Prior to conception it is wise to visit your physician for information and a checkup. Problems can be minimized and healthier babies obtained with a little fore-thought.

It is obvious that any woman with a special health problem (such as diabetes or heart disease) should plan carefully before conception, but it is also true that *all* husbands should educate themselves as much as possible about this life-changing event. Excellent books are available that deal with the emotional aspects of childbearing, the development of the child, and the many other facets of pregnancy.

Before pregnancy is the time to establish a systematic and enjoy-able exercise program, which is the start of a generalized plan of good health. Brisk walking, indoor stationary bicycling, swimming, and low-impact aerobics are among the myriad of activities that are appro-priate for women to pursue throughout pregnancy. More strenuous ac-tivities can be considered as long as they have been part of a daily routine beforehand.

Contrary to what our mothers thought, exercise during pregnancy helps improve muscle tone, strength, and the oxygen supply to mother and baby. Feeling better physically and mentally is an additional bonus. Moderate exercise is dangerous only when unusual pain or fatigue occurs and continues. Just as important as the establishment of an exercise routine is a healthy plan of nutrition. The teenage mother's dependence on junk food often leads to maternal or fetal complications. The best diet is one that includes all the major food groups in balanced proportions. Fad dieting or fasting is out of the question, so prepreg-nancy is the time to get weight under control. In extreme cases there are programs for dieting that are approved by the College of Obstetrics and Gynecology as long as they begin after the three-month mark.

Pregnancy requires an increase of 200 to 300 protein calories a day. Everything that is eaten crosses the placental barrier, which means the baby is indulging too. The importance of getting one's diet under control before conception is therefore obvious.

Taking vitamins before and during pregnancy is more a matter of the personal preference of the physician than of any set medical recommendation. Because we can never be certain of the freshness of the food we purchase (and thus its vitamin content), I recommend that all women take a good multivitamin product whether they are pregnant or not. Vitamin deficiency during pregnancy is primarily revealed by numbness, tingling, and weakness in the hands and feet. Iron-deficiency anemia is also common. Sometime the fatigue seen in the first three months of pregnancy is relieved by vitamins even when the blood work appears normal. Minimally sufficient supplies of iron, vitamins, and minerals can quickly be depleted by the growing fetus.

An overlooked area of prepregnancy preparation is the modification of one's lifestyle to a more balanced pattern. Rest, cessation of smoking and drinking, and decreasing the consumption of caffeine and aspartame (Equal/NutraSweet) are all essential measures to ensure a healthy mother and child.

Prenatal Care

In the past, missing a period was the first clue to pregnancy. Today chemical testing of the blood or urine can verify a pregnancy three to five days from conception. The most sensitive urine test is as accurate as blood tests. Knowledge of pregnancy enables a woman to avoid harmful substances or practices at a very sensitive time of fetal development.

Upon confirmation of pregnancy, the decision must be made as to who will supply the prenatal care (the medical care which the mother receives before the birth). Usually that individual will be the one who will assist in the delivery. Since continuity of care provides a safety factor, and since there are numerous philosophies on delivery, selecting someone whose ideas are compatible with those of the pregnant woman is extremely important.

Who Is At Risk?

The belief that women over the age of 35 are subject to more problem pregnancies has not been well-founded in my experience. A mature woman is more likely to take care of herself physically and to follow the physician's instructions. Maternal deaths in this age range have dropped 50 percent in recent years. Bleeding following delivery is the leading cause of death.

For me, the most difficult and high-risk patients are teenagers. Often their nutritional habits are deplorable, they do not educate themselves, and they do not follow instructions. Embolism and hypertensive conditions are the number one cause of death in this age group.

There are a number of physical and/or medical history factors that can make a pregnancy "high risk." A woman under five feet in height and more than 20 percent over or under ideal weight has an increased risk of complications. A history of previous problems increases the possibility of difficulties still more. Diabetes, Rh factor, high blood pressure, and stillborn births are all red flags to the obstetrician. Although difficult to prove, high-stress situations seem to adversely affect the mother, the fetus, and the course of the pregnancy.

The United States has one of the highest perinatal death rates in the Western world. This fact is traceable to the lack of free or inexpensive maternal care and our high rate of teenage pregnancy. Failure to visit a doctor (or erratic attendance of appointments) radically affects pregnancy outcome.

A new risk is found with women who attempt vaginal birth after cesarean section. This procedure is referred to as TOL, trial of labor, or VBAC, vaginal birth after cesarean section. In less than 1 percent of the cases, the uterine scar may rupture. Vaginal birth after a classical cesarean incision—a vertical incision—is more likely to cause rupture and therefore should not be attempted. (If the obstetrician is new, the old records are essential to ensure what type of incision was actually done.) A low horizontal incision can better withstand the pressure of labor, and in 60 to 70 percent of the cases vaginal birth is accomplished. A trial of labor is not recommended if a severe wound infection occurred with the previous C-section.

Even if the probability of a successful vaginal delivery seems high, new complications or a reoccurrence of the previous complication may require a repeat C-section. Recently a woman appeared on a national talk show who was suing her Ob-Gyn for abandonment because she felt forced to change doctors when he refused to guarantee her a vaginal delivery after a cesarean. The only doctor who would take her (and one would assume, promised her a vaginal delivery) was 300 miles away. She ended up needing a second C-section. Changing preset plans is sometimes necessary. The goal must always be a healthy baby.

What's Happening to Me?

Most women are well aware of the first signs of pregnancy: breast sensitivity, fatigue, and increased urination. The missed period merely confirms their suspicion. It is not until five to seven weeks after conception that the physician can verify, through his or her physical findings, that a pregnancy is indeed present.

The cervix becomes soft (Goodell's sign) and there is asymmetrical growth of the uterus at the site of implantation (Piskacek's sign). The uterus changes from a pear shape to a more round configuration. The enlarging uterine artery can be felt pulsating (Oslander's sign). The breast veins dilate, becoming more visible, and a corpus/luteum cyst, the remnant from which the egg came, may be felt.

The woman may have begun to experience nausea, leg cramps, anxiety, and ambivalence in addition to her first symptoms. In many women these signs continue throughout the first 12 weeks. By eight weeks the blood sugars fluctuate, causing mood swings. The doctor notices a bluish tinge to the vagina and vulva (Chadwick's sign) and finds that the uterus has risen out of the pelvis. At around ten to 12 weeks the fetal heart tones (FHT) may be heard with a hand-held ultrasound device. (It may be seen and heard by six to eight weeks with more sophisticated equipment.) The breasts begin to enlarge and there is increased salivation and vaginal discharge. A three-pound weight gain is appropriate during this 12-week period.

As the hormone level decreases during weeks 13 to 16, many of the more bothersome symptoms of pregnancy fade away. Worry shifts from the health of the fetus to more practical concerns of the mother: "Will my husband find me attractive?" and "Will I get fat?" The uterus is now halfway between the pubic bone and the umbilicus.

Seventeen to 20 weeks is an exciting time for husband and wife as they feel fetal movement and listen to the strong heartbeat. This moment is also shared with any siblings who accompany their mom on her visit. Young Jeremy was particularly intrigued. He listened carefully as we speculated on whether the heartbeat was that of a girl or boy (always a 50-50 chance!) and took his turn listening. As we continued the exam, Jeremy experimented with the ultrasound, placing it on his arm and announcing with alarm, "Oh no! I have a baby boy in my arm!" Needless to say, we used the experience as a teachable moment—after we recovered our composure!

These weeks produce less pressure on the bladder, so urinary frequency is temporarily relieved. Mapping out a route of all the restrooms between home and the grocery store is no longer essential!

The fundus is finally above the umbilicus by 21 to 24 weeks. Measurement is taken from the top of the pubic bone to the top of the uterus. The resulting number in no way relates to the weeks of gestation, but it does provide proof of a normal growth pattern. Backaches are common, and nosebleeds (epistaxis) and gum-bleeding (gestational gingival hyperplasia) occur because the hormones cause an overgrowth of gum tissues and stimulate the vascular supply to the nose. Obvious treatments include gentle nasal care and switching to a soft toothbrush soaked briefly in hot water.

The expectant mom is tired but eager (and approximately 15 pounds heavier) by 25 to 28 weeks, and the fundus is halfway to the breastplate. Some women find that their tummies begin to resemble a road map as stretchmarks appear. Colostrum, the precursor to milk, is excreted from the breast. The plagues of pregnancy, varicose veins and hemorrhoids, occur in many women, increasing in severity with each pregnancy. With the abdomen filled with baby, breathing becomes shallow.

Once the fundus reaches the breastplate (xiphoid process), one knows that weeks 28 to 32 have been reached. Breasts are full and tender. The black line that appears up the center of the abdomen, dark splotches on the face, and darkening of moles and freckles are all caused by the hormones stimulating the pigment cells of the body.

Once again the restroom map to the grocery store must be utilized. The increasing weight and size of the baby, 18 inches and up to five pounds, compresses the bladder.

The remaining time of pregnancy, weeks 33 to 40, is primarily a time of baby growth and of the mother's physical and mental preparation for labor. For some reason it seems to be a time of unusual questions as well. A weight gain of 24 to 30 pounds is normal, and most of this weight is accounted for by the baby, placenta, and changes of pregnancy. Getting back to the prepregnancy weight should not be difficult with this amount of weight gain.

The thrill of being pregnant gives way to the multitude of physical discomforts: "I'm tired of waddling!" "I feel like a whale!" "What I'd give for one good night's sleep!" Pregnant women have been known to scrub floors, rearrange furniture, and eat large amounts of birthday cake and spaghetti in order to stimulate labor to begin. Their efforts make them sore and give them heartburn, but no labor!

The actual time of spontaneous labor is between the baby and God. Not all of the factors that trigger labor are known. The estimated date of confinement (EDC) is at best a "guestimate." A common way to figure the EDC is to subtract three months from the first day of the last period and add seven days. Basically, the length of gestation is 267 days from conception or 280 days from the first day of the last period.

Anyone who claims a ten-month pregnancy is probably calculating from ten 28-day lunar months. A nine-month pregnancy is based on calendar days. Labor usually occurs after the due date with most first pregnancies. Even with infertility patients who know precisely when they conceived, the EDC can be missed.

Preparing the Expectant Father

A six-foot-four muscular Marine refused to attend the prenatal visits and Lamaze classes with his wife. Having convinced himself that the slogan "When the going gets tough, the tough get going" applied to childbirth, he was positive he was prepared. But he began to falter when his wife suddenly bit his shoulder during a particularly painful contraction. The end came when a very blood-covered baby emerged. He simply disappeared. It took six stitches above the right eye to repair the physical damage; he still hasn't recovered from the emotional embarrassment.

I encourage all fathers to attend as many appointments as possible, but especially the first one. It is important that they understand the teamwork involved in enabling the pregnancy and childbirth process to proceed smoothly. The wife they know and love is apt to have days when a "Jekyll-and-Hyde" personality appears. His empathy and understanding are enhanced when he realizes the vast hormonal and physical changes that are occurring.

Attendance at childbirth-preparation classes is highly recommended. Not only does this bring the couple closer, but it enables the father to feel that he is a real part of the unfolding drama. A study on adjustment to motherhood found that the type of delivery, whether C-section or vaginal, did not relate to the mother's satisfaction with the birth process. Instead, adjustment was highly related to what she thought her husband was feeling.

The expression of love and affection is just as important during pregnancy as before. Some fathers withdraw sexually just when their mate needs the expression of their love the most. Among the excuses used in avoiding sex are fears of hurting the child. "I'm afraid I might put the kid's eye out." "Maybe I'll cause a skull fracture and brain damage." "I might cause labor to begin."

Most couples can continue their usual pattern of sexual activity during pregnancy. Oral sex and douching, by introducing air into the vagina or fluids under great force, have the potential to cause air or fluid embolisms to the lungs. Death can result, so caution is advised.

For a woman with a history or threat of premature labor it may be advisable to cease having orgasms, since there is some evidence that the uterine contraction of orgasm may cause labor to begin. Additionally, it is believed that a substance in the semen, prostaglandins, can cause uterine spasm, which could initiate premature labor. A properly used condom is suggested for couples who are at risk. If the uterus remains contracted for more than five minutes after orgasm, orgasm should be avoided. (This does not mean that intercourse should cease.)

Precautions of Pregnancy

Most pregnancies progress along as they have done through the ages—with minimal problems. Pregnancy is a normal variation within a woman's life. With our increased knowledge and awareness of agents that can cause problems for the pregnant mother and her child, far greater attention is being given to avoiding anything that might be detrimental.

Soon after our move from the Eastern medical school I attended to the Western university setting for internship and residency, my wife made a liberating discovery: The feeding schedule she had been adhering to at the instruction of our original pediatrician (despite the three-month-old protestations of our son) was totally revised by the new physician. Joey was much more content and Mary Ann learned an important lesson: Medicine is not always an exact science. She rightfully reasoned that being an intelligent, conscientious person, she could risk trusting her best judgment in areas of controversy or when her own insight and experience seemed to contradict what the pediatrician or baby book said.

What follows is a series of cautions, some which no responsible person would ignore and others requiring the discernment and best use of one's common sense.

There is no conflict of opinion about the harmful effects of smoking on mother and baby. The evidence clearly reveals that smoking mothers have more complications during pregnancy than nonsmokers. They miscarry more frequently and have more premature deliveries (one-half pack a day increases the risk 80 percent) and stillborns. The effects last beyond birth, causing babies to be more susceptible to respiratory problems and diseases of early infancy. Lower birth weight in these babies is caused by the absorption of nicotine, tars, and carbon monoxide into the bloodstream, interfering with the absorption of nutrients and the expulsion of waste.

The newest studies reveal as much as a 50 percent increase in any form of cancer in children born to mothers who smoke at least ten cigarettes per day. And one must not dismiss the effect of passive smoking by the father or other housemates. Studies clearly indicate that such "passive smoking" affects the fetus by causing low birthrates and premature labor.

Equally dramatic effects result from consumption of alcohol while pregnant. Every time the mother takes a drink, the baby does too. Experts do not know the minimal dose at which damage occurs. The effects could vary with each child. As a result, pregnant women should not drink at all. Fetal alcohol syndrome (FAS) causes low birth weight, birth defects, kidney disorders, and heart defects. Mental retardation, learning disabilities, and tendencies toward hyperactivity and irritability may also occur.

Clearly, alcohol and smoking are two practices which no conscientious mother should continue. Using medications for illness calls for discernment. Staying away from all medication is preferred, but if it is necessary for your health your physician may prescribe a particular drug. This is not the time for self-treatment even with over-the-counter drugs. The most critical time for concern is the first three months, when foundational development is occurring.

Drugs that should always be avoided are acutane, sulfa, and tetracycline. Acutane, used in control of acne scarring, is responsible for severe birth defects. Sulfa drugs in the last six weeks of pregnancy can cause jaundice, and tetracycline results in permanent staining of the infant's teeth.

A common substance that should be avoided or at least severely reduced is caffeine. A recent study from Yale University revealed that women who injested 150 milligrams of caffeine a day had a miscarriage rate twice that of those who used no caffeine at all. This is equivalent to one very strong cup of coffee a day or three to four weak cups. Coffee also contains benzopyrene (known to cause human birth defects) and chlorogenic acid (suspected of causing mutations in genes).

There are suggestions that excess caffeine itself may be linked to birth defects. We know that the stimulant effect which the mother experiences is also felt by the child. Sometimes the use of drinks known to be high in caffeine—coffee, tea, and cola drinks—causes one to neglect more healthful eating patterns. Unfortunately, chocolate is also high in caffeine!

The search for easy ways to control weight has led to the use of artificial sweeteners. The use of Aspartame (Equal and NutraSweet) has become extremely widespread. There is some concern that excess amounts of these substances can cause dizziness and subtle brain changes in some people. At this time avoiding aspartame whenever possible is probably the best course.

Certain medical and dental procedures also present risks, although today's improved X-ray and ultrasound machines present minimal risk in comparison to the older equipment. If an X-ray is justified medically, it should be done. No serious problems have been demonstrated with the use of modern ultrasound techniques.

Because the chemistry of the mouth changes with pregnancy, women who are expecting are more prone to have cavities. Dental work is perfectly acceptable and in fact is recommended in order to avoid tenderness and inflammation of the gums. X-rays, if necessary, are permissible after the fourth month.

In California all pregnant women are tested for immunity against German measles (rubella). If immunity is absent, they are cautioned to avoid situations in which measles may be present. Upon dismissal from the hospital after the birth, a rubella vaccine is given to prevent problems with future pregnancies. If a woman develops rubella within the first three months of pregnancy, there is a a 50-50 chance of severe birth defects occurring. Fortunately, there are fewer and fewer outbreaks of rubella.

Old motion pictures always show the pregnant woman fainting. Today we rarely speak of this, although it does occur. Fainting may be caused by low blood pressure, low blood sugar, or anemia. Caution is advised when getting up from a reclining position. Rising in stages enables one to avoid dizziness and fainting.

We have spoken of the precaution of avoiding medications. Clearly, drug-dependent behavior, whether with legal or illegal drugs, presents risks not only of birth defects and addicted babies but also of drug-dependency behavior problems in the mother. Improper diet and missed appointments increase the chance of complications in child-bearing.

Specifically, marijuana use involves all the precautions given for cigarette smoking, but with an even stronger link to irritability and hyperactivity of the newborn. Cocaine addiction (in a typical pattern often involving several days of heavy use) is particularly detrimental to the fetus due to poor hydration and nutrition. Cocaine overdose produces serious complications for mother and child. Like any substance injested by the mother, it crosses the placental barrier and is "taken" by the child.

More mundane hazards can also cause concern. It is hard to think of giving up the family cat when a woman becomes pregnant, but some women may opt to do so. The problem is due to a disease found in cats called toxoplasmosis. It is transferable to humans when they handle the feces of an infected cat. Some people are immune due to previous exposure; but for those who are not, if during pregnancy they contract the disease, the fetus may suffer from pneumonia, a small head, delayed growth, and serious eye problems.

Opting to keep a cat requires other people handling the litter box, hand-washing after pet contact, and curtailing the cat's outside ventures. There is less concern if the cat has always been indoors. The same precautions are required in a friend's home who owns a cat.

The fantasy of a nice long soak in a hot tub or sitting in a sauna to ease the pains and strains of pregnancy looms large in many a pregnant woman's mind. But soaking in water of over 100 degrees (Fahrenheit) may harm the baby. The opportunity to soak in a hot tub or sit in a sauna must be turned down during pregnancy. Even tub baths are hazardous if the water is too hot or if a fall occurs while trying to maneuver an unbalanced body. With ruptured membranes, the possibility of infection exists. To be on the safe side, tub baths should be avoided.

Lest you begin to think that life is no longer worth living (having been denied your Cokes, chocolate, and hot tub), driving is not denied the pregnant woman as long as she can reach the pedals! Seat belts have not been shown to harm the unborn child and should be worn, including the shoulder harness. Maternal death is the major cause of death to the unborn child in auto accidents.

Although some women long for the days of greater restrictiveness, especially when it comes to housework or doing the dishes, working outside the home has no deleterious effects on the baby or the working pregnant woman as long as her working environment is safe. There is an obvious precaution against becoming overtired.

Surviving at Home

One often hears of the "normality" of pregnancy. Indeed it is a natural and normal process of a woman's lifetime. But the multitude of changes in a woman's body appears to challenge the definition of "normal." More than one woman has been distressed by the stranger she sees in the mirror. Many of the changes can be minimized by keeping weight in control, decreasing salt intake, and participating in proper exercise (begun prior to pregnancy).

Mrs. Diamond complained that she was so tired she felt her day consisted of 23 hours of sleep and one hour of eating and taking care of bodily functions. Setting aside extra time to rest is especially essential during early and late pregnancy. In some cases prenatal vitamins provide relief.

Morning sickness is a classic symptom of pregnancy. It can occur at any time during the day or night. Symptoms often subside prior to the fourth month, but may resume in the last few weeks. High levels of hormones, low levels of vitamin B_6, and too little glycogen (the natural sugar stored in the liver) are the probable causes.

In the morning, prior to arising, it is sometimes worthwhile to eat two or three dry crackers. Eating small and frequent meals throughout the day, selecting cold foods over hot, and taking 50 milligrams of vitamin B_6 at morning and night can give relief. In severe cases hospitalization is required.

As body shape changes, the center of gravity is thrown off and there is a tendency to sit and stand improperly. The result is backache. Keeping the muscles in good tone and paying attention to body alignment is beneficial. Flat shoes are both helpful and safer.

By the end of the pregnancy most women experience hemorrhoids, which are varicose veins of the rectum. Heredity is a decided factor in their occurrence, but the weight of the baby, the pooling of blood, and constipation are also factors. A high-fiber diet, warm sitz baths, stool softeners (not laxatives), and commercial hemorrhoid preparations may help, but relief through simply lying flat on the left side should not be overlooked.

This position also helps to relieve swelling (edema) in general. Tight clothing and prolonged standing aggravate swelling. Many women attempt relief by cutting down on liquids. This is a mistake; the fluid intake should not be limited. Instead, salt, the real culprit, should be restricted. Eating adequate amounts of protein is also helpful. Elevating the foot of the bed three or four inches will not interfere with sleep, but it will provide relief. Stacking pillows under one's legs should not be done because it places the body into a jackknifed position that hampers circulation in the legs.

Slowed circulation overloads the veins, and with the pressure produced by the enlarging uterus causes varicose veins. These tend to worsen with each pregnancy and are influenced by one's genetic propensity. The ultimate treatment for varicosities is surgery, but surgery should never be performed until the woman is sure she has had her last child.

Normal vaginal discharge increases during the later months of pregnancy. This is due to increased blood supply and hormones, and the tendency of some women to spill sugar into their urine (glycosuria, a normal occurrence not necessarily indicative of diabetes), which can increase the chance of yeast infection. This discharge may convince some women that their "bag of water" has ruptured. A minipad may be required to prevent soiling clothes, and cotton panties and skirts help reduce the risk of yeast infections.

Leg cramps are related to calcium and pH imbalances. A balanced diet is beneficial, whereas too much milk or too many carbonated beverages can contribute to calcium depletion. This discomfort is primarily seen in the latter part of pregnancy, when the baby begins to require more calcium for its own bone growth. Immediate relief can be obtained by lying flat and having a friend push the balls of the feet toward the head.

Even severe muscle spasm or abdominal pain should not always be a cause for alarm. The cause may be serious only if rest, a low-temperature heating pad, massage, and mild pain medication do not result in diminishing symptoms. Chances are that the pain is either a strained muscle, false labor, or round ligament pain. If pain increases or there is no relief, a physician should be consulted.

Diet obviously affects the incidence of heartburn and intestinal gas. Spicy and fatty foods stimulate acid production. During pregnancy the stomach secretes more acid and has a slower emptying time. The growing uterus causes distortion and a change of position of the stomach. Heartburn results when excessive acidic fluid finds its way into the lower esophagus, which has no protective lining. Antacids are safe, and many women find comfort by elevating the upper body at night by sleeping on two pillows.

Confirming Healthy Pregnancies

Mrs. Wingerd was larger than one might expect for a four-month pregnancy. "Large for dates" suggests to the obstetrician the possibility of a multiple pregnancy. Since ultrasound is a quick and safe way to verify this, I recommended that the procedure be performed the next week. Mrs. Wingerd became very pensive, and with eyes filled with panic she asked, "Will this cook my baby?"

Ultrasound or sonogram (the use of high-frequency sound waves to provide pictures of the baby, placenta, and other components of a pregnancy) has numerous purposes. The most common use is to confirm the due date. It can also reveal abnormal placenta locations, multiple births, and certain birth defects. Occasionally the sex can be determined.

Although it does not "cook" babies and has a history of safety, ultrasound should be used only when medically indicated. Another test recommended with discretion is amniocentesis.

The major reason for ordering this test is to check for chromosomal disorders (such as Down's syndrome) and genetic defects (such as spina bifida and hydrocephalus). Sickle cell anemia, metabolic disorders, and hemophilia can also be diagnosed. However, other birth defects and diseases can go undetected with this test.

With the use of ultrasound in locating the baby and placenta, the possibility of spontaneous miscarriage is less than 1 percent. All expectant women over 35 years of age (or with a previous history of the above-mentioned) should have an amniocentesis test done.

The nonstress test is used to determine fetal well-being and healthy placental functioning. Primary candidates for this test are women who are at 42 weeks gestation or greater, are preeclamptic (a complication of pregnancy), or who suffer from intrauterine growth retardation.

The baby's heart is monitored electronically by a fetal monitor machine. A good test requires variability in the heart rate and a rise of at least ten to 15 beats per minute with each fetal movement. Three variations within a ten-minute period would be labeled a "normal" or "reactive" nonstress test. Since babies do sleep, drinking orange juice can cause a rise in both mother's and baby's blood sugar, thereby stimulating fetal activity.

A "nonreactive" test requires a follow-up procedure called a stress test (oxytocin challenge test). Uterine contractions caused by intravenous Pitocin help the doctor decide if the baby is healthy and if placental insufficiency exists. It gives the doctor the information he needs to decide whether to allow the pregnancy to continue, to induce labor, or perform a cesarean section.

Alpha-fetoprotein testing is required in some states at 16 weeks. This blood test will reveal Down's syndrome, spina bifida, and hydrocephalic infants.

A final common test is the RH antibody factor. If the mother is RH positive there is no concern. There is only a problem if the mother is RH negative and the baby is RH positive. Before the discovery of RhoGAM, having more than one child was very risky because antibodies in the mother's blood crossed the placenta and destroyed the baby's blood cells. Today if you are found to be RH negative, your doctor will determine the presence or absence of antibodies in your blood. If no antibodies are found, the test is repeated at seven months, and if antibodies are still not detected, a RhoGAM injection is given. This prevents sensitization of the mother's blood and is repeated at birth or after miscarriage. RhoGAM will not work if sensitization has occurred.

Taking Responsibility

The discipline to change patterns that are definitely unhealthful for the fetus and in the long run not particularly good for the mother can often be mustered during pregnancy. Love and concern for the unborn provides a powerful motivation. The serious responsibility of bearing a child is almost overwhelming to some mothers, although missed completely by others.

Some women see pregnancy as a time to let oneself go, a time to be undisciplined. I have patients whose thirty or more extra pounds per child have virtually hidden the vibrant young girl who first appeared in my office three babies earlier.

Health begins with the parental mindset before conception. Women who would never dream of injecting their newborn with drugs, feeding him or her an inadequate diet, or handicapping the child by sabotaging his opportunity to learn nevertheless maintain practices that do exactly that.

A husband and wife are ready to have a baby when their spiritual house is in order, when they can commit and maintain good health practices, and when they are willing to devote quality and quantity time to a child. Ability to conceive, as we see so clearly in teenage pregnancies, is not what makes a responsible parent.

In God's perfect plan both sexes are essential for this ultimate expression of sexual communication. Having a baby is a shared responsibility for the sexual woman.

"But women will be kept safe through childbirth, if they continue in faith, love, and holiness with propriety" (1 Timothy 2:15).

Chapter Thirteen

The Complete Woman Gives Birth

He delivered them from their distress.

—Psalm 107:6

Mrs. Sever's labor was long and tiring. As I checked her for what seemed liked the hundredth time on this protracted day, her signs of exhaustion were a concern to me. My medical instinct was to offer relief, but I held back. The Severs, like many modern couples, had looked forward to a "natural" delivery. Although they had been well-educated to the severe pain of childbirth, their belief in the method had minimized the reality of a lengthy labor.

Fourteen hours had passed, and although labor was progressing, it was at a snail's pace. If I couldn't give medical relief, I could at least share her discomfort and hold her hand. Her eyes told it all: She was nearing the end of her endurance. She began to cry when her husband left the room. "Please, Doctor, I can't stand the pain anymore. Give me something."

When Mr. Sever returned, I suggested that perhaps the time had come to consider medical assistance. His response was swift: "No woman in the Sever family has ever given in and required medication. My wife will not be the first! *We* can do it!" She was visibly devastated.

With increased obstinancy, he doubled his coaching effort. He demanded that she practice her learned-breathing patterns and that she concentrate on her focal point while he rubbed her vigorously. His coaching became louder and louder, interspersed with "*We* will do this!"

I became more and more distressed as I saw what is meant to be a shared and positive experience change into something that resembled Marine boot camp. Eventually "they" did deliver. My anger lingered as I contemplated the tendency of people to consider method more important than outcome.

The goal of labor and delivery, first and foremost, is a healthy mother and child. The method is secondary, ultimately inconsequential. Mrs. Sever had a healthy baby but her spirit was broken, and physically she was far more exhausted than she needed to be.

I wish I could say this experience happened only once, but I've seen it far too often. I've even found myself admiring a squirming infant by myself while the parents were so busy reveling in their accomplishment of the method that they had forgotten the baby.

We've tried to make couples aware of this tendency in our classes, and I usually discuss it during one of the visits. They are reminded that a big red zero will not be stamped on their forehead should they have to alter their delivery plans.

The Alternate Birth Center

Many communities have been responsive to the need for birth to occur in a homelike setting. Delivery at home, however, may place the mother and child at risk if complications occur. The development of the alternate birth center has sought to eliminate the danger and maintain an atmosphere conducive to family participation and with less of a medical environment. "ABC" rooms may be within the hospital or freestanding. Emergency equipment and personnel are at hand in case they are needed.

Courses are available to prepare the woman and the family for this choice. Only low-risk patients, those with problem-free pregnancies, may use an "ABC" room. The concept includes maximum flexibility and minimum intrusion of the medical staff. Although it is less expensive to use the "ABC" room, patients are expected to go home within 12 to 24 hours.

Is It the Real Thing or Indigestion?

Mr. Loftus got his wife, Betty, to the hospital in record time. It was a costly trip. The doctor had told him to hurry, and it sounded like delivery was imminent, but little Jeffrey did not appear for six hours. The traffic policeman was not impressed.

Trying to determine if someone is in labor over the phone is a habit I have long since eliminated. The only sure way to verify true labor is to place the patient on a fetal monitor. This establishes true versus false labor (Braxton-Hicks contractions) and assesses the well-being of the baby.

Braxton-Hicks contractions are common during the last weeks of pregnancy. Their role is to prepare the uterine muscles for labor. They are commonly felt in the lower pelvis, are irregular, and usually last less than 30 seconds. In many cases they are eliminated by walking. True labor is felt higher in the abdomen and is very regular, with each contraction lasting longer than 45 to 50 seconds; usually, walking does not provide relief.

Old wives' tales perpetuate the idea that labor is heralded by a "bloody show," a mucus plug, or the rupture of the "bag of water." These may or may not occur. If the membranes do rupture and a large volume of amniotic fluid gushes forth and continues, a trip to the hospital is necessary to determine that the cord is not positioned in a way that can decrease the blood flow to the baby. A small leak does not require an immediate trip to the hospital. After three to five hours, with or without contractions, a medical evaluation should be done.

First-time labors are traditionally expected to take 12 to 14 hours. My experience has been closer to seven to nine hours if good education and spousal support are present. Second babies are usually more rapid. After three or more children, labor may be very fast, although some women with five or six children begin to have lengthy labors again.

Although we usually think of labor as being a long process, sometimes it entails only one or two strong contractions. This is called precipitous labor. As a resident I learned what precipitous labor was from a young women whose obesity hid her pregnancy not only from other people but from herself. After a hardy Christmas dinner she excused herself to prepare for bed. On stepping into the tub, one intense contraction resulted in the newborn infant landing unhurt in the water.

Mother and baby were transported to my service. The force of the delivery resulted in extensive tearing. It took three hours to carefully repair the rectal-vaginal area.

What Is the Doctor Checking For?

A patient might wonder what possible information a five- to ten-minute evaluation can produce. For the physician, it is long enough to give him or her considerable vital information on the progress of the pregnancy. Although every physician has his or her personal adaptation of both frequency of visits and content of the examination, basically an informative and lengthy initial visit is followed by monthly checks for seven months, biweekly ones in the eighth month, and weekly checks in the ninth month.

Routine pelvic exams are usually not performed until the ninth month. But in each visit the growth of the uterus is checked to make sure that the baby is continuing to grow. Fetal heart tones are evaluated for regularity and rate. Erratic rates or high or low rates warn of potential problems. The position of the baby is evaluated. This will indicate if delivery is likely to be breech (bottom-first) or vertex (head-first).

It is unfortunate that with our present medicolegal climate more and more breech babies are being delivered by C-section. The art of breech delivery is rarely taught to present-day obstetrical residents. A large percentage of the increase in C-sections is attributed to this fact. Recent research review indicates that over a ten-year period delivering breech babies by C-section did not improve perinatal mortality. If the baby is small there is no indication that problems will be caused by a vaginal birth. In fact the opposite seems to be true.

Physicians tend to recall difficulty with vaginal breech deliveries and forget that breech babies have three times the rate of congenital abnormalities than with head-first presentations despite the method of delivery. They also overlook the complications associated with surgery. In studies in which babies were matched for birth weight there was virtually no difference in the neurological outcome between head-vagina, head-C-section, breech-vagina, and breech-C-section deliveries.

If the breech baby has one or both legs extended downward toward the cervix (footling breech) a C-section is necessary because of the increased possibility of a prolapsed cord and its devastating consequences. Vaginal delivery is considered when the baby is in a "frank" breech position. This means that both of the baby's legs are parallel to his or her body. A vaginal delivery may also be attempted with a "full" breech. In this position the baby's legs are crossed in a sitting Buddha position.

With first babies the head will often drop into the pelvis (engage) prior to labor. When this fails to happen, it may indicate a large infant or an abnormality that could complicate labor. In women who have had two or three children, the abdomen tends to protrude over the pelvic rim because of weak abdominal muscles, and thus engagement is less likely.

During the last six weeks the cervix begins to thin. This is called effacement (thinning out). The cervix is usually two centimeters long, and so 50 percent effaced equals one centimeter. Near the completion of thinning, called 100 percent effacement, the cervix may now begin to dilate (open).

The doctor measures the dilation of the cervix. A completely dilated cervix is ten centimeters in diameter. This means that the baby may now begin to pass through the birth canal, a process that might take minutes or hours.

Stages of Labor

There are three stages of labor. The first stage begins when regular uterine contractions cause the cervix to dilate. It ends when the cervix is completely dilated. This is often the longest period, and toward the end (the transitional phase) contractions are more intense, longer, and more frequent. The urge to push is strong. Not realizing that the end is in sight, some women feel they can't go on.

The second stage lasts from complete dilation of the cervix to birth. Usually a doctor will not allow this stage to exceed two hours without progress for fear of complications to the baby. It is now all right to give in to the urge to push—it can provide relief. In 96 percent of the cases, as the head passes through the birth canal it rotates face-down. The infant is said to be "crowning" when it pushes against the vulvar area.

The decision to have an episiotomy is determined at this time. This common procedure is used to prevent irregular tearing of the vaginal surface and/or perineal area and allows the baby to pass through the birth canal more quickly. If needed, the incision is made under anesthesia between the rectum and the vagina. A clean-cut incision heals more readily than a tear. The need for an episiotomy is less likely after the first child.

It seems that modern life is characterized by application of numbers to everything. The newborn doesn't escape. By the first minute he or she is assigned a number called an Apgar score. This is a quick measure of health. A score of ten out of ten is perfect. At five minutes this evaluation is repeated.

From the time of the delivery of the baby to the removal of the placenta is the third stage of labor. It may last from one to 20 minutes. The uterine contraction helps to expel the placenta, which might be accompanied by a sudden gush of blood.

My first delivery as a second-year medical student made an unforgettable impression on me. I was relieved that everything had gone according to the text and that I was preparing for the delivery of the placenta when a second very wiggly, live infant landed in my hands. It was so unexpected that I shouted, "The placenta is alive!" My mentor was not thrilled with my conclusion. The woman had given birth to undiagnosed twins, something that rarely happens today.

During this third stage the risk of hemorrhage is increased. Although the practice varies among physicians, I prefer to have an IV in place from seven centimeters through the recovery period in labor. This provides quick "insurance" in case it is needed.

When Things Go Wrong

Little Aaron was sure that a disaster had occurred during the birth of his new brother. His dad was proudly reviewing the home movie of the birth process, which included one segment in which his mother expelled a large piece of feces as a result of a powerful contraction. Aaron cried out in alarm, "Oh, no! Baby Billy fell into the bucket!" It took more than a few moments to convince him that baby Billy had not spent his first moments in a delivery room pail.

Although the majority of deliveries proceed as God designed, the complications that can arise with delivery tend to be rapid in onset and serious in nature. Such emergencies can be quite dramatic. The Greens were excited about the birth of their twins. All was proceeding normally with the delivery of the first twin, but as the water bag of the second twin was broken and the head began to settle into position, a pulsating tubular mass appeared in my hand. This meant that a prolapsed cord was present and that the baby's head had it obstructed. An immediate C-section had to be done. Because the anesthesiologist was present and the operating room crew available, we were able to race down the hall, literally holding the head up off the cord, and perform the operation within a matter of minutes. The baby was fine, but with any more time lost the outcome would have been very different.

The most common problems involve tearing of the lining of the vagina or the cervix. The danger of this trauma is excessive bleeding. Occasionally surgical repair in the operating room is necessary, but usually it can be handled in the delivery room. Failure to progress is another common complication. It has numerous causes and may result in a cesarean section.

If the placenta has not been expelled after 20 or 30 minutes, it may be necessary to transfer the mother to the operating room, where the appropriate procedures can be performed. Failure to do so can lead to severe bleeding and shock.

The most frightening occurrences are umbilical cord prolapse, abruptio placentae, and placenta previa. Timing is so critical that mother and baby can be lost within minutes unless lifesaving procedures are initiated. When the cord is prolapsed, dropping in front of the baby in the birth canal, the blood supply can be obstructed. Abruptio placentae is the premature separation of the placenta from the uterine wall prior to birth. The baby no longer receives oxygen and nutrients and is in grave danger. If the placenta has overgrown the cervical opening partially or completely, and if membranes rupture or labor begins, severe bleeding may occur. This is known as placenta previa.

A rare complication is caused by the formation of an embolus of blood or amniotic fluid. As the embolus finds its way to the lungs, the pregnant woman might experience sudden chest pain, shortness of breath, shock, and cyanosis. Less common is uterine rupture, which occurs when the uterus has become thin from other pregnancies or a previous C-section. A sudden, sharp, shooting abdominal pain feels like something gave way, which is exactly what happened.

Delivery at Home

The possibility of these complications lies at the heart of the controversy over home versus hospital delivery. It has been my experience to care for patients whose home deliveries did not go according to plan. It is scary and upsetting for all concerned.

As I was leaving the house for a Mother's Day brunch with my family, I received a call from a frantic emergency room physician. "Dr. Mayo, I have a lady lying in a pool of blood, unresponsive and in shock. Come quickly!"

My assessment was the same as his: This lady was near death. She had to have immediate blood and IV fluids, which we administered in both arms, and surgery for removal of a retained placenta.

Extenuating factors were all in place: I arrived at the hospital three minutes after the call; the emergency room physician had everything in order; and the anesthesiologist was in the hospital and available.

Despite all this, her blood pressure continued to fall to the point that the usually calm anesthesiologist cried out, "Doctor, I can't maintain her blood pressure—there's too much bleeding!" Having called on every protocol that my frantic mind could muster, the bleeding slowed. Her life was spared.

It took seven units of blood to bring her blood level back to a third of its normal volume. I hesitate to say that it is all behind her. The use of blood transfusions still exposes one to a slight chance of acquiring AIDS, despite the blood testing. Of greater concern is the possibility of the destruction of the posterior pituitary gland (Sheehan's syndrome), which is associated with severe postpartum blood loss and shock. Because this is the "master" gland, thyroid, ovarian, and/or adrenal gland function may be severely impaired.

How did this happen? The new mother was not transferred to the hospital after an appropriate amount of time revealed that the placenta was not going to be expelled—this despite reports of massive amounts of blood loss that had turned the birthing site at home into what looked like a disaster area.

I cannot tell you how much such a risk (which this young couple was willing to assume for the intimacy of a home delivery) affects me emotionally. Although complications of this nature do not happen routinely, for me the risk of losing my wife and/or baby would not be worth it, especially now that freestanding or hospital-based "ABC" rooms are available.

The necessity of viewing their decision as right has kept this young Christian couple from assessing the circumstances and judgment of the people with whom they chose to entrust the life of the mother and child. The hospital, County Medical Society, and each doctor involved received a scathing letter denouncing the care and demanding a partial refund. The letter closed with her intention of having her next baby at home with the same midwife. In the emotional atmosphere that surrounded her experience she misread the alarm which the hospital personnel were experiencing and labeled it "uncaring."

This issue is not about midwives and medical doctors. It is about where the delivery takes place and the availability of immediate medical backup. The American College of Obstetricians approves of Certified Nurse Midwife deliveries. (Lay midwives may have no formal medical training.) During my military service, my experience with Certified Nurse Midwives was positive.

A medical doctor's malpractice insurance does not cover any type of home delivery. If a doctor agrees to be the backup of a midwife who insists on doing her deliveries at home, he and the patient must accept the fact that if something goes wrong, there is no insurance. Many doctors are not willing to take this risk. Others bank on the fact that in most cases things go well. There is no problem if the midwife will deliver in a freestanding birthing center or the hospital and has appropriate backup.

My concern centers around the integrity of the arrangements that are made for home deliveries with the backup doctors. It has been my observation that when problems occur the doctor might not be available. Time is lost trying to contact him for this crisis, and all too often a very critically ill mother or child ends up being seen through the emergency room by a physician who has never seen her before. He knows nothing of her medical history and has had no opportunity to establish any rapport.

Preterm Labor

About 10 percent of all infants born in the United States are born prematurely, or before 37 completed weeks of gestation. Fifty percent of the women have no factors that might indicate premature labor. The other 50 percent are at high risk because of previous preterm labor, an abnormally shaped uterus, abdominal surgery during pregnancy, more than one late abortion, an incompetent cervix, or multiple births.

Early-warning signs may include regular uterine contractions, increased vaginal discharge, rhythmic pelvic pressure, menstrual-like cramps, and vaginal spotting or bleeding. The more quickly treatment is received, the more likely the labor can be stopped. Half of all women with premature labor respond to bed rest only. The remainder require medication. Some medications can cause side effects in the mother which may indirectly affect the baby, but most work well and without problems.

The goal is to reach 37 weeks if at all possible. Since the uncertainty can produce great anxiety for the mother, each week should be celebrated as a milestone of encouragement.

The Aftermath of Childbirth

Basic common-sense activities are an important aspect of the early postpartum period. Exercise is fine, though overdoing is not. Anything that causes undue pain or fatigue should be avoided. Getting plenty of rest will speed recovery. (Feeling extra tired is normal, since the body has been under severe stress for many months.)

Afterbirth pains or contractions are common in women who have had more than one child or who are breast-feeding. The pains result from the normal contractions of the uterine muscles. This decreases the amount of bleeding and helps the uterus return to normal size. The pains usually subside in three to five days.

Another normal occurrence is the vaginal flow known as "lochia." At first it will be heavy and include clots, but by four to six weeks it will usually stop. Keeping clean is important. The use of pads with frequent changes is recommended, tampons are not.

Warm-water soaks, "Tucks," and various sprays can be used to relieve the discomfort of the episiotomy. Kegel's exercises (tightening the muscles of the perineum) may be uncomfortable but promote increased blood flow to the area and thereby more rapid healing. The sutures do not need to be removed; they will dissolve within two weeks.

Hemorrhoids and constipation can best be relieved by maintaining regular daily bowel movements. Stool softeners, roughage, and increased fluids keep the stool soft with no harm to the baby. Hemorrhoids can be treated with hot sitz baths, ointments, creams, and/or suppositories.

If a woman chooses not to breast-feed, there are three basic ways to help dry up the milk: binding the breasts tightly so there is no motion for 48–72 hours, receiving hormones in the delivery room, or taking a pill twice daily for two weeks. Binding is by far the most natural and best way to prevent milk production, although the intense discomfort makes this a very difficult choice for some women. The good news is that the worst part is over in one or two days. Expressing milk to relieve the engorgement merely prolongs the process.

If red streaking, fever, and excessively painful engorgement occurs, a physician should be consulted to check for acute mastitis.

The most important thing for successful breast-feeding is keeping the nipple supple and clean. Washing regularly without soap and using lanolin creams is helpful. Contact with other nursing mothers or an organization such as the La Leche League provides encouragement and suggestions that enable a woman to continue nursing. Besides the mother-child bonding that occurs in breast-feeding, antibodies are passed to the baby that give it a healthy start in life.

Postpartum Blues

It was three in the morning and I had just gotten back in bed from the emergency room when the phone rattled me back to full alert.

"Doctor, something's wrong! I must be crazy—I don't love my baby! I don't even think I love my husband anymore!" Mrs. Harris had been home three short days and three very long nights with her newborn. No one had anticipated a birth with greater joy.

Yet she was one of the 50 to 80 percent of women who suffer depression following delivery. I was able to reassure her that her feelings were physically based and that they would improve. After all, her body had gone through nine months of hormonal, physical, and chemical changes. Getting back to normal would take time.

A mild postpartum depression such as that of Mrs. Harris is called "maternal blues" and is usually transient and self-limiting. Reassurance of the normality of this phenomenon is often all that is necessary. However, if the mother continues to feel overwhelmed by the responsibility of caring for her newborn and is anxious, irritable, depressed, and suicidal, she should be hospitalized. Up to 10 percent of newly delivered women may have persistent depressive episodes. A very small percentage suffer a psychotic break which requires intensive psychiatric treatment.

Lovemaking After the Baby

Each woman is the ultimate expert on when she is ready to resume genital sexual activity. If there were no extensive tears in delivery, most will find four to six weeks adequate. By then, although there may still be some discomfort, nothing will rip or tear apart.

Vaginal dryness, especially among breast-feeding women, may require a vaginal lubricant. Husbands are notorious for inventing reasons for early intercourse. This is a time for good communication and an honest assessment of how she feels. It is important to remember that a new pregnancy may occur. If the woman is breast-feeding, condoms, foam, gels, or diaphragms provide adequate protection, since her fertility is somewhat reduced at this time.

Taking Responsibility

It's a good thing that Eve was assigned the task of bearing children. Men seem much more comfortable with "toiling in the fields" than giving birth. I'm afraid I have to number myself among such men. If men had to endure the birthing process there would surely be zero population growth!

Fortunately, today the birthing process is more of a shared process than ever before. Unquestionably, sensitive and loving support from a husband has a positive effect on the length and outcome of labor.

Whatever the method selected, the goal is a healthy child. To this end, cooperation between mother, father, doctor, and nurse is essential. With greater technology, more babies are born healthy than ever before. The benefit of the intimate experience of delivering at home must be countered with the potential risk. Each couple must carefully and prayerfully determine what is most important to them.

God's majesty is revealed with each birth: One egg, one sperm, and thousands of cell divisions result in a healthy new baby. At six weeks after birth the mother's tremendous bodily adaptations to pregnancy have all but disappeared. No human being could orchestrate such a beautiful symphony of life!

"May God almighty bless you and make you fruitful and increase your numbers until you become a community of peoples" (Genesis 28:3).

Chapter Fourteen

The Complete Woman and Her Healthmate

Listen to advice and accept instruction,
and in the end you will be wise.

—*Proverbs 19:20*

Sally first became my patient after she passed by the clinic and saw me "saving" earthworms after a rainstorm by tossing them from the sidewalk to the grass. She concluded that anyone that compassionate had to be a good doctor. I'm not so sure her reasoning was correct, but I have heard of patients who select their doctors with far less consideration.

Although this "earthsuit" we share is only temporary, that does not excuse us from taking care of it. Choosing a healthmate to aid in the personal care process should be a serious matter. Staying healthy enables us to live a fruitful and productive life for the Lord.

Finding a Doctor

The very first thing a woman must ask herself in choosing a personal physician is what specific medical needs she has at this stage of her life. A young woman with no history of a long-standing illness will probably do well with an obstetrician-gynecologist, as long as he has a philosophy of caring for the total woman. This means that he treats more than just female reproductive concerns, and demonstrates a willingness to refer to other specialists as necessary.

The older woman has a much greater potential for developing a chronic illness that should be followed by an internist or family practitioner. Yet regular visits to the obstetrician-gynecologist should still be part of her routine examinations. Frequently other physicians fail to do routine breast, pelvic, thyroid, and rectal exams, thinking the Ob-Gyn has done this.

The menopausal female has special concerns for choosing the correct gynecologist, for she is beginning to undergo the mental and physical changes associated with hormonal depletion. If these are not properly handled she will most likely develop painful intercourse, low-back pain, easily fractured bones, and marital and sexual problems.

The ideal situation is to grow old with your healthmate. After 20 or more years of visits, he or she will know you well. A young physician may have difficulty relating to the older woman's special needs and concerns, particularly her sexual changes.

Should He or She Be a Christian?

The Bible reminds us not to be unevenly yoked. Since in a sense a woman is in partnership with her healthmate, this is an important consideration. Having been both a secular and a Christian physician, I recognize a difference in my attitude toward my patients. There is a unique bond with my Christian brothers and sisters that is hard to define. We share a common worldview that has the reality of God in it, and thus our communication is especially relevant.

Assuming that a particular physician is the correct one for you merely because of his or her Christianity may not be wise, however. Not all Christian physicians are competent, good communicators and listeners, or compassionate to a woman's needs. One danger could be a legalistic interpretation of the need for a woman to submit to a male authority and the consequent discouraging of questions and discussion required for fully informed medical treatment.

Christian physicians may feel strongly about contraception and abortion. It is important that you understand where his or her particular value system intersects with the practice of medicine.

Mom Thought He Was Great

One of the best ways to locate a competent healthmate is to ask women in your church. If you are looking for a general practitioner, make sure the Ob-Gyn is willing to treat all facets of your general health. An initial visit can confirm whether he or she will meet your specific needs.

There can be problems with seeing Mom's physician. He will probably be older and may be practicing gynecology only. Should you be thinking of having children, this would necessitate a change in doctors. Also, he or she may be less familiar or comfortable with the newest medical advances. (On the other hand, maturity and wisdom generally come with age.)

A young physician has the advantage of a more flexible schedule which might suit your needs better. Chances are that he or she has more years to spend with you as well, since retirement is many years away. A young woman who establishes her care with a younger doctor can look forward to lifelong rapport.

She Can Relate to Me

The real choice in whether to seek a male or female healthmate is your comfort level and the physician's commitment to your medical care. Many women feel that another woman may more easily understand their cares and concerns. Some feel that the examination, always awkward under the best of circumstances, is easier to endure when performed by a female.

Yet concluding that a female doctor will better understand treatment of menstrual cramps or the pain of childbirth is as wrong as concluding that a male doctor will be more competent and aggressive in treatment. Each individual must be judged according to his or her record.

The practice of Ob-Gyn is unique in that there is considerable rapport established with the patient, her husband, and the doctor as they share a major event of the couple's life together. An Ob-Gyn can expect interrupted dinners, missed birthday parties and school award banquets, and many sleepless nights followed by work the next day. His or her personal commitment to the specialty must be clear.

Other Considerations

Some studies indicate that a group setting assures superior care for the patient. Having close associates constantly available for consultation and referral is an advantage. The idea of peers being aware of the results motivates the physician to be diligent.

Your personal comfort is not a bad criterion for judging whether a particular physician is the right one for you. Do not be misled by the length of time it takes to get an appointment; a long wait does not always signify better care. Neither does going to the most popular Ob-Gyn in town, especially if you do not feel a personal accord with him or her. Physicians, like everyone else, have their own prejudices and preferences in patients and office management. If you detect a lack of respect or empathy, you are in the wrong office.

Another essential criterion for choosing a healthmate is the ability to ask any question that is a real concern to you. Sexual questions are often the most difficult for both patient and physician. In my junior year of medical school, the university I attended offered the first course on sexuality for medical students. The competition for entrance into the class was intense, but it proved a major disappointment for many of those who attended, since the subject matter studiously avoided any mention of human sexual behavior! Although courses have improved, the individual doctor's comfort level may or may not have advanced.

How are questions handled? What is the reaction to inquiries about fees or professional degrees? Are you encouraged to fully understand the treatment or recommendations?

As you observe the office, look at the degrees on the wall. Are the institutions reputable? Can you tell something about the personality of the person who uses the office? If the individual is married, are there pictures of the family?

Taking It Off

Unquestionably, women find that the worst part of going to the doctor is the physical exam. The physical contortion required for a routine examination is humiliating. Few women are comfortable with their heels elevated in cold stirrups, their knees agape, and their posterior spotlighted.

A sensitive physician will begin the case history in his or her office. This practice is far more comfortable than discussing the details of the visit while sitting partially clothed in the examination room. The physician's mannerisms and attitude can make the situation better or worse.

A thorough examination should include more than a reproductive checkup. Routine lab work and X-rays are usually not necessary in the healthy person until he or she is over 50. The blood pressure, thyroid gland, heart and lungs, breasts, pelvic, and rectal exams comprise a complete checkup. If any annual exam you undergo overlooks any of these areas, ask that they be done. Don't be afraid to be assertive; it's your health and life.

The doctor should not neglect his role as educator. Insist that you receive help by demonstration, verbally or through handouts, on self-examination procedures that should be a normal part of a woman's routine. Keeping aware of typical body changes allows the patient to participate in partnership with the doctor and ensures the best medical care. Additionally, familiarizing oneself with one's own body can prevent those awful moments of panic when something is noticed for the first time. More than one woman has come to my office convinced she is dying of cancer when in reality she is experiencing normal changes in her breasts related to her cycle.

Expectations Fulfilled

It is special when a doctor makes you feel you are his or her only patient. This is the way it should be in the office. But the reality is that you are one of many. Do not be offended when you need to share considerable information before your physician can identify you over the phone.

A major irritation which many physicians share is the patient's expectation of a definitive cure over the phone. Often there is great reluctance to visit an urgent care center or emergency room: "Just give me a pill, Doctor—I'll be fine." No one is able to tell the extent of pain and suffering over the phone. The risk to health and life by such vicarious treatment can be great. A treatable outpatient problem can escalate into a lengthy hospital stay if not attended to promptly.

A good staff screens many common questions. They should know when direct communication with the physician is called for. They may ask the doctor and relay the message to you. At times speaking directly to him or her is necessary. Do not hesitate to insist on this if you feel that the seriousness of your situation is not recognized by the staff or if you feel that you need the reassurance of a direct conversation.

The Ob-Gyn has a greater chance of being called away from the office than most physicians. It is not uncommon for the office day to begin after the Ob-Gyn has been up all night, and for that day to be interrupted by deliveries, emergency room consults, office emergency add-ons, and other disruptions. A well-run office should be able, within reason, to let you know when you will be seen, despite the disorder.

Never forget that, although we still tend to regard physicians with a certain degree of awe, they are human. They have good and bad days, healthy and sick ones, hectic and calm ones. Your prayers and empathy are always in order. Your irritation at his or her lateness only adds to the stress of a sometimes-frustrating occupation.

A competent physician should encourage your questions. Be specific about your problems. A physician will have trouble treating your sexual problem if it has been presented merely as a headache. On days when schedules are especially out-of-line and your questions are lengthy, reschedule for the amount of time you need. For example, time allotted for a Pap smear may not suffice for counseling on a failing marriage.

Mom As a Healthmate

Mrs. Jones brought her four-year-old with her when she came to the office for her annual exam. The child played contentedly in the waiting room as we chatted in the office. Suddenly she realized that her mother was no where in sight. I directed her to the examination room, where her mother was undressing for the physical exam. She opened the door and exclaimed for all to hear, "Mommy, does Daddy know you take your clothes off for other men?"

Mrs. Jones wisely used this incident as a teaching moment to reaffirm for her daughter appropriate times and situations in which being seen nude is acceptable. I never object to a woman bringing her children with her if we can use the visit in a reassuring way. Much fear of doctors and doctors' offices can be alleviated by this early exposure.

Young women vary in their readiness for their first gynecological examination. It always helps if they know what to expect. Coming in for a routine exam in which there are no known problems is a good idea. As in other areas of life, if the mother has a positive attitude, chances are greater that the daughter will share her perspective.

Sometimes girls resist going to the same physician that the mother sees. It is more important that they get off to a good start than that they maintain the family tradition of seeing the same person. Adolescents can benefit by knowing that they have an advocate who is there for them alone.

Whose Body Is This, Anyway?

In the past, physicians would never have been considered "healthmates" by the patient or the doctor. Participating in treatment was a violation of the physician's prerogative. If he was not considered a god, he was the next thing to it. As more and more has been discovered about holistic health and as specialization has increased, fewer and fewer physicians adopt this unrealistically exalted standard of health care. In its place the modern physician gladly relinquishes his former position for a partnership with the patient.

Jesus always ministered to the whole person, and His model is a good one to follow. People are more than their parts: A woman needing a hysterectomy is also a wife, mother, leader in her church, and skilled computer operator. Her illness is wrapped in a complex web of who she is and what she does. The more the healthmate knows of her strengths, pressures, and needs, the better the treatment and result will be.

There is no way the whole woman can be treated without her cooperation. Here again we see the need for taking responsibility. The ideal patient makes an effort to educate herself about her body and its functions. She is inquisitive and willing to ask pertinent and penetrating questions. She accepts the responsibility of understanding the problem and the follow-up care.

Two-Way Street

Entering a relationship with a healthmate is a two-way street. Patients often do not realize the effect they have on their physician. Their attitude can contribute to feelings of hope and can reaffirm faith, especially if their attitude is calming and insightful. Little will happen, however, unless there is a willingness to speak up.

It was the direct question of a new patient that led me to rethink a very important issue. Mrs. Wellington had come to interview me for her prenatal care. She had heard many good things about me but had a serious hesitancy that needed discussing before entrusting herself and her baby to my care. "Do you perform abortions?" she asked. "I find it unacceptable to go to a physician who brings forth life one minute and terminates it the next."

Up to that point I had not explored my sentiments concerning abortion. During my residency I was not a Christian and unquestioningly performed the duties that were required of me. As I maintained my own practice, I found myself unconsciously limiting abortions more and more each year, preferring to refer all except those that were explicitly requested of me.

Mrs. Wellington's poignant comment caused me to examine what I had never allowed myself to face before. There was no reason or justification for my continuing this procedure. From that time onward abortions have not been a part of my practice. Those patients seeking abortion are no longer given an excuse for referring them to alternative care but are presented, in love, with my personal witness on why I do not perform abortions.

Another occasion when a patient's willingness to be open and honest made a significant difference was through a longtime patient, Sharon. Having observed the escalation of my practice to the point where I had to make each moment count, she took it upon herself to remind me of the changes which such a pace had produced in my attitude and the atmosphere of the office. It hurt to hear, but upon thinking about it I concluded that she was correct.

I now appreciate patients who are willing to pray and be open with their spiritual needs. The first time a patient asked to pray in the operating room brought a curtain of silence upon the scene. Yet the witness of an especially smooth surgery could not be missed by those in attendance.

Appropriate techniques, the latest scientific information, skilled hands, and a responsible patient all play a part in helping to recover or maintain health. The ultimate healer, however, is God. To expect results without His inclusion is to accept partial cure.

Board Certification

A final consideration in choosing a healthmate is whether he or she is Board Certified. Once a physician has completed a residency program (usually four or five years after medical school), he or she is declared Board Eligible. At this point the option exists for practice in his or her chosen specialty. The final plateau in the field of obstetrics and gynecology may be obtained after two years in practice. The acme of the profession, Board Certification, is achieved only after taking extensive and difficult oral and written examinations.

Why should this matter to you? The additional effort and study required to pass the Boards says something about the character of the person who will go this extra mile to be tested by his or her peers. The desire to achieve mastery of the specialty is evident and may be displayed within his or her practice.

The Future Is Now

Rarely do we pick up a newspaper, turn on the TV, or look at a magazine without reading about some new medical advancement. If you have reviewed your child's homework or taken the time to look through his or her books, you have become aware of the voluminous amount of new material that was not there when you were in school. Imagine this same phenomenon on the research level!

The ethical consequences of this rapid scientific evolution confronts all of society. In the near future, babies will be able to be specifically ordered. Sex, eye color, intelligence, and freedom from disease will be offered from a menu designed to fulfill an individual's every whim. Should you prefer not to disrupt your schedule for pregnancy, a surrogate mom will take your place—or an artificial placenta.

Separating procreation from sex is bound to change attitudes. The emphasis will be on the recreational aspects of sex, and people not functioning well in this regard will be more demanding in their desire to function well. Artificial insemination and changing attitudes will result in more women (and men) making the decision to be a single parent.

The desire to have a boy first, and the ability to make this happen, is likely to have far-reaching social repercussions. How will women feel, knowing that they are desired second? As costs of education continue to rise, which child will be chosen to go on to higher education?

Undoubtedly the future holds more abortions as genetic diseases are pinpointed. If you think such intervention is far away, the State of California recently passed a bill requiring that the patient be informed about Down's syndrome, spina bifida, and hydrocephalic infants. The law requires a woman at 16 weeks of pregnancy to appear in the physician's office, read a descriptive brochure, and decide whether she will submit to a blood test for alpha-fetoproteins that will reveal if her child is affected with any of the above problems.

Medicine is also changing as a result of an aging population, a tendency toward less intervention (except in the case of death), and financial considerations. Women live longer than ever before, but the price is an increase in diseases of the aging, particularly osteoporosis. On a positive note, the sheer numbers of older women have resulted in greater consideration given their sexual concerns. Younger women will find less intervention in pregnancy, fewer inductions, and avoidance of anesthetics in childbirth.

The malpractice crisis has probably done more to change the face and future of medical practice than anything else. As of the mid-1980's at least 12 percent of obstetricians have either retired or given up obstetrics. In some states up to 20 percent have quit. The same trend is occurring even more rapidly in the field of family practitioners because their fewer deliveries can in no way cover the cost of the liability insurance.

But the most serious repercussion from this crisis has been the loss of trust that has in the past been the cornerstone of medicine. My father was a general practitioner for over 35 years in a small town. The basis of his practice was a mutual, caring relationship based on respect. Until the last two years of his practice, he had not heard of malpractice insurance. He frequently comments that rapport with his patients was a key to treatment.

While no one denies the right of a patient to be compensated for any avoidable adverse outcome, the current climate is one in which anything short of perfection is not acceptable. This is particularly true with obstetrics. The demand is for less intervention and more natural deliveries coupled with the technology and skill to insure a flawless child. The legacy to the physician is to view the patient no longer as a partner in treatment but as an adversary.

The threat of lawsuits is so great among pharmaceutical companies that several drugs which had a history of long and safe use have been taken off the market. In obstetrics, Bendectin can no longer be used for control of nausea and vomiting of pregnancy despite findings that the drug was not harmful, that it was not unfit for its specific use, and that the manufacturer was not negligent in offering the drug for sale. Several trips to court convinced the company that it simply was not worth the trouble to continue production.

Medicine is also changing as the result of increasingly sophisticated and expensive medical technology. One attempt at controlling medical costs is the birth of health maintenance organizations (HMO's). These insurance groups make their profits by carefully policing the efficiency of the participant's medical care. Only the most necessary surgical procedures and medical tests are allowed.

We can all be comforted by the safeguard that any surgery done is truly justified, but problems with the system sometimes arise from the refusal to adequately treat anything not considered life-threatening. (Many conditions that are both painful and limiting are not life-threatening.)

Getting people out of the hospital as quickly as possible is another way of controlling costs. Gone are the days when you were anxious to get home. Now, discharges one and two days after major surgery are not uncommon. Often a decision on the appropriate convalescent time is made by a nonmedical staff.

Unquestionably something must be done about medical costs. More outpatient surgery and freestanding surgicenters will be part of the solution. Be prepared in this transition time to discover a few rough edges as the proper balance between good care and financial considerations is worked out.

Taking Responsibility

The days of expecting the doctor or other health-care provider to always know what is best for you are rightfully over. You are now a partner in your own health-care concerns. Choosing a physician whom you can comfortably relate to and who is right for your specific needs is a first step. Educating yourself as to what you should reasonably expect is a second. The best care will result when the healthmate you have selected knows you well and sees you in the totality of your life.

"Where no counsel is, the people fall; but in the multitude of counselors there is safety" (Proverbs 11:14 KJV).

Appendices

Appendix A

BREAST EXAMINATION

The American Cancer Society recommends the following:

1. Examine both breasts once a month in midcycle.
2. While bathing, carefully feel each breast for thickening or lumps.
3. Look in a mirror for changes or puckering.
4. Lie down, placing one hand under your head, and examine the entire breast in a clockwise direction, progressing toward the nipple. Repeat with the other breast.
5. Squeeze each nipple to check for discharge.
6. Any lump, change, discharge, or other unusual finding should immediately be checked by your physician.

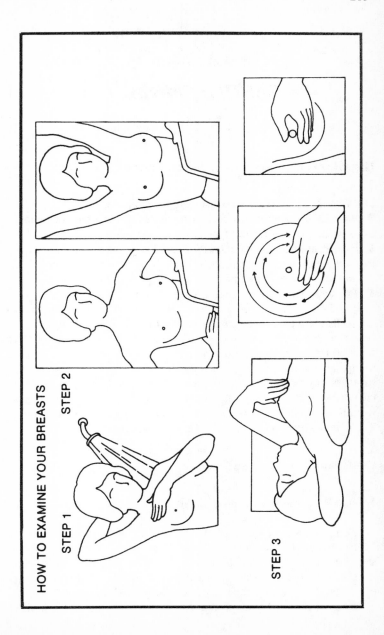

HOW TO EXAMINE YOUR BREASTS

STEP 1

STEP 2

STEP 3

Appendix B

HOME TESTS

Home Pregnancy Tests

1. Advance: Ortho Pharmaceutical Corporation
2. Daisy 2: Ortho Pharmaceutical Corporation
3. Fact: Ortho Pharmaceutical Corporation
4. New E.P.T. Plus: Parke-Davis
5. First Response: Tambrands, Inc.
6. Acu-Test: Beecham Products
7. Answer: Carter Products
8. Predictor: Whitehall

All home pregnancy tests work by detecting HCG (human chorionic gonadotrophin) hormone in a morning urine sample. HCG is released following conception. Many home tests are sensitive enough to indicate the hormone's presence one day past the day on which the menstrual cycle should normally have begun. Although the test procedures vary, they all depend on color changes to indicate pregnancy. Results are available within ten to 45 minutes, depending on the brand. The manufacturers claim 99 to 99.5 percent accuracy.

Ovulation Predictor Test

1. First Response (by Tambrands, Inc.)

This ovulation-predictor test measures the increase in LH (luteinizing hormone) that triggers ovulation. It can help a woman know when she is most likely to become pregnant. A woman must first establish her normal LH level before she can detect an increase. The test consists of six days' worth of testing materials to establish this baseline. This is sufficient for two-thirds of ovulating women. A nine-day test kit is also available that is adequate for four-fifths of all women. The first morning urine is used, and color changes indicate the hormone level.

Gender Predictor Test

1. Gender Choice (by ProCare Industries, Inc.)

The premise of this test is that female-producing sperm are more likely to survive in the acidic environment just prior to ovulation and male-producing sperm in the alkaline environment at the time of ovulation. This has not been scientifically proven. The test itself consists of papers to measure pH and a thermometer to predict ovulation. Our opinion is that your chance of a boy or girl is still 50-50, so save your money!

Appendix C

METHODS OF CHILDBIRTH

Whether or not a couple plan on having natural childbirth, taking a childbirth class has a definite positive effect on the length and tolerance of labor. It is a form of insurance, since labor may proceed so rapidly that there is no time for any anesthesia (or the anesthetic medication may not work). The more the couple knows what to expect, the more adequately they can deal with labor and delivery.

The most popular childbirth preparation method in the United States is Lamaze. Courses are taught in hospitals, clinics, and homes. Lamaze stresses control by training women to learn controlled breathing patterns and special focusing exercises. Husbands or other labor coaches are actively involved and therefore feel part of the process. This is a good method for women who wish to remain in control during labor. It is criticized for its rigidity, the possibility of hyperventilation in some versions, and excessive focus on method (thus minimizing the emotional experience of giving birth).

The Harris Method does not give the husband specific tasks to do but encourages him to give emotional support and encouragement to his wife. Nurses who are Harris instructors serve as labor coaches. The emphasis is on slow breathing and soft-touch techniques. This is an easy method to learn and provides security for those women who choose to rely on professionals during the birth experience. It is not the method of choice for those who want to actively participate in all the decisions affecting their labor.

Most people who use the Leboyer Gentle Birth Method actually use a modified version. The trauma of birth is reduced by delivery into a quiet, dimly lit room with immediate parental contact. Upon delivery the baby is immersed in a warm-water bath and cradled by the father, thereby enhancing parent-child bonding. Critics argue that the bath may cause the baby's temperature to drop and may cause infection via the umbilical cord. Also, some babies do not like baths!

The Bradley Method (husband-coached childbirth) stresses that a woman must trust her instincts to give birth in a "natural" way. The husband gives verbal support. The physician is not seen as an authority figure, and intervention is done only as a last resort. Each couple invents their own method of childbirth. Some feel they have failed if medication is required. The relationship between doctor and patient can easily become adversarial.

Classes are especially recommended for women who know in advance that they will deliver cesarean section. These classes help women understand the surgery and postpartum-recovery aspects of childbirth. The best classes also inform couples of various alternatives, such as types of incisions and different methods of anesthesia.

Today it is possible for C-sections to be done under regional anesthesia, such as epidural, caudal, or spinal. This enables the mother to be awake and the father present, and for both to have immediate contact with the baby. (In the past, the absence of these factors made C-sections a negative experience.) Because women enter the delivery process rested, do not go through labor, and have less reaction to anesthetic, recovery is rapid.

VBAC classes (vaginal birth after cesarean) are controversial if they discourage women from having hospital deliveries. Otherwise they are helpful in encouraging those women who wish to have a trial of labor.

Other Marshall Pickering Paperbacks

RICH IN FAITH

Colin Whittaker

Colin Whittaker's persuasive new book is written for ordinary people all of whom have access to faith, a source of pure gold even when miracles and healing seem to happen to other people only.

The author identifies ten specific ways to keep going on the road to faith-riches, starting where faith must always begin—with God himself, the Holy Spirit, the Bible, signs and wonders, evangelism, tongues and finally to eternal life with Christ.

OUR GOD IS GOOD

Yonggi Cho

This new book from Pastor Cho describes the blessings, spiritual and material, that reward the believer. Yonggi Cho presents his understanding of the fullness of salvation, bringing wholeness to God's people.

THE PLIGHT OF MAN AND THE POWER OF GOD

Dr Martin Lloyd-Jones

The text of the highly esteemed sermons given by Dr Martin Lloyd-Jones, based on verses from Romans, Chapter One, focuses on our need to be entirely committed to the Christian gospel.

Dr Lloyd-Jones highlights the uniqueness of the faith. Because of this he stresses the necessity of our absolute commitment to Christ and his call to us.

This book will be of great interest to all thoughtful Christians and of help to preachers, speakers and students.

THE NATURAL TOUCH

Kim Swithinbank

Some people think of 'evangelism' as knocking on doors, reading your Bible on the train or starting up conversations with strangers in which you get on to the four-point-plan-of-salvation as quickly as possible. Some of these activities we would do, others we'd cringe at doing.

In his first book, Kim Swithinbank says that sharing our hope in Christ is something that we are *all* asked to do. It should be as natural as breathing to us.

Taking us through the most common obstacles which keep people away from Christianity, he shows how we can develop a lifestyle which is attractive and compelling for Christ.

Kim Swithinbank is Director of Evangelism at All Souls, Langham Place.

HIDDEN GOLD
A Spiritual Adventure in South America

Barbara Bazley

Arriving in Chile before 'western sophistication', Barbara records with humour and candour an entire way of life which was soon to pass altogether, and movingly describes the Mapuche Indians' gradual but sure response to the Lordship of Christ.

HEARTS AFLAME
Stories from the Church of Chile

Barbara Bazley

Hearts Aflame is a book suffused with love for the large, sometimes violent country of Chile and joy at the power of the Gospel taking root.

Each chapter is a story in itself, telling of some encounter, episode of friendship that has left its mark on the author's life.

THE TORN VEIL

Esther Gulshan with Thelma Sangster

Gulshan Fatima, the youngest daughter of a Muslim family, lived a quietly secluded life at home in the Punjab. A trip to England began a spiritual awakening that led ultimately to her conversion to Christianity. She has since preached to thousands of Muslims and many have not only found faith but have, like her, found physical healing.

WORKING WITH GOD

Andrew Murray

A new title in the *Evangelical Heritage Series*, *Working with God* is a sequel to the author's well-loved bestseller, *Waiting for God*. The theme is the fulfilling task that Christians are called to in talking about their faith and encouraging others to submit their lives to God.

The book can either be used as a daily devotional book or read in the usual way.